PRAEGER WORLD

# American Art
# Since 1900
A CRITICAL HISTORY

# American Art Since 1900

## A CRITICAL HISTORY

# BARBARA ROSE

FREDERICK A. PRAEGER, *Publishers*
New York · Washington

To Frank

BOOKS THAT MATTER

Published in the United States of America in 1967
by Frederick A. Praeger, Inc., Publishers
111 Fourth Avenue, New York, N.Y. 10003

© 1967 by Frederick A. Praeger, Inc.

Library of Congress Catalog Card Number: 67-20743

Printed in the United States of America

# Contents

6 Acknowledgments

7 Introduction

11 CHAPTER ONE
Apostles of Ugliness

35 CHAPTER TWO
The Largest Small Room in the World

67 CHAPTER THREE
The Armory Show: Success by Scandal

84 CHAPTER FOUR
After the Ball: Cubism in America

114 CHAPTER FIVE
The Thirties: Reaction and Rebellion

155 CHAPTER SIX
Art of This Century

189 CHAPTER SEVEN
The New American Painting

211 CHAPTER EIGHT
After Abstract Expressionism

238 CHAPTER NINE
Toward a Sculptural Renaissance

270 CHAPTER TEN
Toward an American Architecture

295 Notes

298 Bibliography

301 List of Illustrations

316 Index

## Acknowledgments

I wish to acknowledge my special debt to the lectures and essays of Meyer Schapiro, the criticism of Clement Greenberg, and the research and writing of Milton Brown..

I am grateful to Michael Fried, Edward F. Fry, Henry Geldzahler, Richard Meier, Robert Motherwell, John Bernard Myers, Lee Krasner Pollock, Ad Reinhardt, Robert Rosenblum, and William Rubin for their advice and suggestions.

My thanks go also to Leo Castelli, Betty Parsons, and Virginia Zabriskie for their generous cooperation. Finally, I wish to thank Richard Bellamy, John Cage, Philip Pavia, and William Seitz for the friendship and encouragement they provided when it was needed, and Dorothy Willis and Brenda Gilchrist for their work in editing this book.

# Introduction

American artists, in their efforts to achieve independence from European models while maintaining their ties to the European tradition, have had to overcome countless obstacles. Not the least of these has been the standard interpretation of American art. In the past, it has been customary to discuss American art in one of two ways: either as a separate entity, developed independently and divorced from the larger context of European art; or in terms derived directly from the study of European art. Unfortunately, neither interpretation places twentieth-century American art in its proper perspective.

When attempts are made to trace the development of American art without reference to the European mainstream, much art that is mediocre, academic, and provincial is accepted and applauded. Perhaps a young nation in search of its cultural identity might be excused for the way it has extolled its regional manifestations in the past, but the time has indeed come for a reappraisal. Such a review should emphasize the contributions of those Americans who, believing that art transcends national boundaries, have fought an uphill battle to become part of the mainstream tradition. Their efforts, although often ignored, have made it possible for American art to become the powerful international force it is today.

Equally confusing is the incorrect assumption that certain terms, such as "avant-garde" and "academy," which referred originally to specific institutions in the history of European modernism, can have the same meaning when applied to American art. One could not, for example, refer to an American avant-garde movement in the ordinary sense until there was a widespread acceptance in this country of art, not as the servant of some higher power, such as politics or morality, but of art for its own sake. More telling, perhaps, is the "breakthrough" mentality characteristic of many American artists. They seem to share the same driving force, the same competitive instinct, and the same desire for constant innovation that leave their mark on every phase of this country's social and economic life.

Similarly, there is little to be gained from discussing American art in terms of such traditional oppositions as the "classic" versus the "romantic." (One might point instead to a persistent taste for realism, which is evident throughout the history of American art, and consider the attraction of American artists to the literal and the actual as opposed to the allusive or the metaphoric.) Simple oppositions are bound to make little sense in a discussion of a pluralistic society that has produced an art of many styles, an art that often exhibits heterogeneous, even contradictory characteristics. One might, in fact, note that a salient characteristic of American art is precisely its attempt to reconcile its inherent oppositions.

Equally misleading is the assumption that in America, as in Europe, the same clear-cut distinctions can be made between "high" or fine art and applied or commercial art. In point of fact, many American artists, who at one time or another supported themselves as illustrators, commercial artists, sign painters, house painters, etc., did borrow freely from these vocational techniques once they turned to fine art.

Illustration, it should be noted, has frequently been accepted as fine art in America. This may be accounted for by the egalitarian nature of our society, with its lack of fixed traditions and its constant demands for an art that can be understood by the majority. This latter recurrent demand ultimately has acted to erase the boundaries between illustration and high art. Indeed, the identification by a larger public of high art as fine art is a recent phenomenon in America, just as the notion of quality as opposed to mere quantity has only now begun to make inroads on the public mind. Yet some fifty years ago, Alfred Stieglitz and his circle were insisting on the importance of these values.

Clearly, a survey of American art as brief as this one is forced to be selective. Emphasis, therefore, will be placed on those artists who helped unite American art with the mainstream of European art. This study will concentrate on those who labored to achieve an art that challenged both the antivisual bias of America's Puritanism and the narrowness of its political boundaries. One cannot deny, however, that even when American art did achieve international stature, it retained certain constant and distinctive characteristics, which still stamp it as "made in U.S.A." Some art historians, such as John McCoubrey, have tried to define these characteristics. In his *American Tradition in Painting,* McCoubrey views the once vast emptiness of the American landscape as the great protagonist of American art. He attempts to isolate, as characteristic of American painting, spaciousness, rawness, and a generally unfinished quality.

Whether we agree or not, we must consider the uniqueness of the American environment and experience. It is this uniqueness that transformed the art forms and techniques of Europe as soon as they crossed the Atlantic. Equally, we must acknowledge the debt American art owes to those European pioneers who personally transplanted their avant-garde modernism to the new world. Included among these pioneer artists are Marcel Duchamp, John Graham, Hans Hofmann, Frederick Kiesler, and Piet Mondrian, as well as the group of Surrealists, led by André Masson and Matta, that acted as the catalyst in the development of Abstract Expressionism. Their activity reinforced the efforts of American artists whose goal it was to create an international art while still remaining true to their own cultural experience.

# Chapter One

# Apostles of Ugliness

America has yet morally and artistically originated nothing. She seems singularly unaware that the models of persons, books, manners, etc. appropriate for former conditions and for European lands are but exiles and exotics here.

—WALT WHITMAN, *Democratic Vistas*

Nearly two centuries after winning political independence from England, America was still an artistic colony of Europe. Although American literature renounced European models in the nineteenth century, American art did not achieve a similar maturity until the United States emerged as a dominant global power after World War II. Until that time, American artists continued to be torn between their allegiance to Europe's high culture and their wish to initiate a genuinely American style. The struggle to resolve this conflict is the history of twentieth-century American art.

The first American artists to aim programmatically at founding a native style consonant with the American experience called themselves The Eight; because of their humble subjects, they later came to be known as the Ash Can School. Ignoring the revolutionary new art being produced in France, realists like Robert Henri turned back to pre-Impressionist painters—particularly to Manet, the Impressionists' source—for inspiration. Counting on the homely subject matter of the American scene to give their work a native stamp, the Ash Can School instigated a revolt against academic norms that had little or nothing to do with the aesthetic revolution of the French avant-garde a half-century earlier.

Carried out for the sake of democracy in art rather than in the name of art for art's sake, the Ash Can School's revolt was determined not by the strength of the academic tradition but by its weakness. In France, where modern painting took shape, the Ecole des Beaux-Arts and the various private academies provided a solid training, discipline, and tradition from which a new art, still grounded on the principles that made the old masters great, could gradually emerge. In America, the academies were hardly more than organizations that held annual exhibitions. When the American artist rebelled, it was not against the pictorial traditions of Western art (with which he was hardly acquainted in any case), but against the exclusiveness and privilege of the academies and against rules and regulations in general. In other words, the cause of individualism rather than any artistic cause was championed.

In the opening decade of the twentieth century, while this rebellion was taking place, the rapid industrial expansion begun during the previous century did not abate but steadily increased. As the growing cities took on their present identities as great manufacturing centers, demands for labor drew a stream of immigrants, who in turn infused American life with a new energy and diversity. With the inauguration of Theodore Roosevelt in 1901, an age of progressive reform was ushered in. Liberals began demanding labor and social welfare legislation to correct the grosser injustices of the economic system. Women, too, were agitating for reform, demanding suffrage and equal rights.

Celebrating the newly awakened critical spirit, novelists like Frank Norris and Theodore Dreiser and muckraking journalists like Lincoln Steffens attacked existing institutions. Because The Eight treated themes new to American art—the shabby neighborhoods and seamy life of the urban lower classes—and because some, like Robert Henri and John Sloan, were avowed socialists, they have been equated with the American naturalistic novelists and the muckraking journalists. Actually, their taste in literature like their taste in art was for the French realists; their favorite authors were Balzac and Maupassant. Because they described but did not judge, their intentions were in effect much closer to those of Balzac and Maupassant than to those of Dreiser and Norris, who were their contemporaries.

Henri and his "revolutionary black gang," as hostile critics dubbed them, challenged the stuffy discipline of the Academy just as reformers were opposing the authority of the entrenched establishment in other sectors of American life. They were willing to forsake the sacred precincts of high art for the more immediate vitality of popular culture. Their studios were not the plush carpeted ateliers of successful academic artists, but the spare ascetic quarters of brownstone tenements, the forerunners of today's manufacturing-loft studios.

Although the awareness of a national consciousness, of an "American spirit" distinct from European ways of thinking and feeling, came first to such writers as Hawthorne and Melville, Emerson and Thoreau, by the end of the nineteenth century, the painters Winslow Homer and Thomas Eakins had also deliberately begun to turn to native themes. Eakins, responsive to Emerson's and Whitman's pleas for an art that would reflect the unique qualities of the American experience, counseled his students at the Pennsylvania Academy of Fine Arts to "study their own country and to portray its life and types" rather than "spend their time abroad obtaining a superficial view of the art of the old world."[1]

For the most part Eakins' words were not heeded. This was understandable since American art was so little esteemed that when Americans did not purchase from the prestigious French Salon, they bought native imitations of the slick academic works of fashionable Salon painters like Bouguereau and Cabanel.

As the Gilded Age clanked into the twentieth century, American art was cloistered and anemic. Official taste, according to Everett Shinn, the most garrulous member of The Eight, was "swaddled in accessories, fenced in with tasseled ropes and weighted down with chatelaines of bronze name plates." Equally "effete, delicate and supinely refined," painting "lockstepped in monotonous parade in a deadly unbroken circle, each canvas scratching the back of the one in its lead."[2]

It was this vicious circle that Shinn and his friends sought to break. Philadelphia was the scene of this insurrection, whose seeds had already been sown in the musty corridors of the Pennsylvania Academy itself, specifically in Eakins' life class. Eakins' insistence on using nude models for figure studies instead of plaster casts of antique statues marked a break with the spirit as well as the power of the Academy. Eakins' quarrel was not only with the method of academic training as it was retrogressively practiced in puritanical America, but also with the academic mind, which spurned the everyday reality of contemporary life for the empty formulas of a saccharine Neoclassicism, itself a secondhand imitation of the weakest French examples.

Although Eakins was forced to resign in 1886 for removing the loin cloth from a nude male model, his courageous defiance of prudery and convention made him a hero to young Robert Henri. The son of a fugitive from a Nebraska gun fight, robust young Henri, disenchanted with the fig leaves and gauze draperies of the official style, soon gravitated to the life class of Thomas Anshutz, Eakins' most gifted pupil.

Absorbing as much as he could from Anshutz, Henri became impatient with the provincialism of the Academy. In 1888, he left Philadelphia for Paris. But at the height of the excitement of Post-Impressionism, Henri involved himself not in its challenging milieu, but in the academic atmosphere of the Ecole des Beaux-Arts. Although Henri was impressed with Bouguereau, who cautioned him against the heretical ideas of the Impressionists, he regarded his chance to see Manet's *Olympia* and *The Balcony* as the high point of his trip. What he appreciated in Manet, however, was not his modernism, his flattening of forms and advanced pictorial structure, but his flashy brushwork. And throughout his career, the Manet Henri continued to admire was not the Manet who looked forward to Cézanne but the "Spanish" Manet of the somber palette, who looked backward to Velázquez.

In 1891, Henri was back in Philadelphia. Shortly after his arrival, Charles Grafly, an instructor at the Academy whom Henri had known in Paris, introduced him to two young newspaper illustrators. They were William Glackens and John Sloan, who became Henri's disciple and lifelong friend. Soon Henri's studio at 806 Walnut Street, in the heart of downtown Philadelphia, became the gathering place for a group that included George Luks and Everett Shinn, fellow artist-reporters with Glackens and Sloan on the *Philadelphia Press*. At these gatherings, music, literature, and above all, art were discussed—away from the stifling confines of the Academy.

At twenty-seven, Henri seemed worldly and experienced to his friends, who, although working artists, were scarcely out of their teens. Evenings at 806 Walnut differed from meetings of New York artists' clubs like the Tile Club or the Art Club because there were no officers or any set functions. Henri's studio provided the kind of forum for ideas European artists could find in cafés, but which was rare in America. Interspersed with the Tuesday evening discussions were slapstick theatricals, often written by the glib Everett Shinn, whose interest in the theater eventually led him into stage design. The most memorable of these productions was a parody of George du Maurier's *Trilby,* held in 1894 in one of the Academy rooms. It featured Robert Henri as Svengali, John Sloan in a pre-Raphaelite wig as the heroine "Twillbe," and Shinn himself as the expatriate painter "James McNails Whiskers."

But however much Henri and his friends burlesqued Whistler, as they thumbed their noses at everything officially sacred, they were ambivalent in their attitude toward their celebrated fellow country-

I-I. GEORGE LUKS, *The Wrestlers*, 1905.

man. Although they admired Whistler's skill, particularly in handling values, they resented his achieving renown as a Europeanized American. Nevertheless, it was Whistler's technique of washing in the background of the canvas with an atmospheric "soup" before working his rapidly sketched figures into it that Henri imitated in his own paintings.

During the summer of 1893, such discussions were carried on at the Charcoal Club, which had been founded so that artists could sketch informally from life under lighting more adequate than that provided by the dimly lit Academy. At these meetings Henri criticized sketches and encouraged Glackens and Sloan to try oil painting. Glackens, in fact, painted his first oil, a figure study, the following year, while sharing a studio with Henri. In turn, Glackens persuaded Luks, who previously had done only drawings, to attempt pastels and oils. Soon Luks was exuberantly claiming that he could paint "with a shoestring dipped in pitch and lard," a notion compatible with his ignorance of paint chemistry that later caused many of his pictures to crack.

Luks, who was raised in the Pennsylvania mining district, had a firsthand knowledge of the poverty-stricken miners who were the subjects of his early works. His shabby, unbeautified country people with their dirty animals shocked a public accustomed to the neat and tidy landscapes of the Barbizon masters. Later, like Sloan and Henri, Luks was most attracted by the life of the streets. Urging that art have "guts," he chose as subjects the derelicts and urchins of the poorest neighborhoods, or sweat-drenched athletes like *The Wrestlers* (*Ill. 1-1*).

For many years Sloan continued to consider himself a newspaperman who painted only as an avocation. As a teen-ager, he had worked for a print dealer, which gave him the opportunity to examine old-master prints. Finally the skill he developed as a draftsman and his eye for detail (he once copied all the illustrations in the dictionary) gained him a job as a newspaper artist-reporter.

In the decade between 1890 and 1900, before newspapers had adapted the photograph to the requirements of daily publications, artist-reporters, following in the footsteps of Winslow Homer, who had sketched Civil War battles, functioned as photographers do today. Rushing to fires, strikes, murders, mine disasters, and other sensational events, Sloan, Glackens, Luks, and Shinn recorded their perceptions on any available scrap of paper in a kind of visual shorthand. Encouraged by Henri to translate their sketches into paintings, they used to great advantage the rapid execution and spontaneous style they had developed as newspaper artists.

Adopting the reporter's coolness and lack of sentimentality, they considered picturesque details mere embroidery. Of the group, only Luks, in his unbridled admiration for Hals, chose to paint picaresque waifs and sad old crones. Yet despite their sympathy for liberal causes, their works carried no didactic social message other than a feeling for humanity in all of its possible conditions.

No matter how progressive their social views, the painting of The Eight remained essentially conservative: "Art" for them was remote, intellectual, and European, but "life"—vital, changing, and growing— was American. They could thus agree with Oscar Wilde's views on socialism while rejecting his plea for an art for art's sake, proclaiming, like Henri, the superiority of life over art.

Because of their newspaper experience, they were able to capture what the camera could record in a split-second snap of the shutter; they became expert as well at depicting figures in motion and the psychological nuances of gesture. Atmospheric effects, too, were observed and recorded. Gray was the prevailing tone of their paintings because it was the dominant tone of the city.

To John Sloan, the brilliant light of Impressionism, the reflections and momentary effects of sunlight, the optical mixtures of Seurat and his followers, seemed too limited because they appealed solely to the sense of sight. He dismissed such work as "eyesight painting."

Although the realists among The Eight worked often from on-the-spot sketches made during excursions to the country around Philadelphia, they were not *plein-air* painters like the Impressionists. The Americans spurned as "unreal" the light palette and colored shadows of the French. Their own paintings were composed and finished in the studio.

As artist-journalists, they depended a great deal on their ability to recall detail and worked hard at training their memories. Using routines learned from Horace de Boisbaudran's *Training of the Memory in Art,* they would play games to sharpen their perceptions. In a typical game, one member of the group would walk out of a room and then recite its contents from memory. Sometimes they followed strangers to observe and memorize their movements.

When the Charcoal Club disbanded in 1894, talk and sketching continued in Henri's studio. The group at 806 Walnut Street now included James Preston, Edward Davis (art editor of the *Philadelphia Press* and father of Stuart Davis), landscape painter Charles Redfield, and sculptor A. Stirling Calder (father of Alexander Calder). Often in the course of these sessions, Henri referred to *Talks on Art* by the painter William Morris Hunt. Specifically, Hunt's method emphasized the contrasting of highlights and shadows. Hunt insisted on the possibility of an independent American art, a radical notion in its time. Henri also quoted from George Moore's *Confessions of a Young Man* and from his book on art, which criticized those who admired the Salon painter Bouguereau instead of Manet. Many other writers were discussed too, including Whitman, Emerson, Ibsen, and Chekhov. Tolstoy's essay "What is Art?," which dealt with some of the social implications of art, was a frequent subject for discussion.

By 1898, Robert Henri, just married, had returned to Paris on his honeymoon; Glackens and Luks were in Cuba reporting the war with Spain; and Sloan had temporarily taken a job with a New York newspaper. That year the American Impressionists J. Alden Weir, John Twachtman, and Childe Hassam, along with a group of other malcontents, decided to exhibit together as the American Ten. They intended not so much to be revolutionary as to lure buyers who were ignoring native Impressionism in favor of Paris originals.

Henri, who had first painted in Paris a decade before, by now was

1-2. WILLIAM MERRITT CHASE, *An English Cod,* 1904.

reducing his compositions to a series of broadly painted figures, contrasted with equally simple silhouettes of cast shadows. Dramatic lighting provided strong oppositions of light and dark, and broad impasto brushstrokes sufficed to summarize a hand or a sleeve. Often just a single brushstroke could stand for a figure in the distance. Clearly this formula had nothing to do with the brilliantly colored, flat painting of Gauguin and Seurat, nor did it have anything in common with the highly structured compositions being painted by Cézanne. Thus, in 1899, when Henri decided to exhibit a recent painting, *Snow,* he submitted it not to the progressive Salon des Indépendants, but to the official Salon. Although it was rejected, the French Government subsequently purchased the work for the Luxembourg Museum—a triumph for an American.

During his trip, Henri saw the Goyas in Madrid. Goya's ability to capture the textures of flesh and fabrics in a few swift strokes only served to strengthen Henri's commitment to the loose painterly style he had already adopted. On his return to the United States, he settled in New York rather than in Philadelphia. Within the next few years, he was joined there by Glackens, Shinn, Luks, and finally Sloan. By 1904, as work became harder to get on the Philadelphia newspapers, all had migrated to New York. At this time Henri was an instructor at the New York School of Art, also known as the Chase School. Its founder, William Merritt Chase, himself a highly successful practitioner of John Singer Sargent's bravura technique, had a number of pupils, many as distinguished as Henri's. Among them were Charles Sheeler and Morton Schamberg, both of whom were to revolt against Chase's methods; and Charles Hawthorne, who worked for many years in his Provincetown studio, refining and tightening up Chase's slapdash style.

Although Henri's down-to-earth manner of speech and dress contrasted vividly with Chase's aristocratic airs, their painting styles were not very different. They differed mainly in their choice of subjects: Chase painted conventional portraits and still lifes, such as *An English Cod* (*Ill. 1-2*), while Henri chose unglamorized models and action scenes drawn from the life around him. But both Chase and Henri were insistent that the marks of excellence in painting were spontaneity and rapid execution. Chase was famous for his complete figure studies executed in three hours, from start to finish, standing before the assembled student body. Chase, however, emphasized "delicacy of detail," which he claimed was the "essence of art," while Henri believed that the camera could capture detail so well that the artist should concentrate on such subjective matters as the expression of the model and the communication of his own feelings.

Yet despite these differences of emphasis, neither painter had progressed far from the "slashing brush" attack and bravura manner of the Munich School. This broad painterly technique was popularized by Frank Duveneck in America at the end of the nineteenth century. And for Henri, the brushstroke, which could convey so many nuances of feeling, was still the basis for expression in painting. He would categorize strokes according to their function. The single stroke, he noted, might "render form in very wonderful variation"; the charged stroke might carry "the full swing of the body"; and the seemingly effortless stroke might give a look of ease and spontaneity even to a picture that had been "a perfect battle field in its making."[3] (On this score, Henri would often chide Sloan for working so long on a painting that he once described Sloan as the past tense of "slow.")

Much as Henri deprecated the superficiality of Chase's manner and the conventionality of his subjects, he still admired virtuoso painting in which a pyrotechnical display of highlights could mask a faulty if not nonexistent sense of form or structure. As Henri grew older, his technique in fact became looser and less structured, more dependent

1-3. WILLIAM GLACKENS, *Chez Mouquin*, 1905.

than ever on glittering surface effects. Of his former disciples, only Shinn continued to delight in showy effects at the expense of composition and form. The others rejected bravura painting. Around 1910, Glackens turned for guidance to the evenly textured surfaces of Renoir, while Sloan adopted the firm structured modeling of Cézanne. In time, Sloan was to become severely critical of his former mentor. "Facility is a dangerous thing," he warned. "Where there is too much technical ease the brain stops criticizing. Don't let the hand fall into a smart way of putting the mind to sleep."[4]

In New York, Sloan, Glackens, and Henri, together with their wives, often met for dinner at Mouquin's, the restaurant Glackens commemorated in his painting *Chez Mouquin* (*Ill. 1-3*). The restaurant proprietor, James Moore, sits at a table with one of his "daughters." Behind Moore, reflected in the mirror, can be seen Glackens' wife, Edith Dimock, and the critic Charles FitzGerald, who later became Glackens' brother-in-law. Both the mirrored images and the free execution of the painting suggest that Glackens was consciously paying homage to Manet's *Bar at the Folies Bergère*. Often joining the group at Mouquin's was Ernest Lawson, the soft-spoken Scot whom Glackens met just after moving to Washington Square in Greenwich Village. On a typical evening at the restaurant in 1904, they might have been discussing FitzGerald's article in the *Evening Sun* defending the first show at the National Arts Club, which the group, now known as the "New York Realists," dominated. Although their work generally had been dismissed as joyless and unhealthy, these former artist-reporters from Philadelphia were receiving some recognition in New York. By 1905, all had been accepted as members of the Society of American Artists, the year before that organization merged with the more conservative National Academy of Design. In addition, Glackens' *Chez Mouquin* and Sloan's *Coffee Line* won honorable mention at the Carnegie International, while Henri received an award from the Chicago Art Institute for his *Lady in Black*. But even though official acceptance seemed imminent, they still had to support themselves by teaching and illustrating.

When Henri was appointed a judge for the National Academy's 1907 spring exhibition, his friends were understandably elated. Their hopes were soon shattered, however, when they learned that Henri was unable to get the jury to accept any of the paintings by his friends Glackens, Luks, and Shinn or by his gifted students Rockwell Kent and Carl Sprinchorn. The final blow came when two of Henri's own

I-4. JOHN SLOAN,
*Hairdresser's Window*, 1907.

I-5. WILLIAM GLACKENS,
*The Shoppers*, 1908.

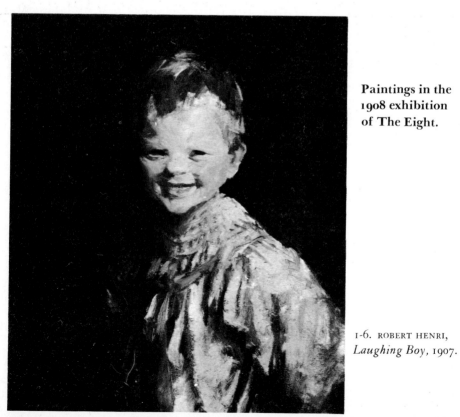

**Paintings in the
1908 exhibition
of The Eight.**

I-6. ROBERT HENRI,
*Laughing Boy*, 1907.

1-7. ERNEST LAWSON, *Winter on the River*, 1907.

1-8. GEORGE LUKS,
*Woman with Goose*, 1907.

canvases were given a "number 2" rating. This meant they were to be hung, not "on the line," which was the preferential position, but either above or below eye level. The furious Henri quickly withdrew his entries. He also gave an interview to *Putnam's* magazine in which he likened those artists who were rejected to other "creators of new art" who had offended official taste, such as Wagner, Walt Whitman, Degas, Manet, and Whistler. In rebuttal, the members of the Academy did not appoint Henri to the jury for the following year. They also denied membership to Ernest Lawson, Arthur B. Davies, and Jerome Myers. Since Lawson, who had studied with Twachtman, was an Impressionist and Davies a romantic in the nineteenth-century tradition, it was difficult to understand the Academy's reason for rejecting them, unless the old guard simply feared to relinquish its privilege to a younger generation.

Sloan and Glackens, angered by the Academy's slight to Henri and realizing that they too would not get their own work shown there, met with Henri to discuss the possibility of a cooperative exhibition to be financed by the artists themselves. An opportunity soon presented itself when William Macbeth, a friend of Davies, offered them exhibition space in his gallery, then the only one in New York that showed contemporary American work. They quickly accepted Macbeth's offer and invited Shinn, Luks, Davies, Lawson, and Maurice Prendergast (a Boston artist whose work Davies particularly admired) to participate with them in the show. FitzGerald, their eager propagandist, was probably responsible for the item that appeared in the *Evening Sun* announcing the exhibit. The item noted it was to be a show of eight artists who were often referred to by those who painted with "T-square and plumb line" as the "apostles of ugliness."

Although some came to jeer, the exhibition of The Eight held in February, 1908, at Macbeth's gallery was at least a qualified success. Macbeth soon ran out of catalogues and sold seven paintings for a grand total of $4,000. Included in the exhibition were Sloan's *Hairdresser's Window* (*Ill. 1-4*) and eight works by Glackens, including *Chez Mouquin, May Day, Central Park,* and *The Shoppers* (*Ill. 1-5*). Among those sold were Henri's *Laughing Boy* (*Ill. 1-6*), a Lawson winter landscape (*Ill. 1-7*), and Luks's *Woman with Goose* (*Ill. 1-8*). Glackens, Sloan, and Prendergast, however, did not sell a picture. For most of their lives, they were to have trouble with sales, although some years later Dr. Albert Barnes of Philadelphia began buying up their works in quantity. Since they were the most progressive artists of the group, their work was the most likely to outdistance contemporary taste.

Most of the criticism of the show related to the subject matter, which many thought not fit for the living room. "Is it fine art," one critic asked, "to exhibit our sores?" Davies' work was described as somewhere "between genius and insanity," while Henri was berated for his "streak of coarseness." Prendergast's bright, evenly lit Neo-Impressionist landscapes were called "explosions in a paint factory." These were more or less the same terms that critics had used some thirty-five years before when the Impressionists were first denounced. But the work the public found most outrageous was Luks's painting of pigs, although apart from its subject matter, it was an entirely conventional work. The exhibition as a whole was condemned for its "clashing dissonances of eight differently tuned orchestras." The works of the group were indeed heterogeneous: they included realistic cityscapes and genre scenes by Henri, Glackens, Sloan, Shinn, and Luks; quiet Impressionist landscapes by Lawson; the idyllic fantasies of Davies; and the strictly patterned compositions of Prendergast. This so-called dissonance was to set the pattern for later groups of American artists who showed together under no other banner save that of nonconformity.

The following year, Henri established his own art school on upper Broadway in the area where Lincoln Center now stands. Many of his loyal students at the New York School of Art followed him there, including Glenn O. Coleman, Guy Pène du Bois, Rockwell Kent, Carl Sprinchorn, George Bellows, and the young Edward Hopper. Among his students were also several artists who would become the first American modernists, such as Stanton Macdonald-Wright, Patrick Henry Bruce, and Stuart Davis, as well as the poet Vachel Lindsay and such realistic painters as Yasuo Kuniyoshi, Eugene Speicher, and Kenneth Hayes Miller. Near Henri's school, in a Bohemian quarter filled with actors, singers, and dancers, lived other young rebels like Walt Kuhn and Walter Pach. Many of the Bohemians were often recruited as models for the school. Even the playwright Eugene O'Neill frequented the quarter and lived in Bellows' studio during the winter of 1909.

As in the old days at 806 Walnut, Robert Henri was a focus for the energies of the young, stimulating them with his vigorous philosophy of freedom of expression. Often Henri quoted from a book Sloan had given him—a copy of Walt Whitman's *Leaves of Grass*—and inspired his students with Whitman's example of independence and courage.

I-9. JOHN SLOAN,
*The Cot*, 1907.

Sometimes he escorted his students to the Metropolitan Museum, where they could see Manet's *Boy with the Sword,* the *Woman with a Parrot* (*Ill. 1-18*), and the then recently acquired *Funeral.* He also took them to the theater to see performances of Chekhov and Ibsen given by the Moscow Art Players. Baseball games with Bellows at shortstop encouraged the spirit of easy camaraderie Henri cultivated at his school, where Teddy Roosevelt's Rough Riders were the ideal of physical fitness and tough virility.

Henri's students and friends, trained to wander the streets in search of subjects, began to paint the various ethnic quarters of New York, which in those years were bustling with new immigrants. Sloan especially was attracted to Coney Island, Union Square, and the Bowery; but he also enjoyed recording the homely melodramas he could observe from the rear window of his 23rd Street studio. In *The Cot* (*Ill. 1-9*), Sloan captures a slice-of-life fragment in a few broad strokes, achieving the economy of style and candor of treatment that were to distinguish his work.

Another typical Ash Can School subject, Everett Shinn's *Sixth Avenue Elevated After Midnight* (*Ill. 1-10*), evokes the forlorn quality of

I-10. EVERETT SHINN,
*Sixth Avenue Elevated
After Midnight,* 1899.

the city late at night. Shinn, the most flamboyant of The Eight, was drawn to music halls and theater scenes. In *Revue* (*Ill. I-11*), he uses a gay sprinkling of highlights to disguise what is an essentially superficial technique. George Bellows, a more solid painter, was also attracted to such spectacles. His painting *The Circus* (*Ill. 3-5*) records a moment of high action in the rapid notational manner of the quick sketch. Glackens, although surrounded by the beggars and low life who loitered around his Washington Square home, preferred, like Prendergast, to paint the happier scenes of the middle class enjoying itself in Central Park. Henri, Sloan, and Lawson loved the rivers in and around New York. Some of their best canvases depict the bleak winter grimness of these rivers and their slush-covered banks. For these

I-11. EVERETT SHINN,
*Revue,* 1908.

I-12. JOHN SLOAN,
*The Wake of the Ferry,*
1907.

painters, the drama of the New York skyline, with its big overhead constructions and steel bridges, so different from the picturesque bridges of the Seine, came to stand for the energy and dynamism of the city, as it would later for many other painters and poets. In *The Wake of the Ferry* (*Ill. I-12*), Sloan dramatically contrasts the dark silhouette of the boat in the foreground against the melancholy gray-

I-13. GEORGE LUKS, *Roundhouses at Highbridge,* 1909–10.

ness of the background sky and water. Luks was also capable of successfully rendering atmospheric effects in terms of tonal harmonies, as he demonstrates in his *Roundhouses at Highbridge* (*Ill. 1-13*).

Unlike the former newspaper artists, who chose their subject matter from the immediate contemporary milieu, Arthur B. Davies turned his back on such realities, inventing dreamy landscapes that were the antithesis of the industrial age. His twilight scenes of nymphs enveloped in mist, such as *Unicorns* (*Ill. 1-14*), are closer in spirit to the lyric allegories of Giorgione, or the reveries of Böcklin, than to any actual landscape.

Henri, seeking a means of exhibiting the work of his friends and pupils, and prompted by a new wave of rejections from the National Academy, set out to organize a second group show of independent artists. He had always been against juries, medals, and prizes because, as he pointed out, "great art cannot be measured." In this spirit, he helped Rockwell Kent plan an unjuried independent show to coincide with the Academy's spring exhibition in 1910. When the Independents' show opened in a large building on West 35th Street, hanging in the place of honor was Henri's portrait of his wife that the Academy had rejected. Exhibitors, in addition to The Eight, included Henri's students Bellows, Davis, Hopper, and Kent, along with more than 200 others. All their entries were democratically hung in alphabetical order. An hour after the opening, 1,000 people were inside the building; while outside in the street, a crowd of 1,500 had become so disorderly that the riot squad had to be summoned.

1-14. ARTHUR B. DAVIES, *Unicorns*, 1906.

I-15. WILLIAM GLACKENS, *Nude with Apple*, 1910.

The paintings were attacked by critics much in the same way that Manet's work had been in 1863. Sloan's *Three A.M.* was considered "too frank and vulgar"; Glackens' *Nude with Apple* (*Ill. I-15*) was called coarse and wooden. And Prendergast, the critics said, couldn't draw properly. But the number of viewers jamming the exhibition demonstrated that the revolt of The Eight had been successful. Because similar attacks had been made on Manet, however, the temptation has been to equate the revolt of The Eight with that of the avant-garde French artists against the French Academy. Actually, the two revolts were not analogous. The revolt of The Eight was not an aesthetic one, as the French avant-garde protest had been. Yet their rebellion was needed to clear the air and to renew American contact with the main-stream of European art, even if it was the mainstream of fifty years earlier.

Henri, blind or hostile to Renoir, Matisse, and Picasso, admired, among the modernists, only Rouault and a few of Cézanne's works. The old masters who inspired him were not the creators of a classical formal order like Uccello or Piero della Francesca, but those like Hals and Goya whose work showed a surface brilliance and emotional sympathy for humanity. Eventually, of course, Henri brightened his murky palette, and the others lightened theirs too. Glackens arrived at a high-colored Impressionism, and Davies converted his idyllic dancers into bright Cubist mannequins. However, with the exception of Prendergast, America's first modernist, only Sloan struggled (unsuccessfully in the eyes of many) to grasp the fundamental concepts of modernism. This was ironic since Sloan was the only member of The Eight who had not studied in Europe. Henri, Prendergast, Davies, Glackens, and Shinn had all worked in Paris. Luks, who studied mainly in Germany, also visited Paris. As their careers progressed, it became clear that the orientation of Shinn, Glackens, and Prendergast was mainly French, while Henri and Luks continued to look to Hals for inspiration. Shinn was indebted to Degas, Glackens to the later Manet and Renoir, and Prendergast—alone among the group—to Cézanne and Seurat.

Of The Eight, only Prendergast, who was never a realist or a pupil of Henri, kept pace with the developments of Neo-Impressionism. First

1-16. MAURICE PRENDERGAST, *Piazza di San Marco, ca.* 1898.

31

impressed by the Venetian painters on a trip to Venice in 1898, he painted sunny water colors of the canals and piazzas, such as the *Piazza di San Marco* (*Ill. 1-16*). In Paris, however, he abandoned these conventional compositions in favor of the flattened, artificial space of the Nabis, whose brilliant, decorative patterns inspired by Gauguin's Pont-Aven paintings were the talk of the Parisian art world. Like the young Vuillard, Prendergast broke up his dry, chalky surfaces into a mosaiclike pattern of spots and dabs. Discarding conventional perspective and modeling through chiaroscuro, in *The Promenade* (*Ill. 1-17*), he united foreground and background in a single continuous plane, as the most advanced French painters were doing. In fact, even before Prendergast saw the work of Cézanne, Seurat, and the Nabis, he was already inclined toward the flat and the decorative. For years he had been a clerk in a Boston dry-goods store and in the process had become familiar with the flat patterns of printed fabrics. And one cannot discount either the impression made upon him by the stylized patterns of the inlaid chests his brother Charles built. (The brothers lived together for many years, first in Boston; then after 1914, in New York.)

More typical of the American misunderstanding of the basic concepts of European modernism with its nonillusionistic space and abstract patterning was Sloan's earnest struggle. Early in his career, Sloan had shown an interest in two-dimensional design as it was applied in Japanese prints. These prints were a main source of the new space and perspective of Impressionist paintings. But Sloan's naive interpretation of the Japanese masters revealed how inadequate his understanding was of their concepts of space and pattern. His interpretations, in contrast with the sophisticated adaptations of Manet and Van Gogh, only clothed the old Western conventions in Japanese guise. They were as modern and as convincing as a Gibson girl in a kimono. Henri, also enthusiastic about Japanese art (he introduced Sloan to the Japanese Commissioner of the 1893 Chicago Fair), was even less adventurous: He went no further than hanging Japanese lanterns in his studio.

Sloan's obtuseness to the way in which Japanese prints offered an alternative to Western conventions was typical of the inability of American artists to grasp what was radical in the European modern movements. In a similar fashion, much as Henri admired Manet, he saw in him only his broadness of technique and a new way of placing a single large figure in a dark void, unbroken by a floor line, so that the figure would appear enveloped in space. In every sense, Henri's

1-17. MAURICE PRENDERGAST, *The Promenade,* 1913.

works based on Manet, like the portrait of his wife, *The Masquerade Dress* (*Ill. 1-19*), are more conventional than their fifty-year-old prototypes.

But if The Eight were not the aesthetic rebels they have been made out to be, at least they were fighters. They introduced a healthy vitality into American art, proclaiming its independence, and raising the possibility of rejecting European models. Against polish, sophistication, contrivance, and finish, they established as their goals candor, immediacy, and directness—the goals adopted by future generations of American

1-18. EDOUARD MANET, *Woman with a Parrot,* 1866.

1-19. ROBERT HENRI, *The Masquerade Dress: Portrait of Mrs. Robert Henri,* 1911.

artists. Tolerant of stylistic deviations from any norm, they were tolerant of eccentric behavior as well. In such an open, unrestrictive atmosphere American art, freed from the hypocrisies of official taste and academic juries, could flourish and develop.

Because the beginnings of American modernism had such popular sources as newspaper illustration and political cartooning, when the time came for a genuine aesthetic revolt, such a revolt was carried out not against any academic notion of style, but against a provincial, illustrational art, which had in turn become officially entrenched.

# Chapter Two

# The Largest Small Room in the World

The idea of Secession is hateful to the Americans—they'll be thinking of the Civil War.

—ALFRED STIEGLITZ, *Twice a Year*, 1942

While Henri and his "black gang" in their successful *putsch* against the National Academy exalted the primacy of life over art, the aesthetic revolution that marks the beginning of American modernism was gathering force under the aegis of art for art's sake. This palace revolt took place in what Marsden Hartley described as "the largest small room of its kind in the world." The room was the attic of the brownstone at 291 Fifth Avenue where the photographer Alfred Stieglitz presided over exhibitions of paintings and photographs. With the painter and photographer Edward Steichen, Stieglitz had founded the Little Gallery of the Photo-Secession in 1905 to show photographs. In 1907 he expanded its program to include paintings with an exhibition of the works of Pamela Colman Smith.

By naming his gallery "Photo-Secession," Stieglitz deliberately invoked the spirit of the modernists who called themselves "Secessionists" in Germany and Austria. According to Stieglitz, "Photo-Secession actually means seceding from the accepted idea of what constitutes a photograph."[1] Similarly, the painting and sculpture eventually shown at 291 seceded from the accepted ideas of what constituted art, especially in America. During the decade in which 291 was a center for avant-garde art, Stieglitz presented the first American exhibitions of Matisse (1908), Toulouse-Lautrec (1909), Rousseau (1910), Picabia (1913), and Severini (1917). In April, 1911, 291 exhibited drawings and water colors by Picasso showing his complete evolution through Cubism, and in March, 1914, Stieglitz gave Brancusi his first one-man show anywhere. Stieglitz was responsible for the first exhibition of chil-

2-1. OSCAR BLUEMNER,
*Old Canal Port,* 1914.

dren's art and the first major exhibition of Negro sculpture. Among the
American painters he introduced were Alfred Maurer and John Marin
(1909); Marsden Hartley, Max Weber, Arthur Dove, and Arthur B.
Carles (in a group show in 1910); Abraham Walkowitz (1912); Oscar
Bluemner (1915); the sculptor Elie Nadelman (1915); Georgia
O'Keeffe (1916) and Stanton Macdonald-Wright (1917).

Although 1908 is remembered as the year in which The Eight held
their historic exhibition, other events mark it as a signal year in
American art. In that year, the socialite sculptress Gertrude Vanderbilt
Whitney, purchaser of four of the seven paintings sold by The Eight at
Macbeth's, opened the Whitney Studio. Here, in her MacDougal Alley
studio, young artists could gather informally to discuss their work.
A friend of Henri and Davies, Mrs. Whitney covered the deficit of
the Independents' show and held exhibitions in her studio and later
at the small museum she opened on Eighth Street in 1914, which
eventually became the Whitney Museum of American Art.

In January, 1908, Stieglitz showed fifty-eight drawings by Auguste
Rodin at 291. This was the first exhibition of a modern artist in
America. Beginning with this show, Stieglitz, aided by Steichen, who
spent much time in Europe acting as his contact, introduced the bewildered American public to European modernism. At the same time
he continued to nurture and promote the emerging American avant-
garde.

During the years just preceding World War I, when Stieglitz sponsored this series of remarkable exhibitions, many of the American
artists he exhibited were in Europe, mainly in Paris. In 1908, for exam-

2-2. ARTHUR B. CARLES,
*L'Eglise, ca.* 1910.

ple, there was a sufficient number of American artists in Paris to warrant founding a New Society of American Artists in Paris. Among its members were Steichen, Max Weber, Alfred Maurer, and Patrick Henry Bruce. Thus, when Steichen reported to Stieglitz on the new developments in Paris, he mentioned not only Picasso's first Cubist works and Matisse's Fauve paintings, but also the work of the Americans Alfred Maurer and John Marin. During the explosive first decade of the century, the young Americans frequented the annual Salon des Indépendants and the Salon d'Automne, where they saw retrospectives of Van Gogh, Gauguin, and Cézanne, as well as the work of Matisse and his friends Braque, Derain, and Vlaminck, who had been called *les Fauves* because of their wild colors. In Gertrude Stein's living room, they could see paintings by Cézanne, Picasso, and Matisse, and perhaps meet Picasso and Matisse, whose works she was among the first to buy. When, in 1907, Matisse inaugurated a painting class, several Americans, including Patrick Henry Bruce and Max Weber, were among his first pupils.

Other Americans in Paris included the figure painter Bernard Karfiol, and the future Fauvists Samuel Halpert, Oscar Bluemner, and Arthur B. Carles. In Bluemner's *Old Canal Port (Ill. 2-1)* and Carles's *L'Eglise (Ill. 2-2)*, one can see how profoundly impressed the young Americans were by Matisse's vision of bold drawing and brilliant color. Also in Paris during the first decade of the century were the future Cubists Maurice Sterne, Marguerite and William Zorach, John Covert, Preston Dickinson, and Andrew Dasburg. The founders of Synchromism, Morgan Russell and Stanton Macdonald-Wright, were there, too, as were Charles Sheeler and Charles Demuth, who would put their knowledge of Cubism to a distinctively American use.

Stieglitz described his mission as "trying to establish for myself an America in which I could breathe as a free man." This was opposite to the point of view of a whole generation of expatriate writers and artists who, rather than face America's philistine hostility to modernism in any form, fled to where the air was already free. Some, like T. S. Eliot, exiled themselves permanently, whereas others, whose careers Malcolm Cowley has chronicled in *Exile's Return,* straggled back when the climate of resistance became less harsh. Stieglitz was constantly in touch with many of the expatriates, often giving them space in *Camera Work* before they appeared elsewhere. He was also in close contact with Gertrude Stein (whom he was first to publish) and her brothers Michael and Leo, who provided a base of operations for Americans in Paris. Those writers who, like the artists Stieglitz supported, sought to treat American subjects in the new language of modernism, were naturally at home at 291 and at Stieglitz' subsequent galleries. These writers were in search of a more direct language, just as the painters Stieglitz showed were in search of a more direct form of visual communication.

In contrast with Henri, whose single cause was American art, Stieglitz was equally devoted to modern art and to American art. That there was rivalry between the leaders of the two main art factions is revealed by contemporary accounts. In April, 1910, when the Society of Independent Artists held their first exhibition, Stieglitz presented his first group show of American modernists at 291. Included were paintings by Dove, Marin, Maurer, and Weber. A review in *Camera Work* castigated the Independents, warning them "you'll never beat the Academy at its own stupid game by substituting quantity for quality!"

To the Stieglitz group Henri and his friends were conventional if not retarded. Henri, on the other hand, found Stieglitz' "ultramodernism" faddish, and since it was unintelligible to the majority, undemocratic. But no one, least of all Stieglitz, would argue that 291 was democratic. "Life" might appeal to the masses, but "art," as Stendhal had pointed out earlier, was for the sensitive, the enlightened, the committed—"the happy few." And it was to the happy few that Stieglitz addressed himself. The audience for the art he showed was miniscule; it consisted mainly of the artists Stieglitz supported and the few writers like Van Wyck Brooks, Waldo Frank, Jerome Mellquist,

Randolph Bourne, and Lewis Mumford, who enjoyed the cozy familiarity of the back room at 291. Perhaps one of the reasons that 291 so little changed the general course of American art was that Stieglitz enjoyed his role of patriarch in a family situation to such a degree that he overprotected his brood from a misunderstanding public. For some, the group spirit of 291 was cultish and arty, whereas for members of the inner circle, 291 was, in the words of the photographer Paul Haviland, "a trinity; a place, a person and a symbol . . . a laboratory where experiments are conducted in order to find out something."[2]

Stieglitz himself aroused similar controversy. An enemy described him as "the kind of man who sits when others stand and stands when others sit"; but Oscar Bluemner spoke of him as the man who had renewed his faith in America, "a missionary in blackest Fifth Avenue, a pioneer battling with the white Indians of obsolete New York." To which Stieglitz replied, not quite convincingly, "I am nobody."[3] For Waldo Frank, Stieglitz was one of the great teachers in line with Socrates, Paul of Tarsus, and Karl Marx. Perhaps more judiciously, Ralph Flint described him as "a master technician, a poet, a seer, a practical student of the humanities, a fighter, a sportsman (without a sport), a rare friend, an acknowledged philosopher and guide."

Messiah or false prophet, in any event, Stieglitz was the antithesis of Henri, and 291 represented a viewpoint at odds with that of The Eight and the Independents. Thus, the polarization of nonacademic painters in America into two groups, a socially oriented faction and an avant-garde faction—which has endured more or less until the present —was already an accomplished fact early in the twentieth century. But both factions played necessary roles. Henri's democratic, nationalistic stance was necessary to give American art a broad enough base from which to work, to the same degree that Stieglitz' insistence on quality was needed in order to set a standard. For, however thoughtful and widely read Henri may have been, he was no intellectual. His notion of culture was closer to that of the American consensus than to Stieglitz' more sophisticated and worldly views. It stopped short at the point at which modern art begins—the point at which the artist, compelled by inner necessity and finding himself no longer in agreement with the values and goals of the society at large, retreats into himself in order to transcribe his own inner vision.

Henri's position made it possible for the artist to reject academic practice and official taste without embracing the modern attitude or any of its implications. It offered a third choice to American artists who were as repelled by Post-Impressionism as they were by Neoclassicism. This middle road, always beloved by the majority, many artists found comfortable and attractive.

Stieglitz, on the other hand, was not only an intellectual, but an aesthete. Like Henri, he too derived his views from nineteenth-century sources. But Stieglitz' sources were precisely those new ideas which supplanted realism. The ideas Stieglitz subscribed to were those of the artist who seceded from society, refusing to address any public larger than himself and his peers. In a sense, Henri's egalitarianism reflected one aspect of the American character: that celebrated by Whitman in his optimistic populist poems. Stieglitz' fierce independence and relentless defense of the extreme and the radical were representative of another, equally important, aspect: the introspective individualism and spiritual intensity of Thoreau, who chose to isolate himself from society, acknowledging no authority other than his own conscience. Like Thoreau, those closest to Stieglitz—Marin, Hartley, Dove, and O'Keeffe—all eventually sought refuge in nature from the superficial materialism of the city and the diversions of social life. For them, Thoreau's *Walden* might easily have served as a handbook for daily living, or even as the philosophic guide Thoreau intended it to be.

In other respects, too, the cosmopolitan group that gathered at 291 differed from Henri's rough-and-tumble band. A number, like Weber, Walkowitz, Bluemner, Nadelman, and Stella, were of European origin. This contrast is intensified by a comparison of Stieglitz' and Henri's backgrounds: Henri, fresh from the frontier just recently closed, became the partisan of democracy in art; Stieglitz, the Berlin-educated son of German-Jewish parents, emerged as the champion of the elite and the avant-garde. Yet in actual practice, Stieglitz was more tolerant than Henri. He insisted that he would show the academicians if they had no other place to exhibit; Henri could never admit the virtues of the "ultra moderns." Yet these two radically divergent personalities who dominated American art in the first decades of the century shared certain ideals. Both encouraged artists to break with the Academy and to work independently; both were uncompromising in their disregard for fashion and public approval and in their encouragement of young artists. And both were artists themselves, as well as educators. However, Stieglitz was an artist of the first rank, an innovator (who changed the history of photography), which Henri was not.

Stieglitz was the first to admit that he had been converted by the

2-3. MAX WEBER, *Figure Study,* 1911.

artists whose champion he became. Under their influence he altered not only his views but also his art. His early photographs are masterpieces of mood and tonal harmony, easily comparable in theme and treatment to the paintings of The Eight. Indeed, Stieglitz' first attacks on the conservative photographic salons resembled Henri's assaults on the Academy to the degree that the photographers of the Photo-Secession were called the Mop and Pail Brigade, as The Eight were later classified as the Ash Can School. Through his conversion to the modernist aesthetic, however, Stieglitz came to believe in the right of the picture to speak for itself, without being subjected to total exhaustion through verbalization. At the same time he conceived of photography as an increasingly abstract medium, in which images are divorced from any other than formal meaning. Inspired by painting, Stieglitz achieved a confluence of the abstract and the concrete which in turn would influence painters.

Although Stieglitz went back and forth to Europe four times between 1904 and 1911, his contact with Max Weber and Abraham Walkowitz, who returned from Paris in 1910, helped to sharpen Stieglitz' eye. Weber, one of the first to recognize the Douanier Rousseau's gifts, had assimilated Cézanne's message almost as quickly as Picasso himself. His nudes of 1910–11 (*Ill. 2-3*), although derivative of Cézanne and Picasso, are remarkable for their acute comprehension of Cubist composition, which was willing to distort reality in the interests of a greater formal coherence. Weber's erudition impressed Stieglitz who remembered that Weber had a knowledge of art only equaled in America by Arthur B. Davies.

Like Georgia O'Keeffe, Weber had the good fortune to study with Arthur Wesley Dow, who taught that art resides in harmonious spacing. In Paris, Weber and his friend Samuel Halpert admired the brilliant colors of the Fauves; Halpert became skilled at imitating Braque's Fauve style in such paintings as *Brooklyn Bridge* (*Ill. 2-4*). Weber was far more original; although he continued to use high color, he embodied it in a Cubist framework. He insisted that "There can be no color without there being a form, in space and in light with substance and weight, to hold the color. I prefer a form, even if it is in black and white, rather than a *tache* of formless color."[4]

Wandering through the Louvre and studying the Oriental art at the Musée Guimet, Weber trained his eye to detect the qualities held in common by Eastern and Western art, by the old masters, primitive artists, and decorative artists. Back in New York, Weber frequented the Museum of Natural History where he found "Chinese dolls, Hopi Katchinas images, and also Indian quilts and blankets . . . much finer in color than the works of modern painter-colorists."[5] These may have been the sources for the abstract patterns of his Cubist paintings on city themes, such as *Chinese Restaurant* (*Ill. 2-5*), and for his original palette of yellows, faded reds, and blacks, and rich full colors. Like most of Stieglitz' artists, Weber was on the edge of poverty. He even

2-4. SAMUEL HALPERT,
*Brooklyn Bridge,*
1913.

2-5. MAX WEBER,
*Chinese Restaurant,*
1915.

camped out for a time in 291. When Stieglitz showed his Cubist figure studies in 1910, Willard Huntington Wright denounced them as derivative. "All the moderns seem to be here," he observed, "but where are the Webers?" After a series of brilliantly evocative Cubist abstractions celebrating the city, Weber began in 1917 to look inward. He moved to Long Island where he painted scenes remembered from childhood, such as *Adoration of the Moon* (*Ill. 2-6*), personal fantasies of grave Talmudists, wistful rabbis, and ceremonial scenes, much as

2-6. MAX WEBER,
*Adoration of the Moon,*
1944.

2-7. ABRAHAM WALKOWITZ, *Bathers*, 1910.

Chagall, in exile in Paris, commemorated the scenes of his Russian childhood.

Abraham Walkowitz was also a product of the immigrant ghetto culture who found his way to Paris. Jerome Myers described him as the "John the Baptist of pre-Armory days, returning from Paris to preach the gospel of modern art." Interested in children's drawings, he captured the naive freshness of the child's vision in his sketches of

2-8. ABRAHAM WALKOWITZ, *New York*, 1917.

2-9. ABRAHAM WALKOWITZ, *Dance Rhythms, ca.* 1920.

subway diggers and workers and in his water colors of bathers (*Ill. 2-7*). After drawing some notice with his restless studies of sky-scrapers effaced in a tangle of lines (*Ill. 2-8*) and of Rodin-like dancers, Walkowitz faded into obscurity during the twenties, when he was do-ing some of his most original work. This consisted of abstract line drawings based on figures in motion which dissolved into disembodied rhythmic swirls of interpenetrating lines (*Ill. 2-9*).

Many years later, Walkowitz described his meeting with Stieglitz, to whom Hartley had introduced him: "I used to come into the Gallery at 10:00 and stay until 10:00 at night. . . . Stieglitz's place was an organization where all the artists, musicians, critics would come together. . . . It was an outlet for all ideas."[6] But, no matter how sympathetic Stieglitz was to the various artists he exhibited, his deepest commitment was to the native Americans in his gallery who attempted to give an indigenous expression to modernism. O'Keeffe, Marin, Hartley, and Dove were to claim his strongest loyalties.

In 1916 Stieglitz was shown a roll of sketches by a young woman art teacher. The delicacy of these charcoal drawings moved Stieglitz to exclaim, "finally a woman on paper!" He included ten of them in a group show in May. But O'Keeffe, who had recently returned to New York to continue her study with Dow, ordered him to remove them. Soon, however, they were able to agree. Stieglitz became her dealer and later her husband, and O'Keeffe became the model for some of Stieglitz' most inspired photographs. Rebelling against her early training at the Art Students League, O'Keeffe developed a highly personal vocabulary of forms derived from nature, and an equally personal sense of color, based on the subtle contrasts and massing of tones that Dow counseled. Although her paintings were praised as embodying the feminine principle, O'Keeffe declined to decipher their literal meaning, in a syntax reminiscent of Gertrude Stein, "I found I could say things with color and shapes that I couldn't say in any other way— things that I had no words for. Some of the wise men say it is not painting, some of them say it is. Art or not Art—they disagree. Some of them do not care."[7] Earlier, Stieglitz had insisted that images were not translatable into words. Dove, too, maintained that painting "should necessitate no effort to understand." Marin may have expressed their attitude most succinctly in advice to a friend: "Don't everlastingly read messages into paintings—there's the Daisy—you don't rave over or read messages into it—you just look at that bully little flower— isn't that enough!"[8]

O'Keeffe, enlarging flowers until they filled the entire canvas with their voluptuous curving petals and tendrils, created a private world in which natural forms were adapted or transformed to express a lyric vision, and real objects became the vehicles for poetic fantasy. Her strange, grayed palette, with its dark greens and muted violets, as well as the degree of simplification and isolation of images from any identifying context, served to heighten the dream-like quality of a work like *Portrait W, No. II* (*Ill. 2-11*). Like Marin, Hartley, and Dove, O'Keeffe found in nature symbolic equivalents for inner emotional states. She did not think of abstracting from nature but of symbolizing nature's generative force. In *Black Spot, No. 2* (*Ill. 2-10*) she evokes landscape without referring to any specific landscape. Stieglitz, too, subscribed to this Symbolist method, calling his photographs "equivalents," in the same spirit that Dove had referred to his series of paintings of 1911–14 as "Nature Symbolized" (*Ill. 2-23*).

Beginning in the late twenties, when O'Keeffe moved to New Mexico and began finding her subjects in the landscapes of the Southwest or in simple architectural forms, her art, like that of Hartley, Dove, and Stella, became more mystical and visionary. In quivering land-

2-10. GEORGIA O'KEEFFE, *Black Spot, No. 2,* 1919.

47

2-11. GEORGIA O'KEEFFE, *Portrait W, No. II*, 1917.

scapes, such as *Red Hills and the Sun* (*Ill. 2-12*), nature is imbued with a pantheistic, transcendental life of its own.

O'Keeffe's later work is increasingly majestic and monumental. A single image—a bleached, desiccated animal skull contrasted with the rich coloration of flowers in bloom, or smooth pelvic bones through which brilliant sky is seen—fills the entire space. Although the strangeness of these images, which deal with death, suggests certain analogies

2-12. GEORGIA O'KEEFFE,
*Red Hills and the Sun,*
1927.

with Surrealism, the images are quite comprehensible within the terms
of her own development as an artist. In more recent paintings, such as
*Patio with Cloud* (*Ill. 2-13*), O'Keeffe has leaned toward a greater ab-
stractness of design, without, however, compromising her original
commitment to nature.

O'Keeffe's independence and personal struggle made her a symbol
of "the new woman." Like Isadora Duncan—the image of uninhibited
womanhood for artists like Sloan and Walkowitz who painted her—
O'Keeffe, too, was seen as the newly liberated, unconventional modern
woman. Modern woman became increasingly popular as a subject for
painters at exactly the moment when American women first asserted
themselves in the Suffragette movement (in which artists like Glack-

2-13. GEORGIA O'KEEFFE,
*Patio with Cloud,* 1956.

ens and Sloan became personally involved). But the reaction was clearly ambivalent; was modern woman, in terms of the dichotomy of Henry Adams, the Virgin or the Dynamo? Davies saw her as the former, elevating her to the majestic status of the "Great Mother," whereas the Dadaists Duchamp and Picabia portrayed her as an animated machine, the bitch goddess of the dynamo.

Like the attitude of artists toward women during this transitional period, the American attitude toward sexuality and its representation in art was at best ambivalent. The Puritan downgrading of the life of the senses—even leisure was considered a sin—had so colored American life that writers like William Carlos Williams studied it as a special problem, perhaps the central problem of American culture. At a time when D. H. Lawrence's radical endorsement of sexual life as a positive good was rocking the literary world, a writer like Lewis Mumford saw Alfred Stieglitz as a secular saviour of the instinctual life in America. According to Mumford, because the "mechanical ideology . . . had limited the provinces of the senses, and confined its operations to a blind world of matter and motion . . . it was necessary to open up once more all the avenues of human experience: to sharpen the eye, quicken the touch, refine the senses of smell and taste, as a preliminary to restoring to wholeness the dwarfed and amputated personalities that had been produced. . . ."[9] In a particularly Lawrencian moment, Mumford saw Stieglitz' photographs of horses as symbols of animal vitality and his women as symbols of animal spirituality. Paul Rosenfeld, too, spoke of "all the intensity of the terrific psychic and sexual conflicts following the multiple appearance of the determinately individual woman."[10]

Stieglitz, and the artists closest to him, O'Keeffe, Marin, and Dove, intended their work to convey a specifically sexual charge, although this aim was not part of a formalized program. They believed that the creative life was tied to the life of the senses. Social progress, they thought, would issue from sensual liberation, without which there could be no aesthetic appreciation. The question of whether the repressive, inhibiting antivisual aspect of the Puritan legacy had permanently crippled the American ability to have an aesthetic experience was asked more than once. For example, the unabashed eroticism of Rodin's drawings caused half the subscribers of *Camera Work* to cancel their subscriptions when Stieglitz published several in 1911. Paul Rosenfeld's description of Stieglitz' "intensely symbolical" photographic images show an understanding of O'Keeffe's, Marin's, and

Dove's intentions as well: "The images are spontaneous, complete transpositions into the visual and tactile field of the ineffable sensuous unities, ordinations, wholes and worlds. . . . In the form of relationships of shape and line and color they symbolize the harmonies of living matter, restlessly yearning, aspiring, struggling to reach beyond itself the cosmic order concurrent with those yearnings, insurgencies, ecstatic leaps. . . ."[11] The sense of the hidden forces in the subconscious and nature struggling to realize themselves, of the "sublime" as an aspect of American romanticism, unites Stieglitz and his friends to later American painters who sought to externalize these hidden forces in their equally romantic art. Similarly, the return to nature of Stieglitz' most devoted followers hints at the future conflicts of nature versus the city, the human versus the mechanical, which would dominate American art for the next two decades.

John Marin, like Georgia O'Keeffe, found his introduction to modernism through the medium of Oriental art. When he left for France in 1905, Whistler's misty, tonal art was his ideal. By the time he returned from Austria in 1911, he was painting transparent landscapes with an economy, airiness, and spaciousness reminiscent of the old Chinese masters of the brush. The ellisions in his paintings, which parallel the elliptical style of his many letters to Stieglitz, are particularly radical in American painting, which errs in telling too much rather than too little. They seem an answer to the critic Sadakichi

2-14. JOHN MARIN,
*Brooklyn Bridge*, 1910.

2-15. JOHN MARIN, *Tree Forms,
Stonington, Maine,* 1919.

2-16. JOHN MARIN, *Region of Brooklyn Bridge Fantasy,* 1932.

Hartmann's plea for an art that is partial, allusive, and fragmentary, an art capable of subtlety and nuance.

Taking as his model Cézanne's sparse, tinted water colors, Marin allowed areas of white canvas to remain bare. Usually the image, a landscape or cityscape, was not painted out to the edge, but floated in the center, adding to the sense of weightlessness and buoyancy. Marin preferred to qualify his works, not as complete statements but as "pertaining to" a particular scene such as *Region of Brooklyn Bridge Fantasy (Ill. 2-16).* In his partial, suggestive views of New York and the Maine coast *(Ills. 2-14, 2-15),* his two principal themes, he modified Cubism; although objects were fragmented and broken into facets, they were not shattered completely.

In 1914, Marin discovered that the Maine coast and the White Mountains could provide a subject as spectacular as the Alps. Moving gradually eastward, by the twenties he was painting the little islands *(Ill. 2-17)* and lighthouses off Stonington. From this point on, Marin's style—remarkable for its unity and light touch—crystallized; although it grew richer, it did not change much in later years as he continued to find new interpretations for his familiar themes.

Unlike Cubist painters, Marin was interested in capturing atmospheric effects. Air circulates through his paintings, waves are churned by wind, lines bordering facets are often rays of sunlight. Both the transparency of his paint—he even used oil with the fluidity and freshness of water color—and the looseness of his structures, which often explode or are tilted expressionistically, differentiate Marin's space from orthodox Cubist space. His notion of space was based on an understanding of spatial tensions and balances. "As my body exerts a downward pressure on the floor, the floor in turn exerts an upward pressure on my body," he observed, and he wished to express the impact of such forces acting against one another in space. The image he chose was thus not static, but one of a restless world of movement and flux. To those who did not understand the emptiness of his canvases, he explained: "a few *seemingly* careless lines—a few seeming daubs of color—if handled so that the whole constitutes a living thing—well—that would be a workmanlike job too. . . ." In his search for pictorial unity, Marin understood structure as a single factor based on a few decisive axes or backbones; "as the backbones bend—the whole structure bends," he maintained.[12]

Marsden Hartley's early works were influenced by the Italian Impressionist Segantini, rather than by the French artists shown by

2-17. JOHN MARIN, *Maine Islands,* 1922.

2-18. MARSDEN HARTLEY,
*Mountain Lake,*
*Autumn, ca.* 1908.

Stieglitz. In landscapes painted in 1908, such as *Mountain Lake, Autumn (Ill. 2-18)*, Hartley began using Segantini's "stitch," a small, even embroiderylike stroke, to fill in a richly colored canvas. However, the darkly brooding "black mountain" landscapes of 1910, exhibited in his first one-man show at 291, seem close to Ryder's melancholy vision and are more prophetic of his later work.

In 1912, Hartley went to Paris, financed by Stieglitz. The following year he found himself in Berlin, where he met the members of the Blue Rider group, the German Expressionists who used Fauve color in an emotional rather than a decorative style. In the turbulent, sometimes violently distorted art of the German Expressionists Hartley found a spirit in keeping with his own intense nature. Although he denied having been influenced by Kandinsky, leader of the Blue Rider group, Hartley's landscapes of 1913, with their jagged forms and floating mountains, are reminiscent of Kandinsky's early abstractions. The symbolic ram in *Forms Abstracted (Ill. 2-19)* reminds one of a similar use of animal motifs by Franz Marc, another member of the Blue Rider group.

As sympathetic as Hartley was to the subjectivity of Expressionism, the notion of abstracting from nature was alien to his outlook. Like many twentieth-century American artists, Hartley tended to view reality either in literal or else in Symbolist terms. Thus even the abstract works, like the series of 1915 landscapes based on the theme of

"Amerika," have an emblematic quality that makes them unlike Kandinsky's abstractions.

After a brief trip to the United States, Hartley returned to Berlin in 1914. He found Kaiser Wilhelm's Germany, on the brink of World War I, in a military mood. In this atmosphere Hartley painted perhaps his most brilliant pictures, a series of still lifes based on German military emblems, such as *Painting, Number 5* (*Ill. 2-20*). Reviving a modified version of the Segantini "stitch," which gave a kind of uniform pulsating beat to the brushwork, he painted arrangements of badges, ensigns like the Iron Cross and the German imperial flag, and epaulettes in strong reds, blues, and greens, set against dramatic blacks and whites. Flattened out and locked together, these objects became the basis for an imprecise, intuitive geometry; the stripes of a flag became abstract bands, and contours were reduced to rough repeated arcs. In such a scheme, more abstract and tightly knit than that of the German Expressionists, yet freer than that of the Cubists, Hartley was able to combine the expressive with the highly structured in a remarkable synthesis, not strictly Expressionist or Cubist. This ability to deal decoratively with patterns such as the checkerboard or the zig-zag was probably aided by his close study of American Indian arts, and perhaps of the Coptic textiles he admired. A constant interest in decorative art may also explain his continued use of the "stitch" stroke which simulates the parallel threads of embroidered textiles.

2-19. MARSDEN HARTLEY,
*Forms Abstracted*, 1913.

2-20. MARSDEN HARTLEY, *Painting, Number 5*, 1914–15.

2-21. MARSDEN HARTLEY, *New Mexico Recollections, No. 11*, 1922–23.

Back in the United States, Hartley abandoned the hot Expressionist palette, and began to paint delicate Cubist abstractions in pastel colors. Executed in 1916–17, these were his last abstract paintings (*Ill. 4-5*). In 1918–20 Hartley produced a series of pastels based on the dramatic mountains, canyons, and gorges of Taos and Santa Fe. After he left New Mexico, these memories of the heroic landscapes and desert sunsets served him as subjects in such paintings as *New Mexico Recollections, No. 11* (*Ill. 2-21*). A wanderer for the next decade, Hartley shuttled back and forth between France, Germany, and New England. In 1926 he settled in Aix-en-Provence, where Cézanne had lived. As if in homage to the French master, he painted several views of Mont-Sainte-Victoire, the mountain painted so often by Cézanne, although the broad broken strokes and raw primaries of Hartley's landscapes are clearly post-Cézanne.

In Mexico during 1932–33, Hartley began to paint in the crude, deliberately primitive manner that marks his late style. Having experimented with Fauvism and Cubism, he found them ultimately alien to his sensibility, and returned to the rough, churning manner that is evocative of Ryder. Early in his career Hartley had explained Ryder's attraction for him, stating that Pissarro, Cézanne, and Seurat were mere "logicians of color" compared to Ryder, who stimulated his "already tormented imagination."[13]

Ultimately, Hartley found the heroic subject for which he had

2-22. MARSDEN HARTLEY, *Fishermen's Last Supper—Nova Scotia*, 1940–41.

searched in the powerful silhouette of Mt. Katahdin and the giant forests and craggy rocks of the Maine coast. Celebrating his return to his birthplace in a poem entitled "The Return of the Native," he insisted on declaring himself "the painter from Maine." In the drama of the simple fishermen, Hartley found the tragic theme of death at sea which inspired such paintings as the *Fishermen's Last Supper—Nova Scotia (Ill. 2-22)*. Like Eugene O'Neill, he was able to extract the tragic from the prosaic realities of American life.

Attributing a higher morality to simple people, Hartley echoed the views held by Millet, Van Gogh, and Tolstoy—true piety was to be found only among the poor who were close to the land, hence to nature, and perhaps to God. In the last paintings done before his death in 1943, Hartley struck a religious mystical note. These fierce landscapes and hieratic figures which he called "archaic portraits," executed in a brutal, painterly style, leave behind any stylistic niceties for the raw directness of the visionary experience.

Arthur Dove, like Marin, was essentially a nature painter of lyrical impulse whose orientation was Expressionist. He differed from the other members of the Stieglitz group in that he viewed nature in abstract terms. A successful illustrator, Dove was attracted to Fauvism

58

as soon as he encountered it at the Salon d'Automne, to which he and his friend Alfred Maurer both submitted works. Typically, a Cézannesque still life, *The Lobster,* praised in the 1908 Salon d'Automne, drew jeers when it was shown in Dove's first one-man show at 291 in 1910.

Dove's 1910 "extractions" from nature, as he called them, are among the earliest abstract works painted in America, and bear the same date as Kandinsky's first abstractions, which Dove could not have known. (Abstractions also dated 1910 by Weber and Walkowitz have recently been found.) In early landscapes, such as *Nature Symbolized, No. 2 (Ill. 2-23),* Dove often opposed the swelling curves of radial forms to the saw-tooth edges of pronged or cog-like forms, using black or white lines as a pulsating, breathing contour for mass. His ambition, he said, was to "take wind and water and sand as a motif and work with them" but, he cautioned, that the motif "has to be simplified in most cases to color and force lines and substances, just as music has done with sound."[14] In color he sought to capture the essential charac-

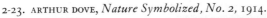

2-23. ARTHUR DOVE, *Nature Symbolized, No. 2,* 1914.

59

2-24. ARTHUR DOVE,
*Sentimental Music,* 1917.

teristic of a form or an atmospheric effect. He called this its "condition of light." In *Sentimental Music* (*Ill. 2-24*) he was able to achieve an effect of incandescence by modulating forms from light to dark and back to light.

Dove's attachment to nature ran deep; for a time he supported himself as a farmer. Even when describing the essence of modernism, with which he appeared to have a natural sympathy, he used an agricultural metaphor: "a good breeder idea . . . goes toward what is meant by modern painting. . . . To save the finest and breed from it is better than saving all. That is what 'Modern' in the real sense means." Dove understood modernism as Stieglitz did, as an experimental, laboratory

2-25. ARTHUR DOVE,
*Fog Horns,* 1929.

2-26. ARTHUR DOVE, *High Noon,* 1944.

situation "making research into life and all human thought and emotion to find young healthy plants that can stand the test of growing among things that are lasting through the ages."[15]

It is hard to know where Dove came by such an adequate understanding, given his limited acquaintance with modern art and its history. But like O'Keeffe, who did not travel in Europe, he seems to have arrived at a spontaneous modern style generated by a philosophy of life which exalted the spiritual in nature. Perhaps he might have arrived at such a formulation as easily from reading Thoreau as from reading Kandinsky's *On the Spiritual in Art.*

Although he never identified it as such, synesthesia, too, interested Dove. He thought he could not only symbolize the forces of nature, but also create concrete images of sounds, like the foghorn whistle he could hear from his houseboat as he floated around Long Island Sound. Like Marin, Burchfield, and other Americans, he invested natural forms and inanimate objects—dancing trees, bug-eyed ferries—with a pulsating energy of their own (*Ill. 2-25*). Gradually purging this tendency to anthropomorphize, Dove arrived at an increasingly pure abstraction which, in its lyric grace and simplicity, appears now as prophetic of the most recent developments in American painting. In the late thirties he began to set areas of color side by side, substituting flatter, more regular shapes for the expanding and contracting organic forms of his early work (*Ill. 2-26*). At the same time, the damp earth colors of his earlier paintings give way to a more abstract palette, still, however, basically tied to nature. In general, Dove's faults were faults in taste and in technique, but not faults in feeling. Even when the illustrator is seen behind the painter, the vigorousness and conviction of the statement are sufficient to identify Dove as a highly original fine artist.

Dove's closest friend, Alfred Maurer, was, of all Stieglitz' protégés, perhaps the most tragic case. His biographer, Elizabeth McCausland, characterizes Maurer's career as typical of the nonconforming artist in America, one of "talent, even genius; success; revolt; long silence, and withdrawal into the solitude of his work."[16] Gertrude Stein, whom he often visited, described him as "a little dark dapper man" with "hair, face, hands and feet all very alive."[17]

Among the first of his generation to go abroad, Maurer was also among the last to leave. In Paris from 1897 to 1914, he witnessed the birth of the modern movement. His early paintings, such as *Evening at the Club* (*Ill. 2-27*), painted in Whistler's tonal manner, were extremely promising. But despite their success, Maurer turned his back on representational art. His conversion was sudden; according to the sculptor Mahonri Young, from the day of his thirty-sixth birthday Maurer "painted like a wild man. He was never again the lighthearted, gay Alfy we had known." His Fauvist still lifes and landscapes, such as *Autumn* (*Ill. 3-1*), brilliant essays in Derain's airy,

2-27. ALFRED MAURER,
*Evening at the Club,*
*ca.* 1904.

2-28. ALFRED MAURER,
*Green Striped Bowl,*
1927–28.

broken-color manner, found favor, it seemed, with no one except Stieglitz.

After his return from Europe, Maurer appeared to lose confidence in his own intuition, and began to cast about for surer means. During the twenties he worked with Jay Hambidge's diagrams which offered mechanical solutions to compositional problems. Abandoning the traditional color wheel, he divided a circle into twenty-four segments; but his preferred palette remained, into the twenties, the light oranges, yellow-reds and pale blue-greens and violets of his Fauve works. In the later still lifes, such as *Green Striped Bowl* (*Ill. 2-28*), the broken stroke is replaced by slab-like planes of paint applied with the palette knife; these planes, however, do not shift cubistically, but remain statically defined. And the extreme, tipped-up perspective counteracts any sense of depth suggested by modeling.

For years after the war forced him to come home to New York, where he moved in with his aging father, Maurer planned to return to Paris. In fact, he kept his Paris studio until 1925, when the paintings were sold for back rent. (Some of these were recovered and exhibited in 1950.) Like Walkowitz, Maurer dropped into almost total obscurity after the Armory Show. In 1924, however, E. Weyhe exhibited his work, which by now had shifted from a semi-abstraction to figurative Expressionism. In the catalogue essay, Sherwood Anderson wrote of the sad-eyed young women who obsessed Maurer during the last decade of his life, "These paintings are . . . plucked out of the life of modern cities. The young girls are like desert flowers, flashing into quick beauty just caught."[18]

Frequently painted on Masonite panels, Maurer's late paintings are scrubbed, scraped, and repainted many times, although the ultimate result is often quite fresh. In Maurer's eyes, a painting was finished when it had a frame. His habit of constantly repainting the same surface led to the effacement of a series of nudes executed in 1927–28.

The few abstract paintings of the early thirties, mainly of the condensed double image of interpenetrating heads, are related to Picasso in their forms, although they are more freely and loosely painted than Picasso's late Cubist works. Like all of Stieglitz' artists, Maurer was desperately involved in finding his identity as a modern American artist, and painted a Cubist George Washington on the occasion of the two-hundredth birthday of the first President, perhaps in answer to those

2-29. ALFRED MAURER,
*Twin Heads, ca.* 1930.

who resented the "foreignness" of his art. Exhibited during the Depression, the painting was offered for barter for the equivalent of $500 worth of clothing.

Maurer's final humiliation, however, occurred when his father, the Currier and Ives lithographer Louis Maurer, famed for his popular recreations of the Old West, held his first one-man show in 1931. In the newspaper accounts, Alfred was mentioned as "also an artist." His father's popular success in the face of his own failure was doubly crushing to Maurer. Maurer's last paintings of interpenetrating Cubist heads (*Ill. 2-29*) have been interpreted as symbolic of his uncomfortable relationship with his aged father, who died at the age of one hundred on July 19, 1932. The following August 4, Maurer, recently discharged from a hospital where he had undergone a serious operation, ended his own life.

Maurer's story, though particularly depressing, is not atypical. Stieglitz' Secession Idea proved to be no bright beginning. When 291 closed its door in 1917, the artists who had exhibited there were exiles in their own land. They dispersed to follow their own increasingly personal directions, communicating with each other by letter or note. They wrote of loneliness, discouragement, the pains of isolation, and sometimes the joys of discovery. Cut off from outside stimulation, some developed an extremely individualized means of expression. At times the art produced was of a high originality, at other times it was tentative, introverted, and personal to the point of being hermetic.

World War I sealed America off from Europe as effectively as any artificial curtain. Stieglitz, unable to get work from abroad, closed 291 with the exhibition of the Italian Futurist Severini. It was the last show he would arrange for a European artist. The rest of his life was dedicated to keeping alive the reputations of Marin, Hartley, O'Keeffe, and Dove. From 1925 to 1929 he showed their work at the Intimate Gallery, a section of the Anderson Gallery, where he also showed Lachaise and Demuth; and from 1929 to 1934 he exhibited it at An American Place. In the forties, Stieglitz' mission of promoting the work of the American modernists was taken over by Edith Gregor Halpert of the Downtown Gallery, who continued to show the artists Stieglitz had supported along with younger American modernists.

Stieglitz did not exaggerate when he proclaimed that 291 was more than a gallery. In the course of its existence, as Stieglitz' evangelistic fervor grew into messianic zeal, 291 became the symbol of a new creative order, which meant to replace the purely mechanical and materialistic values of society with spiritual values derived from art and communal experience. In an era when a new generation was working toward what Malcolm Cowley called "a more passionate apprehension of life," 291 was the embodiment of the progressive vitalist philosophy committed to this goal. Such a philosophy favored the intuitive, the sensual, the experimental, the changing over the cerebral, the purely rational and mechanistic, the reactionary, the inert. As Marsden Hartley remembered, "There was life in all these new things, there was excitement, there were healthy revolt, investigation, discovery, and an utterly new world out of it all."[19]

If the term avant-garde implies more than the historical moment when nineteenth-century French artists broke with the Academy, then the importance of 291 lies in its introduction of the avant-garde attitude toward art, more perhaps, than in its actual presentation of works of art. Like the little magazines, 291 helped to introduce two notions into American art: that of art as experimental research, and that of quality in art. Both went against the American grain; the first because it threatened the status quo and the second because it seemed to negate the principle of democracy. By insisting that there was a superior or "high" art corresponding to what had been the aristocratic art of the past, available only to the noble in spirit, Stieglitz and his friends battled against what Whitman termed "the leveling character of democracy."

But in a country never known for its tolerance of deviation from any norm, whether social, sexual, or artistic, these revolutionary ideas did not receive wide circulation. Nor did they feed into a mainstream of artistic tradition, as the experiments of the modernists did in Europe. Stieglitz' ambition was to defeat the provincialism of American art by uniting it to the mainstream of Western art—without, however, sacrificing its distinctively American qualities. But the time was not ripe for such a fusion. The descendants of the colonial limners were not ready to stand beside the heirs of Boucher or Fragonard, nor would they be until Europe had nearly destroyed itself in yet another devastating war.

## Chapter Three

# The Armory Show: Success by Scandal

Probably in any reform movement . . . the penalty for avoiding the common-place is a liability to extravagance. It is vitally necessary to move forward to shake off the dead hand of the reactionaries; and yet we have to face the fact that there is apt to be a lunatic fringe among votaries of any forward movement.
—THEODORE ROOSEVELT, "A Layman's View of an Art Exhibition," *Outlook,* 1913

Shortly after Woodrow Wilson was sworn in as President of the United States, Theodore Roosevelt visited the International Exhibition of Modern Art held in the former Armory of New York's Sixty-ninth Regiment. The reaction of the ex-President to the estimated 1,600 pieces of European and American painting, sculpture, and graphics on view as reported in the *Outlook* was typical of that of the enlightened but chary layman: admitting the "real good that is coming out of the new movements," he was not yet ready to accept the "European extremists whose pictures are here exhibited." For Teddy Roosevelt, as for most Americans—including even artists as personally concerned with the reforming spirit as Robert Henri—progress was good so long as it did not end in extremism.

The exhibition which Roosevelt viewed with such mixed feelings was the most important event in the history of American modernism. Organized by a group of practicing artists, rather than by museum professionals, dealers, or official academies, it set out to exhibit work "usually neglected by current shows." Mainly this neglected work was by the modernists, both European and American, who previously had exhibited only at Stieglitz' gallery.

The need for another large invitational show on the order of the successful Independents' exhibition had been felt by many. Late in

1911, Walt Kuhn, Jerome Myers, and Elmer MacRae, who were exhibiting with a group called the Pastelists at the Madison Gallery, began discussing the possibilities for an exhibition of larger scope than that of the Independents. The gallery, backed by the unconventional interior decorator Mrs. Clara Potter Davidge, was run by Mrs. Davidge's protégé (later her husband), the painter Henry Fitch Taylor, who was also interested in forming a new society to organize such an exhibition. During the winter, these talks continued in Myers' studio. In December, 1911, others were invited to join the group, now officially known as the Association of American Painters and Sculptors. Of the sixteen charter members, most were conservative, either members of the National Academy or, like Kuhn, Myers, and MacRae, realists associated with the Henri circle. At the first official meeting, the thirteen charter members present included, besides Kuhn, Myers, MacRae, and Taylor, four members of The Eight—Davies, Glackens, Luks, and Lawson; two sculptors—Gutzon Borglum and John Mowbray Clarke; and several academic painters—Jonas Lie, D. Putnam Brinley, and Leon Dabo. In addition, Karl Anderson, James E. Fraser, Allen Tucker, and J. Alden Weir were represented by proxy. Thus the original make-up of the Association was somewhere between conservative and reactionary. By the time that the exhibition, which was called a "harbinger of universal anarchy," opened, however, the viewpoint of the Association had shifted toward the distinctly radical.

Since the Association was to be widely representative, it was felt that the president should be a figurehead, an eminent art-world figure behind whom all could unite. With this in mind, those present quickly elected the respected American Impressionist J. Alden Weir as president. However, when Weir read a news release stating that the Association's purpose was to exhibit anti-academic artists, he declined the presidency of a new society "openly at war with the Academy of Design," of which he had been a member for twenty-five years. Kuhn, envisioning an organization "as big or bigger than the Academy within two or three years," rejected Henri, the next logical choice, on the grounds that he had "queered himself with the Independent show," presumably by including only the work of realistic artists. It was Kuhn's view that "the way to get the confidence of the artists is to give the opposite type a chance,"[1] which represented the first change in the Association's position.

Kuhn, who had refused to accept the praise that he was better than Cézanne because it meant only "the same *damned* provincial loyalty which has hurt us so long," was determined to have someone with a broader, more international view as president. Secure in the positive reception of his recent work, Kuhn was able to prevail, and convinced the others to elect Arthur B. Davies as a compromise candidate. Of the possible choices, Davies was the best for many reasons. He was, for example, the only man who could bridge the various factions in the art world. Respected by academicians and praised by conservative critics, he was the single member of The Eight to frequent 291. In addition, Davies was a perceptive connoisseur with a wide range of taste, who had acquired two paintings from Max Weber's first one-man show at the Haas Gallery in 1909. Well-connected socially, he could gain the financial assistance needed; an erudite man who subscribed to various European art journals, he had a sophistication few of his peers could equal.

Reluctantly persuaded to assume office, the enigmatic Davies (who throughout this period was leading a complex double life as the head of two separate families) was transformed, according to Guy Pène du Bois, from a "perfervid dweller in the land of romance . . . incapable of making the contacts of the real world" into "a dictator, severe, arrogant, implacable . . . [who] governed with something equivalent to the terrible Ivan's rod of iron."[2] With Kuhn as its energetic mouthpiece and Davies as its suave *eminence grise,* the Association had two remarkable and devoted leaders, capable of directing its policy toward a more liberal and international course.

Originally the Armory Show had been conceived as a more ambitious version of the Independents' exhibition. Now Davies had another model in mind. On receiving the catalogue of the Sonderbund exhibition of modern art in Cologne, he proposed to Kuhn that their exhibition emulate this historical survey of the various modern movements. Agreeing, Kuhn left for Cologne in the fall of 1912, where he arrived on the last day of the exhibition. On the way to Paris, where he was to meet Davies, he stopped at The Hague, Munich, and Berlin. Then, for three frantic days in Paris, Davies and Kuhn were hustled around in taxis by Walter Pach, the expatriate painter and critic. As a member of the Stein circle, Pach had many important entrees into the Parisian avant-garde. Through him Davies and Kuhn met the Duchamp brothers: the painters Marcel Duchamp and Jacques Villon, and the sculptor Raymond Duchamp-Villon. As the Association's European agent, Pach performed invaluable tasks selecting, expediting, and shipping works. Alfred Maurer proved another useful contact, introducing Davies and Kuhn to the celebrated Post-Impressionist dealer Ambroise Vollard, who loaned a number of works to the show.

From Paris the two proceeded to London to see critic Roger Fry's exhibition of modern art. Featuring Matisse and Picasso, this exhibition, held at the Grafton Galleries, was the second part of an historical survey organized by Fry, the first having featured Manet and the Post-Impressionists. Like the Sonderbund exhibition, the second Grafton show, from which a number of works went directly to the Armory Show, provided Kuhn and Davies with a model of an historical survey on which to base their exhibition. Ready to outdo Fry, Kuhn wrote to Pach: "We are going to put it *all over it* with our proposition," and ordered Pach to get as many of Matisse's works as possible for the New York show.

Back in New York, Davies and Kuhn were frantically occupied soliciting contributions, cataloguing entries, and preparing publicity. The last was largely Kuhn's task. Acting on the advice of his friend, the lawyer and collector John Quinn, who had volunteered to serve as legal advisor to the Association, Kuhn set out to get as much publicity as possible for the exhibition. Admirably successful, he planted sympathetic stories with FitzGerald, Gregg, and a number of other critics in advance of the opening.

Elated over the exhibition's prospects, Kuhn wrote to Pach in December, 1912: "We want this old show of ours to mark the starting point of the new spirit in art, at least as far as America is concerned. I feel it will show its effect even further and make the big wheel turn over in both hemispheres."[3] This new spirit Kuhn spoke of so glowingly was to do nothing less than marry Henri's democratic "art spirit" with the experimental "Secession Idea" of 291. By including all the various tendencies in American art—from the "soft guys," as Kuhn called them, who painted sentimental genre, to the Impressionists like Weir and Lawson, to the abstractionists Macdonald-Wright and Morgan Russell—the Armory Show followed the nondiscriminatory policy of the Independents. In giving space to the most advanced experimental art, it accepted Stieglitz' point of view.

After a year's hard work, the exhibition was ready to open on February 17, 1913. The enormous Armory on Twenty-fifth Street, rented for $5,500, was decorated with $1,000 worth of banners and pine branches donated by Mrs. Whitney. On opening night, Davies escorted the aging Ryder, who had become a near hermit from abuse, into the crowded hall where ten of Ryder's canvases were hanging.

The homage to Ryder, a neglected American modernist, was pointed. Quinn's opening speech made this clear: "The members of this Association have shown you that American artists—young American artists, that is—do not dread and have no need to dread, the ideas or culture of Europe. They believe in the domain of art only the best should rule."[4] Quinn's bravado, however, may have rung false to those who had already publicly voiced misgivings about the American section.

Looking around, Quinn's elegant audience could see an enormous variety of paintings and, to a lesser extent, sculpture, some of it reassuringly familiar and much of it distressingly strange. Illustrations 3-1 to 3-5 show paintings exhibited by Sloan, Sheeler, Maurer, Glackens, and Bellows; some of the important European works appear in Illustrations 3-6 to 3-11. In all, there were over 1,000 catalogued entries; in addition, more than 1,000 other works, of which a number were multiple entries, were listed in a supplement. One-third of the works were foreign, predominantly French; two Ingres drawings and Delacroix's 1853 *Christ on the Lake of Genezareth* were (with the exception of a Goya miniature loaned by Quinn) the earliest works on view. Although Daumier, Courbet, Corot, and Manet were not well represented, the major Impressionists had good showings. The Post-Impressionists, including Gauguin (with eight oils, several lithographs, and a sculpture) and Van Gogh (with seventeen oils), were seen to advantage. Among the thirteen oils by Cézanne was the 1877 *Poorhouse on the Hill* (*Ill. 3-10*), the first Cézanne purchased by an American museum, sold from the show to the Metropolitan Museum for $6,700. Seurat and his followers, Signac and Cross, represented Neo-Impressionism with several works. Fauvism was remarkably complete in its presentation, with canvases by Derain, Manguin, Marquet, Villon, Friesz, Dufy, and of course, its leader, Matisse, whose thirteen paintings drew the most vitriolic critical blasts. Finally, important Cubist paintings by Picasso, Braque, Léger, de la Fresnaye, Gleizes, Picabia, and Duchamp provided examples of the most advanced European mode.

As an exhibition, however, the Armory Show had a number of flaws. Its limitations were essentially the limitations of the taste of Davies, Kuhn, and perhaps Pach, who also seems to have been influential in making selections. Matisse was well represented because Kuhn, soon to become one of his imitators, insisted on it. In *Dressing Room* (*Ill. 3-12*), Kuhn demonstrates how well he learned Matisse's

## Americans in the Armory Show, 1913.

3-1. ALFRED MAURER, *Autumn, ca.* 1912.

3-2. JOHN SLOAN, *Sunday,
Women Drying Their Hair,* 1912.

3-4. CHARLES SHEELER, *Chrysanthemums,* 1912.

3-3. WILLIAM GLACKENS, *Family Group,* 1911.

3-5. GEORGE BELLOWS,
*The Circus,* 1912.

3-6.  HENRI MATISSE, *The Red Studio*, 1911.

3-7.  FRANCIS PICABIA, *Dances at the Spring*, 1912.

3-9.  GEORGES BRAQUE, *L'Affiche de Kubelick (Le Violon)*, 1912.

3-8.  MARCEL DUCHAMP, *Nude Descending a Staircase, No. 2*, 1912.

3-11. WASSILY KANDINSKY, *Improvisation No. 27*, 1912.

3-10.  PAUL CÉZANNE, *Poorhouse on the Hill*, ca. 1895.

3-12. WALT KUHN,
*Dressing Room*, 1926.

lesson of flattening out shapes and juxtaposing broad simple forms
with more complex patterns to form a decorative unity. Davies, on
the other hand, with his interest in Symbolism, must have been responsible for the concentration of works by Puvis de Chavannes and
the Nabis—Bonnard, Vuillard, Denis, Roussel, and Valloton. Early in
the affair, he had decided to make Redon the star of the show—which
indeed he was; Redon's thirty-two oils were the largest single group
of works in the show. The far more crucial works of the German
Expressionists were represented only by a Kirchner landscape and
Kandinsky's *Improvisation No. 27 (Ill. 3-11)*, which Stieglitz bought for
$500. Apparently, Kuhn and Davies believed that the Germans
were merely imitators of the Fauves. Davies' last-minute decision not
to hang Delaunay's *City of Paris* because it was too large caused the
founder of Orphic Cubism to remove his entries from the exhibition.
Although Max Weber had loaned his Rousseaus, he felt insulted when
asked to submit only two of his own works and did not participate
himself. This was another mistake on Davies' part, since Weber was
the single American painter in America at the moment whose works
could stand comparison with European Cubism. The Futurists, told
that they could not have their own booth, decided not to enter. Although works by Rodin, Maillol, Brancusi, and Lehmbruck were

included, sculpture in general was so poorly represented that the sculptor Gutzon Borglum withdrew from the Association in protest.

Thus, at best, it was an incomplete picture of modernism that the Armory Show offered. Of the hundreds of paintings and sculptures by Americans, perhaps a few dozen could be described as modern. These included the sculpture of Nadelman and Lachaise, and the paintings by Bruce, Burlin, Bluemner, Carles, Dasburg, Halpert, Hartley, Marin, Prendergast, Russell, Schamberg, Sheeler, Stella, Walkowitz, and Macdonald-Wright. More typical of the American entries were the genre paintings of Guy Pène du Bois, Glackens, Luks, Myers, Sloan, and Eugene Higgins, the street scenes of Bellows and Glenn O. Coleman, and the landscapes of James Preston and Van Dearing Perrine. Many entries, like Boardman Robinson's cartoons, were compromises with popular illustration, whereas the work of Leon Kroll, Bernard Karfiol, Carl Sprinchorn, and Jonas Lie represented compromises with academicism.

Once the show opened, an avalanche of publicity descended upon it. Since Kuhn had carefully prepared the way, the early publicity had been mostly favorable, urging viewers to keep an open mind. But after Teddy Roosevelt let it be known that Duchamp's *Nude Descending a Staircase (Ill. 3-8)* reminded him of a Navajo blanket and Lehmbruck's *Kneeling Woman* of a praying mantis, it was open season on modern art. Not until the present "culture boom" have the mass media had such a field day ballyhooing the scandalous goings-on of the avant-garde. A popular photograph of a donkey painting with its tail may have been the ancestor of the painting monkeys who appeared decades later. Cubism was the butt of endless jokes; "futuristic" art, as the modern styles were lumped together by the know-nothing press, inspired cartoons, parodies, skits, and doggerel. The *American Art News* sponsored a contest to find the "nude" in Duchamp's painting. The clever winner discovered "It isn't a lady but only a man." The most popular description was "an explosion in a shingle factory," although it was also seen as a "staircase descending a nude." Disgusted, Walter Pach said the contest was like looking for the moon in the "Moonlight Sonata." Art critic Christian Brinton explained some of the public's reaction by the fact that the awakening of the American public to art was accomplished by a series of shocks from the outside rather than through intensive effort, observation, or participation.

Behind the many statements issued by those involved with the

Armory Show, as well as by those who mocked it, were certain assumptions about the nature of art and culture in America. Sometimes these were veiled behind a transparent rhetoric. For the artists, the "new spirit" was revolutionary. More than that, it was the rebirth of the spirit of the American Revolution. Thus, the pine-tree flag of Massachusetts during the Revolution was chosen as the symbol of the Armory Show. Henri endlessly preached "independence"; Stieglitz called for "a battle cry of freedom without any soft pedal on it." But resurrecting the old Revolutionary War slogans and symbols, which no longer corresponded to any political reality, was sheer nostalgia on the part of the Americans. It was, in fact, an attempt to legitimize revolutionary art in the only context intelligible to Americans, who had no tradition of radical art. That context was radical politics. This confusion between art and politics endured for many decades beyond the Armory Show, and in some minds endures today.

The case against modernism, on the other hand, was also frequently couched in political terms. The editorial in *The New York Times* the day after the show closed called the modernists "cousins to the anarchists in politics." Unrest in art was equated with unrest in politics. But since Roosevelt's and Wilson's administrations were in general liberal and progressive, progress in art was just as often equated with progress in politics. Writing of "Art and Unrest" in *The Globe* in 1913, Hutchins Hapgood exulted, "We are living at a most interesting moment in the art development of America. It is no mere accident that we are also living at a most interesting moment in the political, industrial, and social development of America. What we call our 'unrest' is the condition of vital growth, and this beneficent agitation is as noticeable in art and the woman's movement as it is in politics and industry."

As much as Henri and Stieglitz argued that the values asserted by contemporary art were the basic American values, others, like Frank J. Mather, Jr., argued the opposite. Giving his argument a puritanical twist by confusing art with morality, Mather advised the layman to "dismiss on moral grounds an art that lives in the miasma of morbid hallucination or sterile experimentation, and denies in the name of individualism values which are those of society and of life itself."[5] Like Kenyon Cox, Mather argued that license without discipline results in anarchy. Meanwhile, Charles Caffin was attacking the limitations imposed on American culture by its sentimentality, prudishness, and sexual inhibitions. The issues raised by the Armory Show thus could be generalized to cover not only art, but culture, politics, and morality. And throughout the country, all of these matters were being hotly debated as the old clashed with the new in every sphere.

The moment at which American art attempted to assimilate European modernism coincided with the moment that the American nation was confronted with assimilating 13 million new immigrants. The threat posed by this invasion of foreigners was often expressed in contempt for foreign art. Such a defensive position, ending in political chauvinism as well as cultural isolationism, forced the artist to "Americanize" European art, just as the immigrant was "Americanized" and absorbed into the native population. Consequently, the new painting and sculpture proved an admirable target for the various kinds of insecurities and aggressions thus released. And the anger of the conservatives, as F. J. Gregg described it, was directed most of all against the new generation that "appears to be . . . set on a Nietzschean transvaluation of all values."

From New York, the Armory Show traveled to Chicago, where students at the Art Institute hanged in effigy Matisse, Brancusi, and Walter Pach (who was there lecturing), burning imitations of Matisse's paintings as well. By the time the exhibition closed in Boston, nearly 300,000 people had seen it. Jerome Myers recalls that "Millionaires, art collectors, society people, all were packed in like sardines."[6] During the course of the exhibition, 174 works—132 foreign and 51 American—were sold.

When Quinn predicted that the exhibition would be "epoch-making in the history of American art," he did not exaggerate. But was he equally right that the Americans had nothing to fear from European competition? Not according to Myers, who complained later that "Davies had unlocked the door to foreign art and thrown the key away. . . . we had become provincial . . . while foreign names became familiar, un-American propaganda was ladled out wholesale."[7]

In short, the Armory Show was in many ways a Trojan horse which loosed a band of invaders. Next to the refined, polished, fully realized efforts of the Europeans, the Americans looked tentative, plain, and underdeveloped. For all his sympathy with the cause, Gregg could not help lamenting that the vast mass of American work was a case of "arrested development." If nothing else, the Armory Show established the hegemony of European art for another thirty years.

Aimed at liberating American art from the shadow of European domination, the Armory Show, by displaying more Cubist works than had ever been seen in this country before, provided insecure and un-original artists with a formula that many chose to imitate in a vain search for a fashionable mode. Its other intentions were often frustrated as well. A high-flown statement of purpose revealed that the Association wished to choose, from "all the created Beauty of this Epoch, that which best reveals the individual or group among the creative works, or the contributions of a race."[8] If this meant that some *Volksgeist* or notion of an American style would emerge, then the heterogeneous array of works displayed was hardly calculated to produce such an effect. On the contrary, the diversity, fierce individualism, and lack of focus or common denominators characteristic of twentieth-century American art were made all the more evident.

But the Armory Show was at least partially successful in its two-fold aim of educating the public and enlarging the art market to include the young Americans. Those who troubled to read the four pamphlets published by the Association must have been at least somewhat enlightened. (These were: *Cézanne* by Elie Faure, *Odilon Redon* by Pach, extracts from Gauguin's *Noa-Noa,* translated by Kuhn, and *A Sculptor's Architecture,* Pach's study of the architectural façade by Raymond Duchamp-Villon exhibited in the show.) In addition, the dispersal of the fifty-seven half-tone postcard reproductions on sale must have aided artists and the public to familiarize themselves with modern works. As for the glut of publicity, it acted at least to stimulate awareness of art, although, as Milton Brown dourly observed: "The critical controversy which arose out of the Armory Show served not so much to clarify aesthetic thought, since it was not conducted on a very logical and informed plane, as to extend the area of conflict."[9]

But if few converts were made among curators, critics, or the general public, artists, dealers, and collectors responded with more enthusiasm. Within a year or two of the Armory Show, a number of new galleries were opened. These included the Daniels Gallery in 1913, and in the following year the N. E. Montross Gallery, with Davies as advisor; the Bourgeois Gallery, which Pach advised; and the Carroll Gallery, backed by Quinn. In October, 1915, the Mexican caricaturist Marius de Zayas, who had been associated with Stieglitz, opened the Modern Gallery, financed by Walter Arensberg, with an exhibition of Picasso, Braque, and Picabia.

The Armory Show, for all practical purposes, marks the beginning of American collecting. Those who purchased from it were different from Duveen's clients, men like Henry Clay Frick, Andrew Mellon, and J. P. Morgan, who used their immense wealth and power to plunder Europe of its art treasures. By contrast, the lawyers John Quinn and Arthur Jerome Eddy, the scholars Walter Arensberg and A. E. Gallatin, the society bluestockings Lillie P. Bliss and Katherine Dreier, and the eccentric Horatio Alger hero of science Dr. Albert Barnes immersed themselves in the art of the present and became its evangelists. Through them and the collections they founded, modern art became a permanent fixture of American culture. Among this group of collectors were some of the first to write and talk about modern art in America. A. J. Eddy, for example, produced the first book on Cubism in English. Several, such as Duncan Phillips, a sensitive collector and art writer who became converted to modernism some years after the Armory Show, institutionalized their collections, making them instruments of public education. Thus, the Phillips Memorial Gallery, founded in 1918, was the first public gallery devoted to contemporary art; the Bliss collection formed the nucleus for the Museum of Modern Art, founded in 1929; and A. E. Gallatin installed his "Gallery of Living Art" at New York University in 1927, where it remained until 1942, when it became part of the Philadelphia Museum. Aided by Marcel Duchamp and Man Ray, Katherine Dreier founded the Société Anonyme in 1920, the first modern art museum in America. The Barnes collection, established as a foundation for study and research in Merion, Pennsylvania, was unfortunately open only to those who subscribed to Dr. Barnes's views on art and education. (A recent court ruling, however, has opened the matchless collection of Matisse, Picasso, Renoir, and Cézanne, not to mention Glackens, Sloan, and Prendergast, to the public on a limited basis.) The Eddy collection now forms part of the Chicago Art Institute, and the Arensberg collection, including the sensation of the Armory Show, Duchamp's *Nude Descending a Staircase,* now hangs in the Philadelphia Museum of Art.

These new collectors differed from their predecessors also in that they were advised, not by connoisseurs or dealers, but by artists. Dr. Barnes leaned on the judgment of his boyhood friend, Glackens; Quinn was advised by Kuhn and Pach, and Mrs. Bliss by Davies. Katherine Dreier and Walter Arensberg relied on Duchamp, who would later counsel Peggy Guggenheim as well.

Despite the effect the Armory Show had on molding the taste of these pioneer collectors, it had little effect in other spheres. The universities did not alter curriculum to embrace contemporary art; nor

3-13. GEORGE BELLOWS,
*Stag at Sharkey's,* 1907.

did the art schools become more progressive. The large museums predictably continued to scorn modernism. The single exception was the Newark Museum, directed by Daniel Catton Rich, where a large Weber exhibition was held in 1913. It was the first museum show of a living American artist.

Naturally, the Armory Show had some direct impact on American art, although perhaps not as much as one might assume. A few artists radically altered their styles, choosing to work more abstractly. But such changes might have occurred in any case, since those few had been exposed to modernism through living or traveling abroad. If, however, the Armory Show had a single aesthetic message, it was the message of form. Realists like Kuhn, Sloan, and Bellows began criticizing the lack of structure in their work. Ben Benn recalls that when he saw the modern masters, they "opened my eyes to the necessity for something of more permanent value—interdependence of parts (called organization), pattern (the just disposition of masses), and rhythm to unite these other elements."[10]

A comparison of two boxing scenes by Bellows, *Stag at Sharkey's* (*Ill. 3-13*) and *Dempsey and Firpo* (*Ill. 3-14*), the former painted before the Armory Show and the latter after, may serve to illustrate the new self-consciousness with regard to formal values that enters into Bellows' later work. After the Armory Show, for thoughtful artists like Bellows, Sloan, Guy Pène du Bois, and Edward Hopper, the realism of the "slashing brush" was not enough. Although all remained realists, their realism was relative. Sloan, for example, gave up painting from direct observation in favor of an entirely conceptual approach to

3-14. GEORGE BELLOWS,
*Dempsey and Firpo,* 1924.

art, one which depended on conventions as artificial and arbitrary as those which abstract artists adopted. Seeking a more durable art, Sloan adapted the graphic technique of cross-hatching in order to give his forms a sense of sculptural solidity. Similarly, the others, made aware of the importance of structure, arrived at forms that were generalized into simple volumes. In *Woman with Cigarette (Ill. 3-15),* Guy Pène du Bois derived a sense of substance by firmly modeling the few simple rounded volumes of the women's heads and dresses, eschewing the highlights and other surface effects he had learned as a Henri student. Still others, like the former landscape painter Henry Fitch Taylor and Davies himself, became full converts to the new doctrine of Cubism. But the inadequacies of Taylor's *Guitar Series*

3-15. GUY PÈNE DU BOIS,
*Woman with Cigarette,* 1929.

3-16. HENRY FITCH TAYLOR,
*Guitar Series, ca.* 1914.

(*Ill. 3-16*) and Davies' *Intermezzo* (*Ill. 3-17*) reveal how incomplete
was their understanding of the dynamics of Cubism. Convinced of
the value of modernism, they nevertheless did not have sufficient
background or experience in its fundamental principles. Consequently,
they produced pictures which, however courageous or provocative,
showed only a superficial acquaintance with the vocabulary, not the
grammar, of modern art.

In the wake of the Armory Show, two exhibitions were held which
helped to correct certain of the Armory Show's flaws. The Panama-
Pacific exhibition, a comprehensive survey held in San Francisco in
1916, brought Futurism to America. In the same year, the Forum exhibition held at the Anderson Gallery isolated the best in American
art. Its aim was to challenge the image of European supremacy established by the Armory Show. Because the Armory Show "failed to set
any logical standards by which modern work could be estimated,"
the purpose of the Forum exhibition was "to separate the wheat from
the tares."[11] Selected by a jury including Henri, Stieglitz, the critics

Christian Brinton and W. H. Wright, and John Weichsel, organizer of the first American artists' cooperative, the People's Art Guild, the Forum exhibition included nearly 200 paintings and drawings by seventeen artists. Among them were Marin, Dove, Walkowitz, Man Ray, Sheeler, Hartley, Maurer, Macdonald-Wright, Morgan Russell, and Thomas Hart Benton.

In 1917, another large unjuried exhibition resembling the 1910 Independents' exhibition was held by the Society of American Artists. Marcel Duchamp, vice president of the Society, submitted one of his "ready-mades," a urinal signed R. Mutt. Although the show was presumably open to all who paid the $5 registration fee, *Fountain* by R. Mutt was rejected. In protest, Duchamp resigned from the Society the night before the exhibition opened. Thus the decade of the Armory Show drew to a close: Duchamp, the representative of Europe's avant-garde, challenged the premise of democracy in art, as he would continue for more than a half-century to challenge art's most sacred tenets. For the moment, democracy could not be extended to tolerate extremism. It was safe to say that until it did, modernism would remain an artificial flower, rootless in American soil.

3-17. ARTHUR B. DAVIES, *Intermezzo*, *ca.* 1913.

## Chapter Four

# After the Ball: Cubism in America

It is annoying that there is nothing Gothic about a grain elevator since we have been taught that Gothic architecture is beautiful. It is distressing that the man in the subway in New York is not at all like a Shakespearean or a Rabelaisian or a Cervantic character. But is there any reason to be so angry that we refuse to look at the grain elevator or the man in the subway? . . . As long as the European eye goes on looking for the Gothic cathedral in the grain elevator or for Hamlet in the man in the subway we are not likely to get much forward.

—GILBERT CANNON, "Observations on Returning
to the Remnants of Civilization," *Broom,* 1922

If we accept critic Edwin Avery Park's assessment, American art during the twenties was "the smallest ham sandwich ever unwrapped at the world's biggest and noisiest banquet." The optimistic experimentation that took place in the early twenties ended in most cases in a series of retreats to more conservative and defensible positions, as the reforming spirit of the teens gave way to the complacency of a security-minded, business-oriented society. Cut off from Europe by the war, American artists found themselves in a cultural vacuum that was not encouraging to their art; they were surrounded by a spirit of chauvinistic isolationism that encompassed art as well as politics.

When America emerged from the first European conflict in which she had engaged, she was ready to lose any remaining innocence in the frenzy of the·Jazz Age. The great issues for the moment were political and economic. When submerged minority groups threatened to assert themselves, there was great concern about the evils of Bolshevism, the activities of the Ku Klux Klan, the growing menace of the IWW, and the problem of immigration. As Henry McBride observed in 1920, "The time was out of joint for any great outcry over morality or art."[1]

Nonetheless, both morality and art were undergoing great transformations. With the proliferation of galleries and exhibitions following the Armory Show, the power of the National Academy of Design—mainly its ability to decide what would be exhibited—was rendered negligible. Its spring annual was now just an exhibition among exhibitions. But although the Academy had lost its hold on the art market, academicism as a manner was not dead. It had merely changed guises. The hollow Neoclassicism that The Eight had rejected was brought up to date and modified in favor of a freer technique and more contemporary subject matter. On the defensive now, academic artists were ready to compromise. In 1914, academician Edwin Blashfield argued against the excesses of an unconstrained modernism, counseling instead a compromise between the old masters and the moderns. Such a solution appealed to American artists because it offered a middle-of-the-road course between extremes. Its adoption as an artistic formula accounted for any number of tepid still lifes, figure studies, and landscapes produced from the time the Armory Show made modernism fashionable until the point at which abstraction made realism unfashionable. In the twenties, the desire to compromise, to strike a balance between the old and the new, led painters to concoct an eclectic synthesis that would combine the best of all possible styles.

Not all artists, of course, were in favor of such indiscriminate borrowing. Andrew Dasburg warned that "this idea of combining a variety of forms of perfection into one complete ideal realization prevents any creative work being done which possesses the contagious force of Cubism. . . . Not until it is realized that originality never follows from this attitude of assimilation and refinement can we become innovators."[2] Unfortunately, Dasburg's preachment was better than his practice; the kind of Cubism he and many American artists adopted was just such an eclectic mélange.

For the majority of Americans who called themselves Cubists, Cubism meant little more than sharp lines and acute angles. Cubism was seen, not as a new attitude of mind, but in terms of its surface effects. Thus, many blithely set about superimposing directional lines and fragmented shapes on top of essentially realistic compositions. Some, like Maurice Sterne in his *Bali Bazaar* (*Ill. 4-1*), tried to imitate the shallow space of Cubism. But most accepted compromise solutions, resulting in a kind of semi-abstraction that was still at bottom anecdotal and illustrational. The late work of Davies himself is an example of such unassimilated modernism. Apparently it was not possible to move

4-1. MAURICE STERNE,
*Bali Bazaar*, 1913–14.

from the idyllic romanticism of Marées to the logic of Cubism. Davies' charming failures are just one indication of the confusions that resulted from telescoping art from Van Gogh and Gauguin to Matisse and Picasso into a single style called "Post-Impressionism," the term most critics used as a catch-all to cover the diversity of styles and periods reviewed at the Armory Show.

"The difficulty is not that we are influenced by Europe," critic Lee Simonson observed, but that artists are liable "to make a fad of a particular experiment, without analyzing or understanding the ideas and impulses which are really at the bottom of it."[3] Even the efforts of some artists, such as William and Marguerite Zorach and Konrad Cramer, who had a firmer grasp of Cubism because they had watched it develop in Europe, were remarkable only because they were early examples of modern painting in America, not because they were successful Cubist pictures.

To be an American Cubist was by definition to be an imitator. Like English or Scandinavian approximations of French art, American Cubism was, as Stuart Davis later titled a painting, "Provincial Cubism." As the latest import from Europe in the decade following the Armory Show, Cubism attracted both the serious and the superficial. In the hands of vulgarizers it quickly degenerated into a period style to be paraphrased, like Greek, or Gothic, or Renaissance. This was the case partly because the craft revival, preached as an extension of the Arts and Crafts movement earlier in the century, did not come to fruition in America in a coordinated program of design reform like that of de Stijl or the Bauhaus. Instead, as Simonson complained, modernism became "the stylist's momentary holiday, a manufacturer's fad, a department store novelty," rather than the "business of soundly relating design to machine production and to the capacities of popular taste."[4] If Cubism was transformed, in the hands of irresponsible manufacturers, into the vulgar geometric "moderne" of the thirties, even in the hands of serious artists, it was often misunderstood.

Thus, the real issues at stake in Cubism—the preservation of the integrity of the picture plane, the analysis of both the structure of objects and the means by which objects are perceived, the assertion of the independent, self-referential reality of the work of art—often passed over the heads of even the most dedicated. Those artists who, like Dove, O'Keeffe, Hartley, and Marin, embraced the modernist attitude, usually did so on an emotional, intuitive basis. Significantly, the most intellectual phase of Cubism, its formative analytic period, made little discernible impression on American artists. There is almost no evidence that the analytic Cubist works of Braque and Picasso that were shown at the Armory Show were understood or imitated by American artists. The classical rigor, monochrome severity, and static tranquillity of these works evidently could not serve restless Americans as models. Nor can one find in the works of Americans any consistent concern with the theoretical analysis of three-dimensional forms.

The most talked about and widely imitated artists in the Armory Show were not the major artists, but the minor Cubists—Duchamp, Picabia, and Gleizes. This may be because all three came to America about the time of the show. Picabia's visit was especially publicized. He was widely quoted, and his dogmatic assertion, made at the opening of the Armory Show, that "Cubism is modern painting" which would "supplant all other forms of painting," impressed many.

4-2. PRESTON DICKINSON,
*Industry, II, ca,* 1924.

Even when they chose Cubist models, American modernists preferred throughout the teens and twenties to preserve the high color they had learned from Matisse and the Fauves. On the other hand, conservatives like Henry Lee McFee and Preston Dickinson continued throughout the twenties to remain faithful both to Cézanne's compositions and to his palette. Dickinson's *Industry, II* (*Ill. 4-2*) is an example of such a retrograde solution. Moreover, neither was the most advanced Cubist work that Americans produced much indebted to Braque and Picasso. The dynamic, splintered abstractions of Max Weber, for example, such as *Rush Hour, New York* (*Ill. 4-3*), in their movement and contrasting textures were closer to Futurism than to orthodox Cubism, even though Weber's early figure studies had derived from Picasso. Closer still to Futurism in his approach, Joseph Stella had learned Cubism directly from the Futurists during his trip to Italy in 1910–11. So it is not surprising that the dancing, whirling splinters of light and color in paintings like *Battle of Light, Coney Island* (*Ill. 4-4*) are reminiscent of Severini's ballrooms rather than of French work. In addition, the subjects of analytic Cubism, the narrow world of the studio and the café still life, held limited appeal to the more dramatic and flamboyant Americans, who preferred the urban subject matter of the Futurists or the heroic landscapes of the "epic" Cubists Gleizes and Metzinger.

4-3. MAX WEBER,
*Rush Hour,*
*New York*, 1915.

4-4. JOSEPH STELLA, *Battle of Light, Coney Island*, 1914.

As for the later phase of French Cubism, only two Americans working directly after the Armory Show produced successful synthetic
Cubist abstractions. They were Marsden Hartley and Man Ray. Hartley's *Movement #2* (*Ill. 4-5*) and Man Ray's *The Rope Dancer Accompanies Herself with Her Shadows* (*Ill. 4-6*) are among the few
genuine synthetic Cubist works produced at the time in America.
Their activity in this area, however, lasted only a few years. By 1920,
Hartley had permanently renounced abstraction. Man Ray, under the
influence of Duchamp and Picabia, became a Dadaist, devoting himself more and more to creating Dada objects and to experiments, such
as his "aerographs," the first spray-gun paintings, and "rayographs,"
photographic impressions made on sensitized plates. Moreover, Hart-

4-5. MARSDEN HARTLEY, *Movement #2,* 1916.

ley's and Man Ray's abstractions based on figure studies, although exhibiting the flatness and geometric simplification of synthetic Cubism, were hardly as complex or sophisticated as contemporary French work. Not until the middle twenties did Stuart Davis begin to create flat shapes that were as sharply cut out as Hartley's and Man Ray's, but more complicated and developed in their relationships.

If the Americans did not learn much from classical Cubism, either because they did not have the necessary technical means or theoretical background—or simply because a classicizing style contradicted the romantic American spirit—they found more congenial the branch of Cubism that Apollinaire termed "Orphic," because of its lyric content. Thus, Delaunay, the leading Orphist, was an important stimulus to Synchromism, the only American art movement with a program, a formulated aesthetic, and a manifesto. Even so, as a movement, Synchromism lasted less than a year and took place in Paris. But its ramifications, in terms of the diffusion of modern scientific color theory in America, were considerable.

Synchromism was born as a movement when Stanton Macdonald-Wright and Morgan Russell issued a statement of intentions during their joint exhibitions, first at Munich's Neue Kunstsalon in June, 1913, and then in Paris in October, 1913, at the Galerie Bernheim-Jeune.

4-6. MAN RAY, *The Rope Dancer Accompanies Herself with Her Shadows,* 1916.

Their work was part of a general effort to extend the color theory formulated by Seurat and the Neo-Impressionists from the scientific laws which governed the perception of colors. The main sources of Synchromism were identical with those of Neo-Impressionism: Chevreul's *De la loi du contraste simultané des couleurs,* Charles Blanc's and Helmholtz' studies of optics, and Rood's *Modern Chromatics.* From Chevreul they learned that adjacent complementary colors influence one another—when used in large areas, the colors are intensified and when used in small quantities, they are blended by the eye into a neutral tone. From Rood they learned that the spectrum could be divided into harmonizing pairs and triads of colors which, corresponding to the dominant chord in music, could provide a tonal "key" for a painting.

Arriving in Paris in the first decade of the century, the young Californian Macdonald-Wright and his fellow American Morgan Russell were quickly drawn to these color theories, which Roger Delaunay and the Czech Frank Kupka were beginning to apply around 1910–11 in paintings that rapidly approached total abstraction. Although both knew Delaunay, recently it has been found that Russell's interest in pure color composition antedates his knowledge of Delaunay's experiments. So, despite Apollinaire's dismissal of Synchromism as "vaguement

4-7. MORGAN RUSSELL, *Synchromy,* 1914–15.

Orphiste," evidence points to a certain parallel development of Synchromism and Orphic Cubism. By 1912, for example, Russell was considering painting "solely by means of color and the way it is put down,
in showers and broad patches, distinct from each other or blended, but
with force and clearness, and with large geometric patterns, with the
effect of the whole as being constructed with volumes of color."[5] Yet,
in the 1913 Paris exhibition, all but two of the canvases (both by Russell) were representational still lifes and figure studies, which leads one
to believe that seeing Delaunay's and Kupka's discs of color was nonetheless crucial to the development of Synchromism as an *abstract* style.
In his *Synchromy (Ill. 4-7),* Russell splits discs of color into segments,
each modulated to correspond or contrast with the dominant or key

tone. Similarly, in *"Oriental"* (*Ill. 4-8*), Macdonald-Wright harmonizes the dominant blue-green tonality with its complementary orange.

Although they were partners in their enterprise, Russell and Macdonald-Wright had different interpretations of Synchromism. Russell's work was more clearly abstract; behind Macdonald-Wright's forms there is usually some structure in nature that has been idealized and abstracted. Macdonald-Wright was particularly interested in the rhythmic coordination of the muscular organization of the human body, an interest Thomas Hart Benton was eventually to expand into a complex mechanical system of composition. In place of Russell's opaque planes and sculptural forms—Russell had worked on sculpture with his friend Matisse—Macdonald-Wright preferred the diaphanous quality of intersecting transparent planes. Both, however, were equally insistent on the importance of the tactile sensation evoked by value contrasts suggesting three-dimensional depth. According to Russell, in fact, color was to be seen primarily as a series of value gradations logically and harmonically related by means of a step-by-step progression of tones.

Besides the two who called their movement "Synchromism" (a term

4-8. STANTON MACDONALD-WRIGHT, *"Oriental." Synchromy in Blue-Green,* 1918.

4-9. ARTHUR B. FROST,
*Colored Forms*, 1917.

meaning "with color," derived from Russell's early studio interior
*Synchromie en Vert*), two other expatriate Americans were unofficially
known as Synchromists. Arthur Burdett Frost, whose *Colored Forms*
(*Ill. 4-9*) was exhibited in the 1917 Independents' exhibition, and Patrick Henry Bruce—both former students of Matisse—were friends of
Delaunay as well. Frost, upon his return to New York in 1914, helped
to disseminate Synchromist principles and to explain the work shown
that year by Macdonald-Wright and Russell at the Carroll Gallery.
Shortly thereafter, a group of artists, including Andrew Dasburg,
Thomas Hart Benton, and Morton Schamberg, began painting Cubist
abstractions in which a prismatic shattering of light into its component
spectral colors was the sole subject. (Around 1920 Benton and Dasburg
returned to representational art; but both showed Synchromist abstractions in the 1916 Forum exhibition.) By 1918, abstract color volumes
were the formal basis of the work of Joseph Stella, Arnold Friedman,
Alexander P. Couard, and Arthur B. Davies, although it should be emphasized none of these artists was officially a Synchromist. At the same
time, two formerly academic painters, James Daugherty and Jay van
Everen, were also converted to color abstraction. But the compositional
organization of their works often derived from Picabia's Armory Show
paintings in which flat planes interlocked to create sculptural volumes
(*Ill. 3-7*) rather than from Synchromism.

Remaining in Paris, Russell and Bruce separated themselves from
the Parisian art world. In 1916, Russell returned to figurative paintings,

although from 1920 to 1929, he apparently again painted abstractly. Bruce, on the other hand, now independent of Delaunay, under whom he had worked from 1912 to 1914, became an increasingly original painter. His geometric still lifes of the twenties combined an unusual palette, in which pastel pink and blue were played off against black and white, with an equally original sense of form; three-quarter, profile, and frontal views of objects were presented so as to shift between flat and illusionistic readings without disrupting the integrity of the picture plane, as in *Still Life* (*Ill. 4-10*). Choosing solid forms, Bruce rejected line, which he considered "only the border of surface," insisting that "if line is apparent, it is a drawing."[6]

Discouraged by the lack of interest in his work, Bruce wrote to his friend Henri Pierre Roché in 1928: "I am doing all my traveling in the apartment on ten canvases. One visits many unknown countries in that way. You should be well prepared to appreciate my paintings after Greece."[7] If the reference to Greece can be interpreted as an ambition to produce classical compositions, Bruce was one of the very few Americans of his generation to hold such an ambition. In 1932, Bruce moved to Versailles, gave up painting, and destroyed all but fifteen canvases, which he sent to Roché in a wheelbarrow, along with the note: "You are the only person in the world who likes them." Shortly after a brief trip to the United States in 1936, Bruce took his own life in Paris. Later Roché wrote of his friend: "His slowness, perseverance and seriousness were unbelievable for Paris. His isolation, his irascible modesty, his exclusiveness formed a wall."[8] According to Roché, Bruce's efforts were directed "toward building paintings which would be supported mainly by their four sides having a structural quality. The absence of this quality in other modern paintings made him suffer rightly or wrongly."[9]

There is no question that Synchromism was among the most advanced painting styles that emerged out of Post-Impressionism early in this century. According to Macdonald-Wright's brother, the brilliant, eccentric critic, Willard Huntington Wright, Synchromism represented the apogee of Western art, the culmination of its entire historical development from the Renaissance through Cubism. In many ways—particularly in its emphasis on the central role of color and its insistence on the suppression of line—Synchromism prefigured the concerns of today's new abstraction. But such is the discontinuity of modernism in this country that nothing links the two movements.

One of the effects of the Armory Show, as we have seen, was to

4-10 PATRICK HENRY BRUCE, *Still Life, ca.* 1929–30.

enlarge the art world, and to create multiple focuses of artistic activity. One such focus was the salon kept by Walter Arensberg, who became for New York what Gertrude Stein had been to Paris. Arensberg, who spent most of his own time unraveling Elizabethan riddles and trying to prove that Bacon was Shakespeare, opened his living room on Sixty-seventh Street to a lively group that included Duchamp, Picabia, Man Ray, Marsden Hartley, Joseph Stella, Charles Demuth, Charles Sheeler, Isadora Duncan, William Carlos Williams, Edgard Varèse, and miscellaneous other figures from the artistic and musical avant-garde. From time to time even a few outsiders from the old guard like Bellows and Sloan would drop in.

Within a few months after Duchamp's arrival in 1915, Arensberg's living room became the center of proto-Dada activity in New York. (Dadaism as a movement was not formally founded or named until 1916 in Zurich.) Anti-art, antiwar, antimaterialism, and antirationalism, Dada suited the disenchanted mood of American intellectuals as the country was on the verge of World War I. In a sense, however, when Duchamp and Picabia began their Dada activity in New York, they were working in a prepared context. Even before the Armory Show there had been intimations of a Dada attitude in the negative appraisal

*Camera Work* critics were constantly making of American culture. Later, H. L. Mencken's debunking of the American "booboisie" as hypocritical, cowardly, and stupid was characterized as journalistic Dada. The more serious criticism of American materialism and provincialism by George Jean Nathan, Lewis Mumford, and Van Wyck Brooks reflected a general indictment of American culture by her best artists and critics which could be appropriated to Dada ends.

Indeed, the bizarreness of the American scene and the paradoxes of the American experience continue to lend themselves easily to a Dada interpretation. The unresolved feelings of the Americans toward their industrial civilization (was man the master, slave, or double of the machine?) jibed perfectly with Dada's ambivalence toward the Machine Age. If Western culture was bad, was not the vulgarity and assertiveness of American popular culture that much worse? Because of the prevalence of these negative attitudes among artists and intellectuals, Dada, curiously enough, was the first international art movement in which the Americans had a head start. What Dada served to do in America was to crystallize the antisocial aspects of the avant-garde, but by so doing, to give the avant-garde a sense of its own identity, for better or for worse. Irony was prescribed as a cure for despair, and an aggressive stance counseled as the best defense against a hostile society. Typical of the attitude of the group surrounding Arensberg is Morton Schamberg's sardonic assemblage *God* (*Ill. 4-11*).

Obviously, if the public chose to take modern art as a scandal, the answer was to give them more scandals. Unconventional behavior, sexual liberation, even dissipation were condoned; chess playing and

4-11. MORTON SCHAMBERG, *God, ca.* 1918.

transvestitism took their place as artistic activities. The trappings, if not the living arrangements, of a Bohemia had arrived. If there were not sufficient scandals to suit the public, then scandals were arranged. One of the first of such arranged scandals took place at the opening of the 1917 Independents' exhibition, from which the *Fountain* by R. Mutt had been banned. Picabia and Duchamp invited the boxer Arthur Craven, who had a reputation for outrageous behavior, to deliver a lecture. Craven, not unexpectedly, arrived drunk and began disrobing; the public gasped, and Duchamp pronounced his performance a "wonderful lecture."

Duchamp and Picabia gathered around them a motley group of eccentrics, including the Baroness Elsa von Loringhoven, who dressed in rags, wore sardine cans on her head, and had objects suspended from her clothes on chains. Duchamp's apartment itself was a spectacle; a friend described how it was "strewn with clothes pegs like a forest of wolf traps," while on the glass walls "spirals revolved beside a shovel inscribed, 'Ahead of the broken.arm.'" Perhaps the best explanation of what was behind these activities was offered by the Dada poet Tristan Tzara. Writing in the magazine *New York dada,* he insisted that "we shall see certain liberties we constantly take in the sphere of sentiment, social life, morals, once more become normal standards. These liberties no longer will be looked upon as crime, but as itches." To the critics who cried out that modern art was immoral and anarchistic, the Dadaists answered in the affirmative, and claimed that the rights of the artist transcended morality and politics. In holding that anything goes, they may have discredited art, but they also created a climate of experimentation in which many artists felt liberated for the first time from the repressive aspects of American culture. In such an atmosphere Holger Cahill's Inje-Inje group sponsored concerts in which only per-

4-12. JOSEPH STELLA,
*Collage #11, ca.* 1921.

4-13. ARTHUR DOVE,
*Portrait of Ralph Dusenberry*, 1924.

cussion instruments were played and dances in which the performers were costumed only in mitts.

Often, however, this urge to experiment, without the guidelines of a definite tradition, took artists to the periphery of artistic activity. And in many ways this kind of experimentation remained a characteristic of American art. A number of collages executed by American artists around 1920 might be described as experiments from the periphery. In their literalness and use of objects from the environment, the collages of Stella, Dove, and Maurer have more in common with Schwitters' Dada *Merzbilder* than with Cubist collage. Stella's torn and faded papers and old cigarette packages, and his extraordinary series of abstract collages (*Ill. 4-12*) seem to anticipate the Abstract Expressionist sensibility; Dove's collage *Portrait of Ralph Dusenberry* (*Ill. 4-13*) goes beyond Cubist collage in its literal use of actual materials. And John Covert's string paintings, such as *Vocalization* (*Ill. 4-14*), are an unexpected form of abstract collage. Similarly, Maurer's use of oilcloth and textiles as backgrounds in pictures like *Still Life with Doily* (*Ill. 4-15*) shows original experimentation which takes advantage of the properties of materials.

In a sense this kind of experimental activity becomes more comprehensible when viewed in the context of the Dada revolt against the conventional limits of art. It was an important moment when the American artist discovered that freedom from tradition meant freedom from rules; and that if there was no tradition, at least there were no rules either. Some artists later repudiated this freedom to steer a safer

4-14. JOHN COVERT,
*Vocalization*, 1919.

4-15. ALFRED MAURER,
*Still Life with Doily, ca.* 1930.

course within known boundaries, at times repudiating their experimental work as well. Thus one of the difficulties in reconstructing American art history in the twenties and thirties is that much experimental work of the period was destroyed. Bruce, Benton, Covert, and Burchfield, among others, demolished many of their own paintings. Burchfield was especially contrite. He wrote with distaste of the time immediately following his discharge from the Army in 1919 as "a period of degeneracy in my art that I have never been able to explain . . . the vagaries of the Da-Da school were nothing compared to mine at this time, though I had never heard of Da-Daism."[10] As soon as his native American common sense returned, however, he destroyed these offensive works.

For every artist who turned his back on modernism, there were others determined to find new forms adequate to express the qualities of modern life, "to produce the tickling sensation of a new way of thinking and feeling," in Gilbert Cannon's words. Adapting to the realities of an industrial society was central to America's aesthetic coming of age. The acceptance of the idea that culture could be contemporary and that the breaking with old traditions did not preclude the founding of a new tradition was an important step in this coming of age. In Europe, the Futurists and the Purists had already begun to use machine imagery as the basis for their art. In America, a group of artists who became known as the Precisionists or Immaculates also turned to mechanical and industrial forms as a way of stamping their work as contemporary.

In this context, the machine imagery of Precisionism may be considered part of a general trend toward using mechanical forms, as in the work of Kupka or Léger. Others, however, continued to find the machines not a blessing but a threat. Perhaps only foreigners like Duchamp and Picabia had sufficient perspective to enjoy all the ironies of the situation: America, the most industrially advanced nation in the world, the country of automobiles, airplanes, fast trains, and power engines, should have fulfilled Marinetti's and Tatlin's prophecies for a new machine art. Instead, Americans were just as likely to feel with Rilke that American machines were turning out "life-decoys" to replace the old objects of love and devotion. For them, the machine itself became an object of ironical devotion or equally ironical derision, and man's dehumanization the instrument of the humanization of the machine. Attributing human qualities to the machine, Picabia made the first of his satires on mechanization in his 1913 drawing, *Girl Born Without a Mother.* A year earlier, Duchamp had painted the *Bride,* a complex diagram of a female machine. The project that occupied Duchamp throughout the war and into the twenties was *The Large Glass,* a big, complex group of quasi-human machines connected by means of quasi-mechanical relationships. Picabia's 1915 cover for the magazine *291, Young American Girl in a State of Nudity,* and Duchamp's *Chocolate Grinder (Ill. 4-16),* which appeared on the cover of *Blind Man* in 1917, were prototypes of mechanical objects rendered in a dry, factual manner and placed in an anonymous setting. They provided a point of departure for Precisionist imagery; certainly their

4-17. MORTON SCHAMBERG,
*Machine,* 1916.

4-16. MARCEL DUCHAMP,
*Chocolate Grinder, No. 2,* 1914.

clean, hard edges and simple geometry must have impressed Schamberg, Sheeler, and Demuth, friends of the Dadaists, who were already beginning to work in such a direction. Schamberg was the first to develop these machine forms into the basis for a lucid geometric art, as in *Machine* (*Ill. 4-17*). But shortly after the Armory Show, Sheeler, too, had abandoned his Fauvist manner in order to experiment with Cubist reductions of objects into volumes, planes, and lines of direction. His aim was "to divorce the object from the dictionary." Since Sheeler's studies reveal the underlying structure of objects, they are related to analytic Cubism. But to the degree that their source remains Cézanne, they miss the complex spatial ambiguities of Braque and Picasso, and are not genuinely analytic Cubist works. Beginning in 1917 with *Barns* (*Ill. 4-18*), Sheeler reconstructed his flattened masses into a solidly integrated composition, in which color and texture were arbitrarily added. His analyses consisted mainly of diagramming structure rather than disintegrating it; these reconstructions idealize reality

4-18. CHARLES SHEELER,
*Barns*, 1917.

4-19. CHARLES SHEELER,
*Barn Abstraction*, 1918.

4-20. CHARLES DEMUTH, *Trees and Barns, Bermuda,* 1917.

rather than reformulate it through distortion. In his 1918 paintings of barns, structures are further simplified to a few straight lines and rectangles set squarely and directly in the middle ground, coolly floating in an anonymous setting as in *Barn Abstraction (Ill. 4-19)*. "In these paintings," Sheeler has said, "I sought to reduce natural forms to the borderline of abstraction, retaining only those forms which I believed to be indispensable to the design of the picture."[11]

At about the same time, Demuth seems to have arrived at a similar solution to the problem of unifying abstract design based on Cubist precedent without destroying the recognizability of objects. Two important influences on Demuth at this time were Duchamp, through whom he said he gained an interest in good workmanship, and Marsden Hartley, who was painting his most abstract Cubist works when he vacationed with Demuth in Bermuda in 1917. During this Bermuda trip, Demuth began to paint landscapes, such as *Trees and Barns, Bermuda (Ill. 4-20)*, which exhibit the same clarity, dryness, and geometric simplifications as Sheeler's barns. Demuth, however, made greater use of the Futurist "lines of force"—ray-like projections that crossed and recrossed over objects creating linear patterns that in turn were played off against the mass of the objects. But, unlike Stella, Weber, or Feininger, who also appropriated these lines of force, Demuth did not shatter masses into fragmented planes. This unwillingness to shatter the object is what mainly distinguishes Precisionism as a Cubist style; instead of fragmenting, the Precisionists simplified, stylized, and arranged objects in such a way as to emphasize their purity of line and structure. For this reason, Precisionism has also been called Cubist-Realism.

Obviously, certain kinds of objects lent themselves more easily than others to such treatment. With this in mind, the Precisionists usually chose forms that were geometric to begin with. They found the rectangles of windows and barns, the cylinders of grain elevators, the circular wheels and cogs of machinery best suited to their aims. The cool objectivity of Demuth's *Machinery (Ill. 4-21)* is characteristic of the Precisionist approach.

In the carefully wrought, pared-down shapes of Shaker furniture and utensils, Sheeler found a favorite subject. The plainness of Shaker shapes, their refined finish, and especially their craftsmanship—so precious in an era of mass production—expressed an integrity of workmanship and design Sheeler wished to emulate in paintings such as *American Interior (Ill. 4-22)*.

Sometimes the intermediary of the camera was employed to freeze a scene so that it could be transformed into a static composition. For this reason, many Precisionist paintings have the quality, common to photographs, of the frozen moment. In many respects the hard edges, slick impersonal surfaces, solid shadows, and upward tilted perspectives of Precisionist paintings seem inspired by the study of photographs. In Schamberg's and Sheeler's cases, the relationship is clear; both sup-

4-21. CHARLES DEMUTH, *Machinery*, 1920.

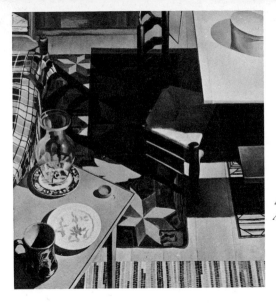

4-22. CHARLES SHEELER,
*American Interior,* 1934.

ported themselves as photographers. Sheeler in fact based specific compositions on photographs he had taken. The 1931 *Classic Landscape* (*Ill. 4-23*), for example, is patterned on the photographs Sheeler took of the Ford Motor plant at River Rouge in 1927. The movie *Manahatta,* which Sheeler made with the photographer Paul Haviland, helped to fix in his mind the image of the skyscraper. Beginning in 1920, he used this image again and again. Although O'Keeffe has denied being influenced by photography, the way that her giant close-ups of flowers fill the frame reminds one of photographic blow-ups. Demuth and

4-23. CHARLES SHEELER,
*Classic Landscape*
(*River Rouge Plant*), 1931.

4-24. CHARLES DEMUTH,
*Incense of a New Church*, 1921.

Stella, too, painted flowers in a manner more related to the photographic enlargement than to conventional still life. Interestingly, one of the rationales for photography as the most modern of the arts was that photographs are the result of man bending the machine to his will.

Because the theme of the factory seemed particularly appropriate to the Machine Age, it soon became a standard of Precisionist iconography. Although Joseph Stella had painted industrial subjects such as factories and gas tanks from 1915 to 1918, Demuth's factories, beginning with the 1921 *Incense of a New Church* (*Ill. 4-24*), were more clearly flattened, stylized, and simplified. Soon other artists such as Stefan Hirsch, George Ault, Louis Lozowick, Edmund Lewandowski, Niles Spencer, Ralston Crawford, Peter Blume, and Preston Dickinson were interpreting native American subjects in terms of their potential as abstract design (*Ills. 4-25, 4-26, 4-27*). Joseph Stella, although painting in the Futurist style, continued to share the Precisionists' concern with finding epic material in urban and industrial images.

Like many American artists of the forties and fifties, Joseph Stella—one of the outstanding draftsmen in the history of American art—rejected his own virtuosity in order to arrive at a more authentic expression of his feelings. Born in Italy, he was an arch romantic who wholeheartedly embraced the American dream. Combing contemporary American experience for viable universal symbols, he arrived at a

4-25. GEORGE AULT,
*Sullivan Street Abstraction,* 1928.

4-26. RALSTON CRAWFORD,
*Grain Elevators from the Bridge,* 1942.

visionary interpretation of the industrial landscape which sought to capture the quality, texture, and tempo of American life. For Joseph Stella, as for Marin, the city was the nexus of explosive, form-shattering power. Fond of quoting Whitman, whose portrait he drew (*Ill. 4-28*), he discovered heroic images in the banal and the prosaic. In the Brooklyn Bridge, Stella, like Hart Crane, found a contemporary subject worthy of elegiac and lyric treatment.

Since his arrival in America, the Brooklyn Bridge had been his ever-growing obsession. He saw it for the first time as a "weird metallic

4-27. NILES SPENCER,
*Erie Underpass,* 1949.

4-28. JOSEPH STELLA,
*Portrait of Walt Whitman, ca.* 1920.

apparition under a metallic sky, out of proportion with the winged lightness of its arch" (*Ill. 4-30*). He was inspired by the "massive dark towers dominating the surrounding tumult of surging skyscrapers with their gothic majesty sealed in the purity of their arches." For Stella the bridge was "the shrine containing all the efforts of the new civilization, *America*—the eloquent meeting point of all the forces arising in a superb assertion of their powers, an Apotheosis."[12] After making a number of versions of the bridge, he later turned inward to a fantastic world of strange images and tropical landscapes (*Ill. 4-29*).

In choosing banal or commonplace themes, the Precisionists were, like the best American critics of the time, beginning to reject the mock

4-29. JOSEPH STELLA,
*Song of Barbados,* 1938.

4-30. JOSEPH STELLA, *Brooklyn Bridge,* 1917–18.

heroics of a grand style. Such a style seemed unsuited to the down-to-earth realities of the American experience. In 1924, Lewis Mumford wrote in *Sticks and Stones* of the greatness of the anonymous architecture of the American countryside, the factories and the grain elevators, as opposed to the pretentious glamour of official architecture. In focusing on indigenous subject matter and relating it to earlier American art traditions, the Precisionists were able to translate the language of Cubism into local usage. Noting, perhaps, that this earlier American art also had been anonymous, like the grain elevators and factories Mumford praised, they sought an anonymity of time and place. But the anonymity they arrived at was less charged with nostalgia and associations than de Chirico's deserted railroad stations, although these paintings may have inspired the Precisionists.

The virtue of much of this work is that it did not transform an abstract substructure into a figurative art in order to give viewers a way into the painting, but instead sought in reality geometric shapes, patterns, and rhythms that expressed a sense of order and permanence. In the hands of these artists, the skyscraper, also a favorite theme of Georgia O'Keeffe from 1926 to 1929 (*Ill. 4-31*), became a heroic subject. In their calm, reflective view, the Precisionists seemed to agree with Sheeler that: "Banging one's fist upon the table until the glasses dance is not as impressive as claiming the same attention by means of a well-ordered statement."[13]

In Europe, F. Scott Fitzgerald's friend Gerald Murphy was also painting abstractions of common objects, like matchboxes and cigarette packages, in a cool impersonal style that had much in common with Precisionism. Murphy's compositions, such as *Wasp and Pear* (*Ill. 4-33*), however, with their complex overlapping of planes which brought the image close to the picture surface, are more reminiscent of Stuart Davis' early abstractions than of Precisionist work.

Although less technically advanced and less ambitious than Synchromism, the Cubist-Realism of Demuth and Sheeler was the more distinctively American version of Cubism. And it had a more lasting

4-31. GEORGIA O'KEEFFE,
*New York Night,* 1928–29.

4-32. CHARLES DEMUTH, *My Egypt*, 1927.

effect on American art. Its modest productions possessed a resolve, finish, and quiet integrity that distinguished them from, as Forbes Watson put it, the "fog-horn chorus of blah" that was American painting in the twenties. In comparison with French painting, Precisionism was conservative, but it was not a compromise with either academicism or illustration. By renouncing the European mold, the Precisionists achieved their own dignity, even if this meant renouncing any pretension to grandeur. The acknowledgment that American subjects were commonplace and banal, and that the American landscape could claim as its monuments, not the pyramids or ruins of antiquity, but only the

4-33. GERALD MURPHY,
*Wasp and Pear*, 1927.

humble utilitarian objects of the here and now, was difficult for sensitive artists to make. To find something worth celebrating with honesty sometimes drove an artist like Demuth to ironic conclusions. Although he was able to discover monumentality in the plain forms of a grain elevator (as O'Keeffe and Sheeler had in barns and skyscrapers, and as Stella had in the bridge), Demuth expressed his sense of loss by comparing the grain elevators with the pyramids of antiquity, ironically titling them *My Egypt* (*Ill. 4-32*).

In their programmatic return to American sources, to the art of the Shakers, the Indians, and the colonial primitives, American artists of the twenties clarified their relationship to the American tradition. In general, despite the provincialism that continued on some fronts, there was a gradual advance toward a more sophisticated outlook. The little magazines continued to print defenses of modernism; the *Dial*, for example, published articles by the leading European critics, Clive Bell, Roger Fry, and Julius Meier-Graefe, as well as a regular column by Henry McBride. In 1921, the Metropolitan Museum held an exhibition of modern art, and in 1923, W. R. Valentiner organized the first full-scale American exhibition of German Expressionism at the Anderson Gallery. Between 1921 and 1930, sixty new museums were founded, a further indication of how greatly the art world had expanded. In addition, the American public could see abstract art at the Carroll and Montross galleries, and at the exhibitions of the Société Anonyme, where Kandinsky, Klee, Léger, Villon, and Archipenko had their first one-man shows. There, Schwitters, Miró, Mondrian, Ernst, and Malevich also had their first shows anywhere. The work of these artists was proof of the society's motto: "Traditions are beautiful—but to create them—not to follow." Besides these exhibitions, Katherine Dreier and her friends sponsored lectures on the psychology of modern art and a symposium on Dada, and published the English translation of Apollinaire's work on Cubism.

Summarizing the new attitude toward modernism, Christian Brinton wrote in 1926: "Modernism as a definite, specific issue has entered into the consciousness of the public at large, and modern art today is recognized and accepted by the leading museums of the country, and by our more astute and progressive professional dealers. We do not need another Armory Show, for the days of the Circus Maximus are over."[14]

Despite Brinton's optimism, the twenties were not an altogether happy epoch for American art. During the disillusioning postwar period, many artists felt that their only choices were to give up abstraction, give up art, give up society, or give up life. In many ways this mood coincided with the conservative European retreat from abstraction and experimentation; that is, with the time when many progressive European artists returned to tighter, more realistic styles. But the collapse of American modernism in the twenties was more complete, tragic, and inevitable than the European *détente*.

By 1920 O'Keeffe, Hartley, Weber, Macdonald-Wright, Dasburg, and Benton, to name the most prominent examples, had renounced abstraction. Of the major painters, only Dove maintained his commitment to abstract art. Stieglitz' gallery, 291, had closed, and the artists associated with it had disappeared. When *Camera Work* suspended publication in 1917, its circulation was thirty-six subscribers. Walkowitz was forgotten, and Frost, unable to pursue his friend Craven's career of dissipation, was dead of a tubercular hemorrhage, four days before his thirtieth birthday. Morton Schamberg had died at the age of thirty-seven, a victim of the 1918 flu epidemic. John Covert had given up painting to return to business. Throughout the entire decade, only one major painter, Stuart Davis, emerged to take up the cause of modernism. With the coming of the Depression, what little serious interest there had been in art would soon be distracted by the more pressing issue of the country's economic collapse.

## Chapter Five

## The Thirties: Reaction and Rebellion

Revolution is possible only in instances and domains where tradition is present. No tradition, no revolution.

—John Graham, *System and Dialectics of Art,* 1937

Discovering the futility of reconciling the old with the new in a compromise with modernism, artists of the twenties had attempted to end imitation and to create a style that was both modern and American. The Depression years, however tragic and difficult they may have been otherwise, saw the birth of such a modern style in America. During the thirties the search for the roots of an American tradition took on an even more urgent character. The political and economic crisis seemed to augment the need to define the nation's cultural identity.

The crucial years of the Depression, as they are brought into historical focus, increasingly emerge as the decisive decade for American art, if not for American culture in general. For it was during this decade that many of the conflicts which had blocked the progress of American art in the past came to a head and sometimes boiled over. Janus-faced, the thirties looked backward, sometimes as far as the Renaissance; and at the same time forward, as far as the present and beyond. It was the moment when artists, like Thomas Hart Benton, who wished to turn back the clock to regain the virtues of simpler times came into direct conflict with others, like Stuart Davis and Frank Lloyd Wright, who were ready to come to terms with the Machine Age and to deal with its consequences.

America in the thirties was changing rapidly. In many areas the past was giving way to the present, although not without a struggle. A predominately rural and small town society was being replaced by the giant complexes of the big cities; power was becoming increasingly centralized in the federal government and in large corporations. As a result, traditional American types such as the independent farmer and the small businessman were being replaced by the executive and the bureaucrat. Many Americans, deeply attached to the old way of life, felt disinherited. At the same time, as immigration decreased and the population became more homogeneous, the need arose in art and literature to commemorate the ethnic and regional differences that were fast disappearing. The incursions of government controls on the laissez-faire system, acting to erode the Calvinist ethic of hard work and personal sacrifice on which both the economy and public morality had rested, called forth a similar reaction. Thus, paradoxically, the conviction that art, at least, should serve some purpose or carry some message of moral uplift grew stronger as the Puritan ethos lost its contemporary reality. Often this elevating message was a sermon in favor of just those traditional American virtues which were now threatened with obsolescence in a changed social and political context.

In this new context, the appeal of the paintings by the Regionalists and the American Scene painters often lay in their ability to recreate an atmosphere that glorified the traditional American values—self-reliance tempered with good-neighborliness, independence modified by a sense of community, hard work rewarded by a sense of order and purpose. Given the actual temper of the times, these themes were strangely anachronistic, just as the rhetoric supporting political isolationism was equally inappropriate in an international situation soon to involve America in a second world war. Such themes gained popularity because they filled a genuine need for a comfortable collective fantasy of a God-fearing, white-picket-fence America, which in retrospect took on the nostalgic appeal of a lost Golden Age.

In this light, an autonomous art-for-art's sake was viewed as a foreign invader liable to subvert the native American desire for a purposeful art. Abstract art was assigned the role of the villainous alien; realism was to personify the genuine American means of expression. The argument drew favor in many camps: among the artists, because most were realists; among the politically-oriented intellectuals, because abstract art was apolitical; and among museum officials, because they were surfeited with mediocre imitations of European modernism and were convinced that American art must develop its own distinct identity. To help along this road to self-definition, the museums were prepared to set up an artificial double standard, one for American art, and another for European art. In 1934, Ralph Flint wrote in *Art News,*

"We have today in our midst a greater array of what may be called second-, third-, and fourth-string artists than any other country. Our big annuals are marvelous outpourings of intelligence and skill; they have all the diversity and animation of a five-ring circus."

The most commanding attraction in this circus was surely that of the American Scene painters, a category that may be broadened to accommodate both the urban realists, like Reginald Marsh, Isabel Bishop, Alexander Brook, and the brothers Isaac, Moses, and Raphael Soyer, and the Regionalists, like Thomas Hart Benton, James Steuart Curry, and Grant Wood. American Scene painting was, to a degree, a continuation of the tradition of Henri and the New York realists, which had by no means died out. Its stronghold was the Art Students League, where John Sloan was elected director in 1931, and Kenneth Hayes Miller and Yasuo Kuniyoshi, also former Henri students, per-

5-1. KENNETH HAYES MILLER,
*The Shopper,* 1928.

5-3. REGINALD MARSH,
*Bowery and Pell Street—
Looking North,* 1944.

5-2. RAPHAEL SOYER,
*Office Girls,* 1936.

5-4. ISABEL BISHOP, *Nude*, 1934.

5-5. YASUO KUNIYOSHI, *I'm Tired*, 1938.

petuated Henri's approach. Here, too, Thomas Hart Benton preached the gospel of Regionalism.

Sloan, of course, continued Henri's great liberating influence, stressing individual expression, in whatever form, as long as it was authentic, rather than insisting on any doctrinaire adherence to formula. But Sloan was exceptional in his convictions—so exceptional in fact that he resigned his position during a controversy over hiring foreign teachers, in this case, the distinguished German Expressionist George Grosz. Also unusual was Sloan's position on social consciousness in art. Criticized for not propagandizing for social reform, Sloan, an active socialist since his youth, countered: "They may say that I am now fiddling while Rome burns, but I question whether social propaganda is necessary to the life of a work of art."[1] Earlier he had been subject to similar criticism when he and Stuart Davis resigned from the *Masses* in 1916; the magazine, edited by Floyd Dell, had attempted to dictate the subject matter of their art and direct it toward a more socially critical orientation. Significantly, the unsentimental objectivity that distinguishes Sloan's work from the acrid or maudlin genre produced by the majority of American Scene painters was viewed in its time as an irresponsible refusal to take sides.

Like the paintings of The Eight, Kenneth Hayes Miller's *The Shopper* (*Ill. 5-1*), Raphael Soyer's *Office Girls* (*Ill. 5-2*), and Reginald Marsh's *Bowery and Pell Street—Looking North* (*Ill. 5-3*) depict familiar urban scenes. Similarly, *Nude* by Isabel Bishop (*Ill. 5-4*) and Yasuo Kuniyoshi's *I'm Tired* (*Ill. 5-5*) are typical of the modest, careful figure studies turned out by the faculty and students of the Art Students League. Yet although American Scene painting appropriated Ash Can School subjects, its practitioners often lagged behind Henri technically. The wholesale attempt to revive Renaissance techniques of draftsmanship, composition, and execution, such as the use of tempera as a medium, may be seen as yet another aspect of the search for a tradition. But among insecure or conservative artists, this search was often translated solely into a quest for a set of rules for the artist on which the bewildered public could base standards. Toward this end the American Scene painters revived all of the old tricks of academic illusionism long discarded by the modernists. Chiaroscuro, foreshortening, perspective, and fine detail were enlisted in the service of an art that was contemporary only in depicting contemporary settings and costumes.

American Scene painting arose partially out of the same growing conviction that the American experience was tangibly different from the European experience that had inspired the art of O'Keeffe, Dove, Hartley, Marin, Stella, and the Precisionists. Artists came to realize that American art required not only its own subjects, but also its own forms and means of expression. Many believed that the homely style of the American Scene painters provided these. Some artists, however, although they painted typically American subjects and scenes, renounced the concept of an "American Scene" as too restrictive.

Discussing American painting with Maurer, Dove criticized the shortcomings of a literary interpretation of the American scene: "When a man paints the El, a 1740 house or a miner's shack, he is likely to be called by his critics, American. These things may be in America, but it's what is in the artist that counts. What do we call American outside of painting? Inventiveness, restlessness, speed, change." Suggesting a broader conception of a national style than the mere rendering of indigenous objects, locales, or types, Dove held that the means of expression took priority over subject matter, observing that "a painter may put all these qualities in a still life or an abstraction, and be going more native than another who sits quietly copying a skyscraper." Dove found particularly objectionable the popular attitude that "the American painter is supposed to paint as though he had never seen another painting."[2]

Stuart Davis, too, condemned provincialism, but declared, "I paint what I see in America, in other words, I paint the American Scene." Despite the fact that he painted abstractions, Davis still called himself a realist: "I want to paint and do paint particular aspects of this country which interest me," he stated. "But I use, as a great many others do, some of the methods of modern French painting which I consider to have universal validity."[3] Davis was among the first publicly to prescribe an accommodation with modernism that would not compromise American art, or rob it of its national stamp, but, nonetheless, would extract it from the provincialism which was the core of American Scene painting.

The group of artists who became known as Regionalists, which included Benton, Wood, Curry, Aaron Bohrod, Joe Jones, and by association, Charles Burchfield, aimed at capturing the image of America's heartland, and a nostalgic interest in preserving disappearing local types and scenes soon monopolized their art. Although New York has been the center of American art throughout the twentieth century, many native-born artists maintained strong attachments to the insular farms, midwestern towns, and coastal hamlets where they were born. Hartley's New England fishing villages fit the Regionalist iconography as easily as Curry's prairies and farms, Wood's steepled towns and villages, and Benton's plantations and corn fields. The difference, however, is that Hartley presented his themes in terms of the conventions of modern art, specifically Expressionism, whereas the Regionalists by and large wished to escape the art of their time, just as they wished to turn their backs on contemporary reality in order to preserve the atmosphere and life styles of times gone by.

As leader and spokesman of the group, Benton attacked the internationalism of the modern movement and focused his criticism particularly on Alfred Stieglitz, whom he saw as the personification of all the evils of the decadent Old World. In his attacks on Stieglitz, he displayed the typical virulence of a convert to a new religion against his former beliefs—and with good reason. Benton's hard-nosed individualism, though it had taken a reactionary turn, was cut from the same cloth as that of Hartley, Marin, and of Stieglitz himself. For Benton, in fact, had been a frequent visitor to 291, and his early paintings, although based on Renaissance compositions, were nonetheless Synchromist abstractions. As he confided later to his friend and apologist, the critic Thomas Craven, "I wallowed in every cockeyed ism that came along and it took me ten years to get all that modernist dirt out of my system."[4] Like Burchfield, upon seeing the light, he repudiated his brief fall from grace into the degeneracy of modernism and was rabid in his denunciation of heretics. The Stieglitz group he dismissed as "an intellectually diseased lot, victims of sickly rationalizations, psychic inversions, and God-awful self-cultivations."[5]

As for Benton's diatribes against urban life, they seem now the last outcry of midwestern populism, the defensiveness of the country boy afraid of being taken by the city slickers. In his autobiography, *An Artist in America,* Benton voiced his many frustrations. Suspicious and chauvinistic, he gloried in the fact that "the people of the West are highly intolerant of aberration." Appalled by the corruption of the urban milieu, he thundered, "The great cities are dead. They offer nothing but coffins for living and thinking." He and Craven, analyzing the state of moral decay about them, saw Marxists and homosexuals wherever they looked. Opposed to the aestheticism of the "curving wrist and the outthrust hip," they embraced a hairy-chested masculinity that was a vulgarization of the Henri stance, much as Regionalism was a vulgarization of Ash Can School subjects.

Benton began to be suspicious of "political and aesthetic doctrines drawn from middle European philosophizing" during World War I when he worked as an architectural draftsman in a Norfolk naval base. Away from New York and its subjective theorizing, his interests changed, and became "in a flash, of an objective nature." At this time, "the mechanical contrivances of buildings, the new airplanes, the blimps, the dredges, the ships of the base, because they were so interesting in themselves" tore Benton away from his "play with colored cubes and classic attenuations, from aesthetic drivelings and morbid self-concern." Curiously, the very subjects that had inspired Malevich to invent non-objective art brought Benton back down to earth.

5-6. THOMAS HART BENTON, *City Scenes,* 1930.

5-7. GRANT WOOD,
*Stone City, Iowa,*
1930.

After the war, Benton describes how he, Wood, and Curry revolted "against the general cultural inconsequences of modern art," separately arriving at the belief that "only by our own participation in the reality of American life . . . could we come to forms in which Americans would find an opportunity for genuine spectator participation."[6] In the name of democratizing art, Benton conceived a grandiose new monumental, public art, whose program was not much removed from those espoused by the totalitarian "people's governments." As part of such a program, he planned a comprehensive, pictorial history of the United States in sixty-four panels, sixteen of which were completed. Such a narrative sequence was in a sense but an up-dated version of the popular art form, the cyclorama. In 1930, when he was commissioned to paint a series of murals at the New School for Social Research, Benton interpreted contemporary Americana in a crammed, churning panorama filled with bulging, muscular figures, drawn from Michelangelo and combined with popular images (*Ill. 5-6*). If these murals are vulgar in spirit and crude in technique, nonetheless they are bursting with energy. Their enormous popular appeal must be attributed to their ability to satisfy that aspect of American popular taste which applauded the flamboyantly tasteless murals of Sorolla earlier in the century while spurning the "ugliness" of The Eight. If Benton's compositions strike the viewer as false or contrived, it is because they are first plotted as abstractions, and then turned into figurative motifs, and not vice versa, as is the case with Hopper or Sloan. The figures are often unconvincing as figures, although Benton's ability to render the plasticity of three-dimensional form is such that they are charged with a seething vitality.

Grant Wood's cardboard-stiff forms and dry, laconic style, as shown in *Stone City, Iowa (Ill. 5-7)*, are quite the opposite of Benton's rolling, bulging forms and rhetorical expression. With its slick surfaces, hard edges, and sharp focus, Wood's work, like that of the Magic Realists, was related to Precisionism. Finding a "quality in American newness," he perversely attempted to express this quality in the terms of the meticulous detail of the German and Flemish primitives, whom he had studied during a trip to Munich in 1928. A designer of model houses and stained glass interiors, Wood also made some little-known surrealistic objects.

Like Wood, Curry chose to celebrate the achievement of legendary American folk heroes. In the saga of John Brown, he found a theme he considered sufficiently heroic, and clumsily attempted to paint it in the style of the heroic painting of the past, in the swelling forms of

5-8. CHARLES BURCHFIELD, *Noontide in Late May,* 1917.

5-9. EDWARD HOPPER, *Early Sunday Morning,* 1930.

Rubens and the soft light of Turner. The result was a naive and inept travesty of heroic painting. Just as Benton and a large part of the great public that admired his work had confused the folk tradition with popular culture, Curry too confused the two by introducing Charlie Chaplin and Walt Disney creatures into his Pageant of America. Like most Americans of his generation, Curry resented that art "as a reality was as foreign as Chinese."

Charles Burchfield never set out to confine himself to Regionalist themes; he was a Regionalist only by association. His earliest surviving paintings were composed of florid, curvilinear, two-dimensional patterns based on exotic plant motifs. These were the symbolic motifs that he called "conventions for abstract thought." By 1917, in such works as *Noontide in Late May (Ill. 5-8),* Burchfield had retreated to a more conventional interpretation of landscape motifs. After his rejection of modernism, his later works became less decorative and more bizarre. In these paintings of strange haunted houses, inanimate objects are invested with a life of their own. In his many variations on a number of standard themes—the deserted street, the empty house, the haunted wood—Burchfield exaggerated the quality of fantasy and unreality, his object being "the expression of a completely personal mood." An admirer of Sherwood Anderson's *Winesburg, Ohio,* Burchfield himself lived in Salem, Ohio. Like Anderson, he used the modest, undramatic houses and streets of his town as the inspiration for richer fantasies.

123

Although he praised Burchfield's work, Edward Hopper dismissed the less imaginative versions of American Scene painting as mere caricature. Hopper was more interested in the psychological investigation of the characteristics of American experience—its loneliness, barrenness, and lack of variety or high moments. Instead of the grandiose themes of the Regionalists, Hopper chose the genuine pathos of daily life. Whereas his contemporary Stuart Davis found the city a subject for abstract transformation, Hopper saw only the doomed yearning of lonely figures in cold offices and desolate hotel rooms. To the clamorousness of Davis' collective and synthetic experience, he opposed melancholy single figures, isolated in anonymous, depersonalized surroundings.

Returning from Europe in 1910, where Bruce had introduced him to the Impressionists, Hopper soon moved to Washington Square, admitting that he liked the neighborhood because it gave him a sense of continuity with The Eight. After he showed a small painting, *Sailing,* in the Armory Show, he devoted himself mostly to etching everyday scenes and rural landscapes. Around 1920, Hopper began to paint more oils. Like Bellows and Guy Pène du Bois, during the twenties Hopper learned to generalize forms, treating them summarily, and eliminating trivial detail in such paintings as *Early Sunday Morning (Ill. 5-9)*. In 1930 he bought a house in Truro, and most of his landscapes after that time were based on Cape Cod scenes. In these studies of rooftops and architectural forms, Hopper achieved a new sense of solidity and weightiness. Approving of Burchfield's interpretation of the American landscape, Hopper called the United States a "chaos of ugliness," but admired Burchfield's ability to find the "hideous beauty" of native architecture with its "fantastic roofs, pseudo-Gothic, French Mansard, Colonial, mongrel or what not," and of the houses with their "eye-searing color or delicate harmonies of faded paint, shouldering one another along interminable streets that taper off into swamps or dump heaps."[7]

Hopper defined his goal as making "the most exact transcription possible of my most intimate impressions of nature." Because this goal remained constant, Hopper did not feel compelled to alter drastically the means he had acquired early in his career. For that reason, the pictures of the fifties and sixties, such as *Second-Story Sunlight (Ill. 5-10)*, resemble those of the twenties, with the exception perhaps that they seem starker, barer, and more frontally oriented. As Hopper's art matured, one noted also an increasing ability to give solidity to mass

5-10. EDWARD HOPPER, *Second-Story Sunlight*, 1960.

and to integrate patterns of theatrically focused light and shadow within a highly organized compositional structure. Hopper differed from most of the other realists of the thirties in that he was able to maintain realism as a viable mode by choosing a subject compatible with his style and by refining his style to fit the needs of his subject. In such a coincidence of form and content, he achieved an honest and harmonious unity.

As a style, the illustrational realism of American Scene painting gained a large audience, partially because it appealed to popular taste and partially because it was widely disseminated throughout the country by mural painters, such as Mitchell Siporin, Boardman Robinson, George Biddle, and Anton Refregier. These artists were commissioned to decorate local banks, railway stations, and public buildings like post offices, as part of the public works program inaugurated by the New Deal to employ those out of work because of the Depression. Artists, who were living on the fringes of the economy in the best times, were particularly hard hit. To give them relief, the Public Works of Art Project, administered by Edward Bruce and Forbes Watson through the Treasury Department, was set up in 1933. Abandoned in June, 1934, it was replaced a year later by the Federal Art Project, within the Works Progress Administration. The project was supervised by Holger Cahill, who also organized the *Index of Ameri-*

5-11. GEORGE BIDDLE, *Sweatshop,* Study, *ca.* 1935.

5-12. WILLIAM GROPPER, *Suburban Post in Winter,* 1934-36.

*can Design,* a vast record of the history of decorative arts in America.

Through the Federal Art Project, painters, sculptors, and graphic artists were employed by the government at a monthly stipend. Among the artists who worked for the WPA mural and easel painting projects were Stuart Davis, Yasuo Kuniyoshi, Marsden Hartley, Jack Levine, Hyman Bloom, Loren MacIver, and Morris Graves. Younger artists included de Kooning, Gorky, Pollock, Gottlieb, Reinhardt, Rothko, and Guston. By the time the Federal Art Project was abandoned in 1943, 3,600 artists had participated in creating 16,000 works of art in over 1,000 American cities. The murals illustrated familiar scenes considered appropriate to their settings in bus and airline terminals, radio stations, schools, and housing projects; their subjects included trains pulling into stations, crowds at work, and events in the history of communications and transportation. Unfortunately, many have since been destroyed or painted over. Among the murals created for the Federal Art Project were George Biddle's *Sweatshop (Ill. 5-11),* William Gropper's *Suburban Post in Winter (Ill. 5-12),* and Arshile Gorky's *Aviation: Evolution of Forms Under Aerodynamic Limitations (Ill. 5-13).*

When the WPA muralists were not inspired by the master fresco painters of the Renaissance, they often took as their models the Mexican mural painters, particularly Diego Rivera and José Clemente

Orozco, both of whom were working in the United States during the thirties. The vigor of the Mexicans' style, and their protest against economic and social injustice in forceful expressionistic images, often couched in allegorical or religious terms, impressed the Americans, who were still convinced that art should serve a higher purpose than itself. At a time when American painters were so involved in finding an authentically American means of expression, the Mexicans' successful marriage of native Indian art with modernism seemed a particularly attractive solution.

The WPA is a unique but crucial chapter in American art. This is so despite the fact that, outside of a few murals known only through sketches or reconstructions, such as Gorky's Newark Airport mural and de Kooning's sketch for the Williamsburg housing project, the WPA programs produced almost no art of any consequence that has survived. Nevertheless, it radically altered the relationship of art and the artist to the art audience and to society. By making no formal distinction between abstract and representational art, the WPA supported the budding avant-garde's contention that both were equally "American." (However, it must be admitted that far more commissions were given to representational artists.) By affording artists the opportunity—which most had never had—to paint full time, the WPA gave them a sense of professionalism previously unavailable outside the academic context. By giving artists materials and time, it allowed them to develop their skills and technique to a new level. Throwing artists together in communal enterprises, the WPA experience provided an esprit de corps that carried over into the forties. Not the least of its contributions was the sponsorship of exhibitions and classes

5-13. ARSHILE GORKY, *Aviation: Evolution of Forms Under Aerodynamic Limitations,* Study, *ca.* 1936.

which served to arouse a consciousness of art in the far reaches of the country, where many people had never before seen an original work of art. On another level, the muralists' practice of creating for the large area of the wall rather than for a limited space of the easel picture helped to prepare artists to paint large-scale pictures a decade later.

Many of the WPA artists played an active role in politics, and many sought to convey a specifically political message through their art. These artists were often referred to as social realists. Even the artists who did not paint social protest themes were often politically active during the Depression. In 1936, between 300–400 painters, designers, photographers, and sculptors formed the Artists' Congress, dedicated to propagandizing antifascism. At the first meeting, Lewis Mumford announced that "The time has come for the people who love life and culture to form a united front . . . to be ready to protect, and guard, and if necessary, fight for the human heritage which we, as artists, embody."[8] Among its members were Peter Blume, Moses Soyer, and William Gropper, and the photographers Paul Strand, Margaret Bourke-White, and Ben Shahn, whose Depression photographs supplied him with many subjects for painting. Stuart Davis, Executive Secretary of the Congress, complained how the "prevalence of meetings, petitions, picket lines, and arrests" left him little time to work. Similarly, fine artists were even organized into an artists' union.

It is not surprising, then, that the theme of the worker and his plight was one of the principal subjects of the social realists. However, the "realism" of the social realists, it should be pointed out here, was twice removed from the realism of Courbet or Daumier. Although it often claimed them as ancestors, social realism in America emerged, not from the painterly tradition of nineteenth-century French realism, as the realism of The Eight had to an extent, but directly from the graphic tradition of magazine illustration and poster art. Often the paintings of the social realists were little more than stylized drawing in which paint was merely a fill between contours. Typical of social realism was Shahn's indictment of the treatment of the Italian anarchists Sacco and Vanzetti, who were condemned to death for murder in a trial that was the cause célèbre of American intellectuals in the thirties (*Ill. 5-14*). Shahn's series of paintings commemorating the trial are animated by the same sense of outrage that impelled Grosz to satirize the industrialists of postwar Berlin, but lack Grosz's sophistication and wit.

The "realism" of painters such as Shahn, Evergood, Hirsch, and

5-14. BEN SHAHN,
*The Passion of Sacco and Vanzetti,*
1931–32.

Jacob Lawrence, who saw art primarily as a means of communicating a social message, ought not to be confused with the realism of artists like George Bellows, Reginald Marsh, and Edward Hopper, who continued the best of the Henri tradition. If, as Hopper suggested, the American Scene painters were engaged in caricature, then the social realists, who editorialized in paint, were often not far removed from political cartoonists. A typical example, William Gropper, worked mainly in the graphic medium as an illustrator for the *New Masses,* and not surprisingly, his paintings are little more than translations of his cartoons of tycoons and bread lines.

For some artists, the reality of the thirties—the poverty, the joblessness, and the threat of the coming war in Europe—was too oppressive to deal with realistically. Many chose to escape reality through personal fantasy. Like the Surrealists, such as Dalí, they presented the inner world of the imagination in the precise, detailed realism of the photograph. Because they combined the factual with the fantastic, they were known as Magic Realists. However, the images used by artists like Ivan Albright, Peter Blume, Louis Guglielmi, Henry Koerner, and Alton Pickens were not, by and large, the monstrous or nightmarish images of Surrealism, but the factual, everyday images of the American Scene painters turned upside down.

Ivan Albright's *horror vacui* results in a hyper-realism which fills the canvas with a writhing, pulsating mass, reducing all textures to the same unpleasant common denominator, as in *That Which I Should Have Done I Did Not Do (Ill. 5-15)*. In the forties and fifties, artists like Honoré Sharrer, George Tooker, and Paul Cadmus continued to work in a manner that could be characterized as Magic Realist, in that it married a highly cultivated, precise technique and slick, polished surfaces with a perverse version of the everyday.

The most sophisticated of its practitioners, Peter Blume, offered a rationale for the unabashedly literary content of Magic Realism: "Since I am concerned with the communication of ideas I am not at all ashamed of 'telling stories' in my paintings, because I consider this to be one of the primary functions of the plastic arts. Visual or pictorial images are as much a part of the material of a painter as the color, shapes and forms he uses."[9] In *South of Scranton (Ill. 5-16)*, he presents surreal images in a matter-of-fact, realistic manner. Blume, whose early work was inspired by the Precisionists, insisted on the primacy of a highly developed technique capable of capturing fine detail. Admiration for his technical skill was of the same order as that which now greets the extraordinary technical accomplishment of Andrew Wyeth's more reticent and story-telling art, shown in *Christina's World (Ill. 5-17)*.

5-15. IVAN ALBRIGHT,
*That Which I Should Have Done
I Did Not Do,* 1931–41.

5-16. PETER BLUME,
*South of Scranton*,
1931.

Blume's search for the "permanent values in painting" led him, as it led many others, to attempt to restore the pictorial ideas of the past. Finding fault with this practice, the critic George L. K. Morris stated, "The plastic language requires a broader definition of 'technique' for sustenance than the mere ability to follow boundary-lines on a smooth gesso panel. . . . The painting 'looks like' the Quattrocento, but one will search in vain for an internal vitality such as the Italian masters produced throughout their struggle with the shapes of their new expression."[10]

Several artists who did not use the sharp focus or photographic detail of the Magic Realists are allied to them through their use of fantastic or bizarre images. Philip Evergood, whose anger at social injustice relates him to the social realists, often used the combined or

5-17. ANDREW WYETH,
*Christina's World*, 1948.

5-18. PHILIP EVERGOOD, *The New Lazarus*, 1927-54.

fantastic images of Magic Realism. Evergood's *The New Lazarus* (*Ill. 5-18*) is a complex religious allegory which translates the theme of the raising of Lazarus into contemporary terms. In the forties, a number of American artists painted religious or allegorical themes with surreal overtones, probably under the influence of Max Beckmann, who was teaching in America at the time. Younger members of this group, such as Stephen Greene, later turned to abstraction. Like Evergood's representation of the Lazarus episode, Greene's *The Burial* (*Ill. 5-19*) treats the theme of resurrection after death.

Other artists whose realistic paintings have a mystical or surreal

5-19. STEPHEN GREENE, *The Burial*, 1947.

5-20. EDWIN DICKINSON, *The Fossil Hunters*, 1926–28.

quality are Edwin Dickinson and Morris Graves. Dickinson's layered fantasies, with their superimposed images and meanings, and Graves's strange birds and landscapes defy strict categorization. Dickinson, a sophisticated romantic who spent much of his life in isolation in Provincetown, worked in a sensitive, highly developed, realistic style of a higher order than that of the Magic Realists, in order to explore the world of his private fantasies. In *The Fossil Hunters* (*Ill. 5-20*), for example, bodies tumble down on one another, entwined in drapery, smoke, and haze, evoking ghostly images, effecting mysterious transformations. Dickinson's constant reworking of the same themes, often

5-21. MORRIS GRAVES, *Bird in the Spirit*, 1940–41.

5-22. ADOLPH GOTTLIEB, *Sun Deck,* 1936.

5-23. MILTON AVERY, *Baby Avery,* 1932.

on the same canvas, gives his work an obsessive fascination; his decaying images are echoes of the Gothic themes of nineteenth-century romantic painters. Graves, a painter of the Pacific Northwest like Mark Tobey, shares with Tobey an interest in Zen Buddhism. His fragile transparent *Bird in the Spirit* (*Ill. 5-21*) seems a metaphor for the fragility of human experience.

During the thirties, figure painting per se, devoid of literary or social content, was not a popular mode, although artists like Lee Gatch and especially Milton Avery were able to find a fresh approach to painting the figure. Although both Gatch's and Avery's interwoven patterns of flattened figures and landscapes are essentially a departure from Fauvism, Avery's paintings show his grasp of Matisse's direct use of color and his treatment of the figure and landscape as flat patterns with rhythmic contours. Avery's work was one of the main channels through which Matisse's decorative color painting survived in American art in the forties, when much painting took on the pallid chalkiness of tempera or the lurid rotogravure tonalities of commercial illustration. Avery's ability to eliminate detail and to organize masses as flat areas of pure color, dividing the canvas into transparent yet brilliant zones, mark him as one of the outstanding American painters of recent years. Admired by younger painters like Rothko and Gottlieb, Avery's work became the model of an art of subtle, close-valued color. *Sun Deck* (*Ill. 5-22*), a painting Gottlieb executed for the easel painting section of the WPA, is reminiscent in its sensitive paint application and muted palette of Avery's paintings of the thirties, such

5-24. MILTON AVERY, *Mother and Child*, 1944.

5-25. JACK LEVINE, *Gangster Funeral*, 1952–53.

as *Baby Avery* (*Ill. 5-23*), the first of many portraits of the artist's daughter. In the forties and fifties, in such paintings as *Mother and Child* (*Ill. 5-24*), Avery's use of color became bolder as his formal inventiveness and assurance increased.

In the forties, important figure painting was also done by "the two kids from Boston," Hyman Bloom and Jack Levine. Encouraged by art educator Harold Zimmerman and Harvard professor Denman Ross, Bloom and Levine left the world of the ghetto to develop their considerable talents. Bloom acquired a masterful technique, rich in sensuous surface effects (all the more remarkable because it was so rare in previous American painting). Bloom was a moralist like Rouault and a mystic like his hero Blake; he painted fantastic visions in brilliant, visceral colors, whose smeared impasto and writhing, melting forms are reminiscent of Soutine.

In contrast with Bloom's other-worldly mysticism, Levine's works are very much of this world. His bejeweled dowagers and grossly corpulent businessmen are stereotypes of capitalist corruption which descend from Grosz through the left-wing cartoons and paintings of American social-protest art. Like Pascin and Kuniyoshi, Levine was able to use line to give a convincing sense of plasticity. His *Gangster Funeral* (*Ill.* 5-25) is a searing indictment of human corruption as personified by gangster-tycoons.

Fewer in number than the realists and more insecure in their position, abstract artists during the thirties could look to few American precedents for their work. Only Stuart Davis seemed capable of reconciling the diametrically opposed currents of American Scene painting and Cubist abstraction. Davis' career, like Hopper's, spans half the century, and represents a straight line of continuous development from the origins of twentieth-century American art. Like Hopper, Davis was a Henri student who exhibited in the Armory Show. Otherwise, however, the two stand for the antithetical currents in American art which were dramatically polarized in the thirties. Although both artists were engaged in defining a specifically American tradition in art, the solutions they arrived at were mutually exclusive. In a sense, Davis and Hopper may be taken to represent the two faces of the thirties: Hopper looked backward in order to record the plain virtues and undramatic pathos of life in small-town America, or to find poignant beauty in the homely, sometimes grotesque, American landscape; Davis celebrated the present, transforming the American scene into symbols and signs charged with the electricity of the moment. Hopper, like Sloan, was the detached reporter—with perhaps a more poetic bent than Sloan—who hardly altered his technique or subject. Davis, the restless experimenter, constantly recast and enlarged his repertoire of images in order to distill more intensely and succinctly the reality of the present.

For Hopper, contact with Europe meant little, even though he visited Paris three times between 1906 and 1910; but Davis called the Armory Show "the greatest single influence I have experienced." Hopper's emphasis on structure and coherence of pictorial design, however, suggest that he, like Davis, reacted against the casualness of Henri's surface effects. But in Hopper's case, the rejection of bravura painting appears to be based on a puritanical rejection of the glamorous. In contrast, Davis had specific complaints about Henri's approach, which he felt repudiated academic rules without establishing "new ones suitable to the new purpose." That there was a new purpose was clear to Davis as soon as he saw the Armory Show.

5-26.  STUART DAVIS,
*The President*, 1917.

Davis' criticism of Henri is applicable not only to Henri's teaching, but also to American art education in general: Davis complained that the "borderline between descriptive and illustrative painting, and art as an autonomous sensate object, was never clarified."[11] To clarify this distinction was the task Davis set himself, although he admits, "I did not spring into the world fully equipped to paint the kind of pictures I want to paint."[12] Davis' struggle to acquire the technical means of painting was arduous. As he gradually expunged crudeness, awkwardness, and laboriousness from his paintings, he was able to reach the level he sought, and in so doing, to raise the general level of American painting. It is hardly exaggerating to suggest that Davis was the first American artist to appropriate successfully the means of French art toward the end of making distinctively American pictures.

Like many in the Henri circle, Davis began as a cartoonist and illustrator, and his attitude remained that of the wandering sketch hunter, even when he began to transform his impressions of the city into abstract signs and symbols. Shortly after his conversion to "the new purpose," Davis met Demuth in Provincetown. During the period following the Armory Show, while Demuth and Sheeler worked to create a native version of Cubism, Davis painted a number of precocious abstractions, such as *The President* of 1917 (*Ill. 5-26*), as well as experimenting with collage, in which he sometimes incorporated *trompe-l'oeil* labels. Beginning with the 1921 *Lucky Strike* (*Ill. 5-27*), the labels alone became the subjects for a series of paintings. In these, Davis first introduced words and lettering, using them as the Cubists had done, to emphasize the actual two-dimensionality of the painting by identifying the flat letters with the flat surface plane. In his later works, these words would be transformed into a lively calligraphy of cut-outs which functioned as abstract shapes themselves. The flattened, reorganized packages of commercial products of the twenties are related to Demuth's work, not only in their clear, hard-edged forms and use of commercial lettering, but also in their choice of banal subjects.

Like the Precisionists, Davis began by searching for abstract patterns in real objects. Gradually, he concentrated his attention on logical elements, as he explains it, "groping towards a structural concept." In 1927, concluding that "a subject had its emotional reality fundamentally through our awareness of . . . planes and their spatial relationships,"[13] he began his first abstract paintings. These were the brilliant "egg beater" series (*Ill. 5-28*). Revealing the attitude of the

5-27. STUART DAVIS, *Lucky Strike*, 1921.

5-28. STUART DAVIS, *Egg Beater, Number 2*, 1927.

modernist who strives to refine and purify a single theme, Davis used
a still-life arrangement of an electric fan, a rubber glove, and an egg
beater as his exclusive subject for a year. "The act of painting," he
had decided, "is not a duplication of experience but the extension of
experience on the plane of formal invention."[14]

In the paintings of the next few years, such as the street scenes inspired by a trip to Paris in 1928–29, figurative elements re-emerged; but
the men and houses were definitively flattened out and stylized into
patterned shapes. Later, these elements were recaptured in *The Paris
Bit (Ill. 5-30)*. In the thirties, Davis continued to paint landscapes
made up of many small, jagged elements locked together like the
pieces of a complex jigsaw puzzle. He appears at this time to have
been influenced by Léger's bold assertive shapes and thick black lines.
As editor of *Art Front*, the magazine of the Artists' Congress, from
1934 to 1939, Davis found his painting time curtailed. Nevertheless, he
managed to paint four major murals during the thirties: *Men Without
Women* (1932), in the men's lounge of Radio City Music Hall; *Swing
Landscape* (1938), now at the University of Indiana; an abstraction

based on musical and electronic symbols for radio station WNYC (1939); and a huge *History of Communication* for the 1939 New York World's Fair (which was later destroyed).

In the following decade, Davis' ability to translate the sights and sounds of American life was solidly established. He was one of the first artists to appreciate jazz as a distinctly American idiom. The technical means he had disciplined himself to master were now by and large in his grasp; his color, evidently stimulated by Matisse, became increasingly active and brilliant. To the primaries he favored in the thirties, he added hot, fully saturated oranges, pinks, and magentas, and the black and white which Matisse had used as a foil for color in his *Jazz* cut-outs. Like Matisse's *Jazz,* Davis' paintings, such as *Hot Still-Scape for Six Colors* (*Ill. 5-29*), contain an astonishing variety of lively, dancing shapes, sharply contoured and smoothly fitted together in a sequence of syncopated rhythms. But in the tension of their relationships, and in the sheer quantity of nervous energy discharged by their coordinated activity, they express Davis' concern with ordering the frenzy he found in the American scene.

5-29. STUART DAVIS, *Hot Still-Scape for Six Colors,* 1940.

5-30. STUART DAVIS, *The Paris Bit,* 1959.

Despite their degree of abstraction, Davis claimed that all his paintings have their origin in things seen. Describing his method of working on *The Paris Bit,* a 1959 recapitulation of the Paris street scenes of the twenties, Davis revealed that he composed his paintings first as line drawings, because this method was "most amenable to inspiration and change." Drawing until he felt that the "all-over configuration has reached a degree of complexity and completeness satisfactory to the impulse that initiated it," he increased the visual impact "through the use of stimulating color intervals."[15] In the sense that Davis stored up from observation innumerable images which he could later draw on, he remains, like Hopper, the heir of Henri. But by transforming the context and form in which these impressions and memories will reappear, he points forward to the new American painting.

Davis represents the crest of the first wave of American modernism. His friendship with Arshile Gorky was one of the few bridges between the pioneer modernists and the new American painting. Among the

first to recognize his unique genius, Gorky admired Davis' understanding of the canvas "as a rectangular shape with a two-dimensional
surface plane," into which he refused to "poke bumps and holes."
When Gorky wrote about Davis in 1931, he wrote also of the em-
battled role of the abstract artist, condemning the "critics, artists, and
public suspended like vultures, waiting in the air for the death of the
distinctive art of this century, the art of Léger, Picasso, Miró, Kandinsky, Stuart Davis." These were the gods of the young American
abstract artists. They shared Gorky's conviction that "for centuries
to come artists of gigantic stature will draw positive elements from
Cubism."[16] Already, in works of the early thirties, such as *Organization* (*Ill. 5-40*), Gorky had begun to adapt the means of Cubism to his
own more painterly ends. Other artists, too, such as the Russian
émigré John Graham, from whom Gorky's generation learned to appreciate the finer lessons of Cubism, were painting fully developed
Cubist works in New York in the thirties. Graham's 1932 *Anschluss*
(*Ill. 5-31*), for example, shows an understanding of the dynamics of
synthetic Cubism which was rare, if not nonexistent, in America before that date.

By 1936, the year in which Alfred H. Barr, Jr., organized the historic
survey "Cubism and Abstract Art" at the Museum of Modern Art,
the younger abstract artists had banded together in an association
known as the American Abstract Artists. The importance to young
artists of Barr's vision of internationalism in art and his application of

5-31. JOHN GRAHAM, *Anschluss,* 1932.

5-32. JOHN FERREN, *Multiplicity,* 1937.

art historical methods to the study of contemporary art should be noted. Soon the annual exhibition of the American Abstract Artists was the focus for the energies of the emerging. American avant-garde. The group was formed at that moment when the international abstract movement, in which French Purism, Dutch de Stijl, Russian Constructivism, and Bauhaus abstraction, having briefly coalesced in the Paris-based Cercle et Carré and Abstraction-Creation groups, was dis-

5-33. KARL KNATHS, *Maritime,* 1931.

5-34. CARL HOLTY, *Of War,* 1942.

5-35. GEORGE MCNEIL, *Green Forms Dominant*, 1938–39.

persing as Hitler menaced Europe. Among the artists who originally exhibited with the American group were Carl Holty and John Ferren, both recently back from Paris, Karl Knaths, Jean Xceron, Charles Shaw, Balcomb and Gertrude Greene, Ad Reinhardt, Byron Browne, Giorgio Cavallon, and George McNeil.

Ferren's *Multiplicity* (*Ill. 5-32*), Knaths's *Maritime* (*Ill. 5-33*), Holty's *Of War* (*Ill. 5-34*), McNeil's *Green Forms Dominant* (*Ill. 5-35*), and

5-36. GIORGIO CAVALLON, *Untitled*, 1938–39.

Cavallon's untitled abstraction (*Ill. 5-36*) are examples of the high quality achieved by members of the association during the thirties and forties. By 1938–39, the group also included Josef Albers, Ilya Bolotowsky, Fritz Glarner, Burgoyne Diller, Alice Mason, Albert Swinden, I. Rice Pereira, Lee Krasner, Willem de Kooning, and David Smith. Most association artists tended to work within the conventions of Purism or Neo-Plasticism. Bolotowsky's *White Abstraction* (*Ill. 5-37*), a study in cool Purist terms, is typical of their work. However, others, such as de Kooning, Krasner, and Gorky, chose Picasso as their mentor; three abstract paintings by these artists (*Ills. 5-38, 5-39, 5-40*) recall Picasso's studio interiors of the late twenties (*Ill. 5-41*) and his expressionistic surrealizing Cubism of the later thirties.

Although the American Abstract Artists was international in character, its aim was to make New York a center for abstract art. (Glarner and Albers, recent arrivals from Europe, were frankly oriented toward geometric abstraction; and a number of the members also belonged to Michel Seuphor's Abstraction-Creation group.) The association's annuals were still dominated by strict geometric abstraction based on the

5-37. ILYA BOLOTOWSKY,
*White Abstraction*, 1934–35.

5-38. WILLEM DE KOONING, *Untitled*, 1937.

5-40. ARSHILE GORKY, *Organization*, 1932.

5-39. LEE KRASNER, *Untitled*, 1939.

5-41. PABLO PICASSO, *The Studio*, 1927–28.

horizontals and verticals derived ultimately from de Stijl or Constructivist prototypes. Typical catalogue essays were "On Simplification" by Albert Swinden, "The Quest for an Abstract Tradition" by George L. K. Morris, and "On Inventing our Own Art" by Ibram Lassaw.

In the late thirties abstract art in America was a voice crying out in the wilderness. With no hope of winning a mass audience away from the realistic styles, abstract art also was spurned by the museums as hopelessly out of date—the modern style of the twenties. Although the Whitney had lent impetus to the movement by holding an exhibition of abstract painting in America in 1935, when the Abstract Artists wished to hold its annual showing there in the late thirties, it was refused. In 1940, members of the Abstract Artists picketed the Museum of Modern Art demanding that the museum show American art.

The small but militant avant-garde was fortunate to find a few supporters like the critic George L. K. Morris and the collector A. E. Gallatin, both also abstract painters. Morris wrote about their work, and Gallatin showed some young Americans, along with the latest work of Picasso, Braque, Gris, Léger, Arp, and Masson, at his Museum of Living Art, installed at New York University's Washington Square College. Further uptown, abstract art could be seen at the Dudensing Gallery, the Pinacotheca (later Rose Fried) Gallery, and at Curt Valentin's, where Matisse's large 1916–17 *Bathers by a River* showed what open areas of saturated color could do in a large format. At the Solomon R. Guggenheim Museum of Non-Objective Art, founded in 1937, Kandinsky's freely painted lyric abstractions provided another alternative to the hard linear contours and architectonic compositions of late Cubism. With the gradual influx of the leading artists of France, Holland, and especially Germany, examples of the most ambitious European art were more plentiful in New York than ever before. Even more important, perhaps, was the opportunity for direct contact with these artists whose standards the Americans now felt that they could— and must—measure up to.

Certain of the Europeans were, of course, more influential than others. Jean Helion, one of the leading French Purists, who came to America during the mid-thirties and later left to join the French Resistance, was influential in disseminating the fundamental principles of abstract art. In interviews, lectures, and statements, Helion presented the argument, well-known in Europe but not in America, that abstract art was best suited to express the abstract thought of the technological age. Helion's compositions, based on the juxtaposition of flat shapes with modeled shapes, influenced a number of American abstractionists. Léger's visit in the late thirties also helped to stimulate native abstraction; in their audacity and directness, his bold mechanistic images held great appeal for the Americans. Albers became an important force in American art from the moment he took over the art department at the experimental Black Mountain College in North Carolina in 1933. Here he raised art instruction to the sophisticated level it had reached at the Bauhaus, stressing the principles of abstract composition and design that were the core of the Bauhaus curriculum.

5-42. ARSHILE GORKY, *The Artist and His Mother,* 1926–29.

In the forties and fifties, Black Mountain became an important center of avant-garde activities; Buckminster Fuller, de Kooning, Kline, Motherwell, Tworkov, Clement Greenberg, and John Cage, at one time or another, were on its faculty. Among the students were Robert Rauschenberg, Kenneth Noland, and John Chamberlain.

Although Picasso was respected by the young members of the American Abstract Artists, it was rather the late Cubist geometry of Helion, Léger, Herbin, and Mondrian that the majority chose as their models. In the meantime, a few of the most gifted young painters were already beginning to rebel against the dryness and rigidity of geometric art. Gorky, de Kooning, and Pollock, never attracted by non-objective or Purist art, went straight to Picasso himself. Their position vis-à-vis geometric art was that articulated by Picasso: "Abstract art is only painting, but where is the drama?"

Gorky had looked to Picasso since the late twenties. His 1929 *The Artist and His Mother* (*Ill. 5-42*), a haunting and sensitive study based on a photograph taken when he was a boy in Armenia, has many affinities with Picasso's 1906 *Self Portrait,* which Gorky could have seen at the Museum of Living Art. Throughout the thirties Gorky continued to study Picasso, taking as his model the angular forms of Picasso's more recent expressionist Cubism, which he adapted with singular ingenuity in his mural for the Newark airport. But toward the late thirties, he began to demonstrate an impatience with Picasso's strict Cubist structuring. Earlier, Gorky had described how "clumsy painters take a measurable space, a clear definite shape, a rectangle, a vertical or horizontal direction, and they call it blank canvas." Now he was ready to apply his observation that "every time one stretches canvas he is drawing a new space."[17] Gorky's realization that the painter was free to determine the actual space in his work was an important step in liberating his compositions from the fixed structural armature of the Cubist grid in order to open the limited, shallow space of late Cubism into an infinite atmospheric continuum. Both Miró and Kandinsky had hinted at such a possibility. But in Gorky's work are the seeds of a new style. This revolutionary style, which constitutes the first major American contribution to world art, could not, however, have come into being before the European tradition had been thoroughly assimilated. The presence of older European-born artists such as Jan Matulka, John Graham, and Hans Hofmann, who had witnessed the rise of Cubism in Europe, and were willing to transmit its principles to young Americans, was of inestimable value in aiding this assimilation. In addition, the example of painters like Hartley, Marin, Burlin, and above all Arthur B. Carles, whose painterly expressionistic styles had provided earlier alternatives to Cubism within the modernist context, took on new significance. In his last painting, Carles allowed his fluid brushstrokes to break the barrier of the Cubist armature of black lines, releasing explosive energies in a manner prophetic of Abstract Expressionism (*Ill. 5-43*).

Thus, for the first time in America, there was the basis for a genuine avant-garde, capable of absorbing not merely Dada's destructive impulse to shock the bourgeoisie, but also the constructive forces gathering throughout the twentieth century in America which offered an alternative to middle-class conventions and popular taste as they were

5-43. ARTHUR B. CARLES, *Abstraction,* 1939–41.

expressed in academic and commercial art. The members of this avant-garde, which inherited Henri's disdain for the official and the established along with Stieglitz' insistence on an art-for-art's sake, had many battles still before them. Their refusal to use their art for political ends alienated many intellectuals and reformers. Yet they had precedents for such a stand in Sloan's and Davis' earlier refusal to compromise their art. Sloan had explained, "I hate war and I put that hatred into cartoons in the [old] *Masses.* But I didn't go sentimental and paint pictures of war." Davis, on the other hand, maintained that "the Painting itself is the responsible Social Act of the Artist, and is one of the surest, most direct forms of Communication known to man." One of the problems was that modernism had never taken root in America to the extent of evolving a utopian program tied to revolutionary social reform. Thus, Gorky could argue against the fine artist attempting to make popular art by claiming that "poor art is for

151

poor people." But no American artist would maintain with Léger that there was the possibility of realizing a new collective art.

The emerging American avant-garde held no such hopes for a rapprochement between art and society. Its base was in the dingy lofts and tenements of downtown Manhattan; its cafés were sordid all-night cafeterias. In this area below Fourteenth Street, where WPA classes were conducted, and Hans Hofmann had opened his school on Eighth Street, a small but committed fellowship developed. In these unpromising circumstances, American art, through the stimulation of direct contact with the European avant-garde, matured to a vigorous adolescence, and found itself prepared at last to challenge its parent for independence. In the process of defining their own cultural identity and tradition, the best American artists of the twenties and thirties had come to make virtues of their limitations. Boldness, lack of refinement, and even a certain crudity were sought, along with a literalness that tied art incontrovertibly to its environment, and a directness which eschewed subtleties and nuances. These characteristics, it became clear, were what distinguished American art from its European parent.

Disdaining the provincial themes and illustrational approach of the American Scene painters and the social realists, the rebels were most interested in the abstract art coming from Paris, which they could read about in art journals such as *Cahiers d'Art, Plastique, Verve,* and *Minotaure* or in occasional reviews like *transition.* Hofmann, from whom, according to Clement Greenberg, "you could learn more about Matisse's color . . . than from Matisse himself," gave lectures in the late thirties in which Greenberg remembers he stressed that "there was more to high painting than Cubist design."[18] Even had the concept of a "high art" been current among American artists, which clearly it was not, this would have been a radical position. Cubist design was at that point perhaps the only aspect of high art that Americans like Davis had been able to master; they were still struggling with the painting culture behind it. This is what the Europeans, and, above all, Hofmann could teach them. Hofmann had directed an influential art school in Munich from 1915 until 1932, when he settled permanently in the United States. At his Eighth Street school, opened in New York in 1934, he introduced the most advanced concepts of European painting to his students. He taught, as he had in Munich, that "creative expression is . . . the spiritual translation of inner concepts into form, resulting from the fusion of these intuitions with artistic means of expression in a unity of spirit and form." "Imitation of objective reality," Hofmann warned, "is therefore not creation but dilettantism, or else a purely intellectual performance, scientific and sterile."[19]

Painting, for Hofmann, was "forming with color," and nature was the great teacher of painters. Hofmann's method stressed oppositions— of contrasting colors, of positive planes floating in negative space, of expansion versus contraction, of the dynamic opposed to the static. "Every movement [in space] releases a counter-movement," he maintained. "A represented form that does not owe its existence to a perception of movement is not a form, because it is . . . spiritless and inert."[20] The compositional tension he considered most vital to a living work of art was the opposition created by the simultaneous assertion of the two-dimensional surface plane and that of three-dimensional depth. This tension, he felt, could be harmonized by the balance of "push and pull." Push-pull was his celebrated principle of composition, by means of which the various oppositions within a painting were resolved. In sum, Hofmann stressed the active line, intense color, and assertive paint application.

Although the audience Hofmann addressed was larger than Stieglitz' audience, it was still a minority group, made up mainly of the artists themselves and a few sympathetic writers. Describing the time, Gorky called it the most spirit-crushing period of his life. Of the paralyzing poverty, he said that "if a human being managed to emerge from such a period, it could not be as a whole man."[21] From such a struggle for survival, he maintained, there was no recovery.

In this bleak milieu, two young painters attempted to come to terms with their own compelling visions as well as with the art of their time. Beginning from opposite points of departure, they were to consolidate, each in his own manner, the dynamic impulses of the new world with the painterly tradition of the old. Jackson Pollock, Benton's student and an admirer of Orozco and Siquieros, would transcend the provincialism of the former and the banality of the latter to achieve an art that was universal in its range, and international in its significance. Gorky's young Dutch friend, Willem de Kooning, denying his own extraordinary virtuosity, would bend the refined tradition in which he was steeped toward the end of capturing the explosive tensions and ambiguities of the American experience.

Arriving in New York in 1929, Wyoming-born Pollock was perhaps almost as much a foreigner as de Kooning, who had arrived in 1926 from Amsterdam, where he had studied at the Fine Arts Academy.

Pollock's turbulent, dark, romantic seascapes of the mid-thirties are reminiscent of Ryder's possessed visions. De Kooning's paintings of these years were finely wrought melancholy figure studies, distinguished by the fluid line of the master draftsman. For both, the decisive encounter was with Picasso's expressionistic late Cubism. For Pollock, experience with Picasso's sophisticated, highly-structured compositions was a disciplining agent; for de Kooning, who was in the process of rejecting realism, it was a liberating force, which enabled him to distort his own figures to gain a more intense form of expression. Each in his own manner struggled with the genius of Picasso, and in his struggle, helped to free American art permanently from its European ancestry.

# Chapter Six

# Art of This Century

The Surrealists had the laudable aim of bringing the spiritual to everyone. But in a period as demoralized as our own, this could lead only to the demoralization of art. In the greatest painting, the painter communes with himself.
    —ROBERT MOTHERWELL, "The Modern Painter's World," *DYN*, vi, 1944

The Kwakiutl artist painting on a hide did not concern himself with the inconsequentials that made up the opulent social rivalries of the Northwest Coast Indian scene, nor did he, in the name of a higher purity, renounce the living world for the meaningless materialism of design. The abstract shape he used, his entire plastic language, was directed by a ritualistic will towards metaphysical understanding. . . . Not space cutting nor space building, not construction nor fauvist destruction; not the pure line, straight and narrow, nor the tortured line, distorted and humiliating; not the accurate eye, all fingers, nor the wild eye of dream, winking; but the idea-complex that makes contact with mystery—of life, of men, of nature, of the hard black chaos that is death, or the grayer, softer chaos that is tragedy. For it is only the pure idea that has meaning. Everything else has everything else.
    —BARNETT NEWMAN, *The Ideographic Picture* (Catalogue, Betty Parsons Gallery, January 20, 1947)

Abstract Expressionism was born of two catastrophes: a depression and a world war. The first, by means of the WPA, provided new opportunities for professionalism and cooperative ventures among artists; the second brought the leading figures of the European avant-garde to America, where their attitudes and their works served as an example to American artists. During the strife-torn years of the late thirties and early forties, the center of world art moved from Paris to New York. It is no wonder, then, that an art maturing in such circumstances should be marked by signs of anxiety, emotional stress, even despair.

In addition, the American artist faced the problem of extricating his art from a debilitating provincialism as well as from the demands of leftist politics, which required that art serve a social purpose. To make

6-1. LYONEL FEININGER,
*Gelmeroda, VIII*, 1921.

matters more difficult, the time when American art prepared to join
the mainstream of Western painting was precisely the moment when
abstract art was undergoing the general crisis that accompanied the
decline of Cubism.

Between the two wars, the only major international art movements
to arise were Dada and its offspring Surrealism. Neither contributed
to the continuing evolution of pictorial form which the pioneers of
modernism had envisioned. Disillusioned with the myth of political
progress through the triumph of reason, Dada and Surrealism set out
to destroy the concept of progress in art. By the time World War II
broke out in Europe, art had polarized into two camps: Cubist-derived
abstraction, including the purist geometry of the non-objective styles,
de Stijl and Constructivism; and Surrealism. To synthesize Cubism
and Surrealism in an entirely new pictorial style became the goal of
American artists.

Certain tentative moves toward imbedding Surrealist forms in a
Cubist structure had been made in the thirties, mainly by Gorky and
de Kooning, who were inspired by the works of Picasso. However, it
was not until the forties, when a sufficient number of refugee artists,
both abstract and Surrealist, had arrived in New York, that such a
synthesis was accomplished. To the dingy proletarian loft culture of
New York came the glittering celebrities of modern art, whose names
had been legend and whose reproductions were already tacked to
downtown studio walls. Joining Josef Albers were other former members of the Bauhaus faculty: the American-born Cubist Lyonel Feininger, who had lived in Germany until the war's outbreak; the designer Laszlo Moholy-Nagy; the sculptor Naum Gabo; and the
architects Walter Gropius, Marcel Breuer, and Mies van der Rohe.
*Gelmeroda, VIII* (*Ill. 6-1*) is typical of Feininger's modified semi-

abstraction, which he continued to practice on his return to the United States. Albers, a far more influential artist, chose the geometric severity of the square as his principal motif, creating innumerable subtle variations on the theme generically called "Homage to the Square" (*Ill. 6-3*). Respected throughout the postwar period, Albers came to new prominence in the sixties when his studies on the interaction of colors served as part of the background of the "new abstraction." Amédée Ozenfant, co-founder with Le Corbusier of Purism, which sought to restore to Cubism its classical purity by basing forms on the clean lines of machinery, set up a Purist school in New York. Fernand Léger, who had visited in the United States briefly in the thirties to paint a never-completed French Line mural, returned to teach at Yale and at Mills College during the early forties.

However, the most important abstract artist who came to America during this period was Piet Mondrian, founder of Neo-Plasticism and the leading member of de Stijl. Like the Surrealists, he had attracted considerable attention during the thirties in America, where his cool, geometric abstractions, composed of intersecting right angles and flat planes of color, were highly esteemed. While he had been largely ignored in Europe, his work had been purchased by American collectors such as A. E. Gallatin and Katherine Dreier, as well as by the Museum of Modern Art and the Guggenheim Museum. Among his admirers were American artists like Ilya Bolotowsky, Burgoyne Diller, and I. Rice Pereira, whose work in the thirties had been closer to Constructivism in its use of free-floating planes on a colored ground. Persuaded by the American Neo-Plasticist Harry Holtzman to leave London (where the flat next to his had been bombed out), Mondrian arrived in New York in 1940. Immediately he was surrounded by a devoted circle of abstract artists, some of whom had already been painting in the Neo-Plastic manner before his arrival. Among the

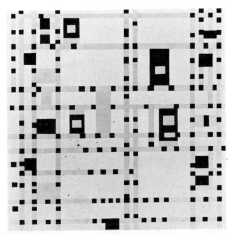

6-2. PIET MONDRIAN,
*Broadway Boogie Woogie*, 1942–43.

6-3. JOSEF ALBERS, *Homage to the Square: Frislan,* 1955.

group were Holtzman, Bolotowsky, Glarner, Albert Swinden, and Charmion von Wiegand.

Mondrian's contribution to American art was a strengthening of the current of geometric abstraction. This movement, which had been active in the thirties, was to run submerged in the forties and fifties, and become more central once again in the sixties. Supporting and exhibiting with the American Abstract Artists, Mondrian proved a symbol of selfless dedication to art, and his work acted as an important stimulus to the development of the artists around him. Along with Kandinsky, Klee, and Malevich, Mondrian was one of the major theoreticians of modern art; in America he became the source for the diffusion of the principles of pure plastic design.

Like Malevich, Mondrian was convinced that abstract art was the form of expression appropriate to the twentieth century. New York City, with its indomitable energy, swift tempo, flashing lights, and its strict grid of streets with skyscrapers shooting upwards, became for

6-4. BURGOYNE DILLER,
*First Theme*, 1955–60.

Mondrian the essence of the modern age. The power of abstract art to express feeling is forcefully demonstrated in Mondrian's last works, executed in New York just before his death in 1944. In contrast to some of the refugee artists, such as George Grosz and Marc Chagall, who were relatively untouched by the American environment, Mondrian underwent a profound stylistic change during his last years. Like the young New York artists, Mondrian became interested in the syncopated rhythm of jazz—not in the cool, poetic improvisations of Charlie Parker or Miles Davis, whose music would find sympathy among New York painters somewhat later, but in the measured beat of boogie woogie. In his last masterpieces, *Broadway Boogie Woogie* of 1942–43 (*Ill. 6-2*) and *Victory Boogie Woogie* of 1943–44, which

6-5. FRITZ GLARNER,
*Relational Painting:
Tondo #43*, 1956.

were regularly on exhibition at the Museum of Modern Art during the forties, he replaced the static primary-color rectangles and black grids on a white surface, which had characterized his works since the twenties, with small, irregularly placed rectangles of red, blue, and yellow which flash to a syncopated beat. A new energy and movement, and an optical flicker, give these works an active quality that is radical for Mondrian.

Mondrian received from America perhaps as much as he contributed. His exhibitions at the Dudensing Gallery continued to inspire artists like Glarner, Diller, and Bolotowsky, whose work of the late forties and fifties became more closely tied to Mondrian's. Diller, for example, began breaking up his canvas into a field activated by a complex, ladder-like configuration of narrow, intersecting horizontal and vertical bars. In later paintings, such as *First Theme* (*Ill. 6-4*), Diller returned to the simpler compositions of a few rectangular elements suspended freely on a colored ground that had characterized his early work. In the later paintings, however, these elements tend to be similar and their placement more rigorously symmetrical.

Fritz Glarner remained close to Mondrian, although he departed from Neo-Plasticism in using diagonals and circular compositions and in introducing colors other than the primaries. Eschewing the grid in favor of interlocking planes of color wedged together, he repeated equivalent planes or wedges which set up a series of echoes. Glarner termed his method of composing "relational painting" (*Ill. 6-5*), as Mondrian had called "relationships" the basis of abstract art.

Although the abstract artists from abroad were important to the future of American painting, the Surrealists-in-exile had an even greater impact. Matta, the first Surrealist painter to arrive, came in 1939; in the early forties he was followed by Dalí, Max Ernst, Kurt Seligmann, and André Masson. The poet André Breton, who in 1924 wrote the first Surrealist manifesto, became the center of the transplanted movement. Resuming his Surrealist court in New York, where artists and poets played Surrealist games like *cadavre exquis* and made automatic poems and drawings, Breton helped stage exhibitions, publish magazines, and hold events which scandalized the public.

As Max Ernst's wife and hostess to the Surrealists, Peggy Guggenheim played an important role by introducing young American artists to the exiled artists. Miss Guggenheim had been living in Paris at the start of World War II; her earlier plans to open a modern art museum in London had not materialized. In Paris she made purchases based on a list compiled by Marcel Duchamp, Sir Herbert Read, and Petra van Doesburg, widow of Mondrian's collaborator, Theo van Doesburg. During this time, she became active in a committee to send artists to America, through which she met Breton and Max Ernst. By 1941, all three were in New York, where Miss Guggenheim decided to start a combination gallery-museum. Called Art of This Century, it opened in 1942 with an exhibition of her collection. Decorated by the unpredictable architect-designer Frederick Kiesler (who also designed an extraordinary set of furniture with multiple functions), the gallery was arranged so that pictures were suspended in mid-air or projected a foot outward from the walls. The catalogue included a history of Surrealism by Breton, essays by Mondrian and Arp, and statements by the artists. The collection was divided into two groups: abstract and Surrealist. The abstract section included works of the critical years before World War I by Léger, Picasso, Duchamp, and the other leading Cubists; Futurist paintings by Balla and Severini; abstractions by Kandinsky, Delaunay, Mondrian, Malevich, Lissitsky, and Arp; and sculpture by Arp, Archipenko, Brancusi, Lipchitz,

6-6. HANS HOFMANN, *Effervescence,* 1944.

6-7. HANS HOFMANN, *Cathedral*, 1959.

6-8. RICHARD POUSETTE-DART, *Desert, 1940.*

Giacometti, Gonzalez, Pevsner, and Vantongerloo. The Surrealist section was called "Fantastic Art, Dada, and Surrealism" (the title of the 1936 Surrealist survey at the Museum of Modern Art); it included works by Chagall, de Chirico, Picabia, Man Ray, Ernst, Schwitters, Klee, Tanguy, Matta, and Magritte.

With the help of her secretary, Howard Putzel, Miss Guggenheim completed her collection in New York. Describing the opening, held for the benefit of the Red Cross on October 29, 1942, she recalls, "I wore one of my Tanguy ear-rings and one made by Calder, in order to show my impartiality between Surrealist and abstract art."[1]

From 1942 to 1947 (the year Miss Guggenheim and most of the Surrealists returned to Europe), Art of This Century showed young American painters along with the Europeans. The young Americans exhibited were Pollock, Motherwell, Baziotes, Rothko, Still, Gottlieb, and David Hare. In addition, Hans Hofmann had his first one-man show there. In his lyric paintings of the early forties, such as *Effervescence* (*Ill. 6-6*), Hofmann achieved an unprecedented degree of painterliness in an abstract style. In later works, such as *Cathedral* (*Ill. 6-7*), he reverted to the more solid structuring of architectonic planes which were balanced by the "push-pull" dynamic of their intricate color relationships. Another artist doing advanced abstract work in the early forties was Richard Pousette-Dart. His *Desert* (*Ill. 6-8*) was a successful attempt to translate the boldness of Picasso's late Cubist style into an entirely abstract decorative context. But among his fellow artists, Jackson Pollock rose the fastest during those years. "Pollock became the star of the gallery and for five years I supported him and launched him by selling his paintings, which in those days was very difficult," Peggy Guggenheim remembers.[2]

The main lines of the revolt of young New York painters in the late thirties and early forties may be followed in the light of what they borrowed from Surrealism. For them, abstract art was mere formalism, empty decoration which could not embody universal themes. Rejecting the narrow chauvinism of Regionalism, they set out to express the general, the universal, and the elemental. Although the nature painters in the Stieglitz group, O'Keeffe, Dove, Marin, and Hartley, had a similar aim, their approach was not programmatic. The younger painters differed from previous generations of American artists in that they valued content over subject matter, and as much as form, if not more so. But spurning the easily communicated content of religious allegory, they also refused to illustrate the tragedies of the moment in literal terms.

Still following the lead of the Surrealists, who had adopted much of their imagery from Freud, these artists turned to the enduring myths of the race as the source for the most profound and universal emotions. In general, Jung's theories of archetypes and the collective unconscious proved sympathetic to artists like Gottlieb, Rothko, Still, and Pollock, who were seeking symbolic equivalents for interior states of mind. Freud's theories seemed too intellectualized, and too exclusively a product of Western European culture to be sufficiently universal. Searching for pictorial equivalents of universal experiences, they appropriated ancient myths, symbols, and signs. Often these symbolic forms were simplified to stand for such Manichaean oppositions as light versus darkness, good versus evil, celestial versus chthonian.

If these universally meaningful forms were buried in the subconscious, then the problem was how to bring them to the level of consciousness in order to express them in art. Surrealism was part of that reaction against the deadening and inhibiting factors in Western culture, which may be traced from Jean-Jacques Rousseau through the self-conscious primitivism of late nineteenth-century art. Surrealism put an even higher store on the instinctual and the archaic than Cubism or German Expressionism had done. But it was the buried primitive in modern man that the Surrealists wished to reconstruct. Inspired by the Freudian method of free association, they invented the technique of "psychic automatism." By means of this technique, the poet or artist allowed his thoughts or hand to wander spontaneously, much as the hand moves at random on the Ouija board, and to meander in strange paths unchecked by the fetters of reason or logic.

The purpose of automatism was to allow the subconscious to generate buried images unavailable to the conscious mind. Ostensibly no attempt was made to control these idle doodlings which then might serve as points of departure for more conscious configurations. In this manner, the Surrealists and American artists who practiced automatic techniques, such as Motherwell, Pollock, Gorky, and later, Bradley Walker Tomlin, hoped to tap the free flow of unhampered creativity. Other semi-automatic methods, probably based on the manner in which Rorschach images are interpreted, were developed, especially by Max Ernst, whose imagination was particularly fertile in this area. Ernst's "frottage" involved rubbing grained textures with a pencil and using the impression as the point of departure for an image; "grattage" was Ernst's technique for manipulating the paint surface, scratching over it with an oiled fork or ruler, so that it yielded forms like those of a fantastic landscape. "Decalomania," another Ernst technique, consisted of crushing paint between two canvases and elaborating the resultant hills and valleys of pigment into crevices and encrustations of lunar or volcanic landscapes. Ernst is also said to have invented a machine for randomly spotting the canvas with paint. Common to all of these methods is the precedence of process over conception. This is the reverse of the creation of abstract art which, although it might undergo alteration during its execution, had a conceptual basis. This aspect of automatism—its stress on process as central to creativity—was taken over by the Abstract Expressionists, who gradually changed the emphasis from the process of inventing and generating images to the process of painting itself.

Because as little control as possible was exercised in automatic creation, accidents of all kinds, random and chance effects, were frequent. These effects were considered the means for achieving greater spontaneity, and the accidental splashes and drips of paint left by the path of a rapid brushstroke were cultivated. The Surrealists' emphasis on the play element in art became a way of preserving freshness for the Abstract Expressionists.

Although the literal symbols of Freudian dream images did not generally appeal to the Abstract Expressionists, the more ambiguous, but equally sexually charged vocabulary of forms invented by Arp and Miró and adapted by the Surrealists remained a source of inspiration throughout the forties. These organic free shapes were called biomorphic because of their similarity to biological forms, such as the

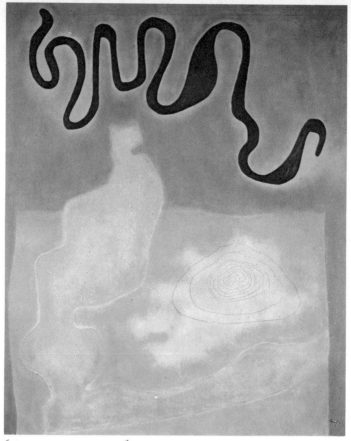

6-9. WILLIAM BAZIOTES, *Congo,* 1954.

amoeba with its pulsating contours and bulbous protrusions. Since these forms are common to all natural life—human as well as plant and animal—they provided the common denominator that the painters sought. William Baziotes, who never developed the fluid painterly freedom of his contemporaries, based his imagery on such biomorphic forms. In *Congo* (*Ill. 6-9*), a work revealing Baziotes' considerable gifts as a subtle colorist, curvilinear biomorphic forms are flattened out into decorative patterns which float in a watery atmosphere. Similarly, Theodoros Stamos used biomorphic forms and turned to the collective unconscious for the mythic content of his *Archaic Vista* (*Ill. 6-10*). Gorky, on the other hand, developed a highly personal formal vocabulary based on biomorphism which influenced de Kooning. De Kooning, in turn, exhausted the possibilities of biomorphism toward the end of the forties in his black-and-white paintings. And both

6-10. THEODOROS STAMOS,
*Archaic Vista,* 1947.

Rothko and Gottlieb, in such symbolic works of the forties as Rothko's *Prehistoric Memories* (*Ill. 6-11*) and Gottlieb's *Voyager's Return* (*Ill. 6-12*), couched mythic content in the forms of biomorphism.

Thus, the crisis in American art engendered by the rejection of formalism in the late thirties was resolved in the early forties through the adoption of Surrealist symbols and techniques. Automatism freed painterly qualities and allowed the expression of universal themes, already implicit in the earlier works of Gorky, de Kooning, and Pollock. However, in the late forties, as the Americans gained confidence and

6-11. MARK ROTHKO,
*Prehistoric Memories,* 1946.

6-12. ADOLPH GOTTLIEB,
*Voyager's Return,* 1946.

6-13. ARSHILE GORKY,
*Garden in Sochi,* 1941.

the Surrealists returned to Europe, there was a reaction against Surrealism which was similar in some respects to the earlier reaction against formalism.

Despite the degree to which American painting is indebted to Surrealism, certain aspects of Surrealism remained distasteful to the Americans. They disdained, for example, the social life and sensational publicity sought after by the Surrealists. Photographic realism, literary content, or perverse overtones were also rejected out of hand. Interest in the meticulously detailed style of Dalí and Tanguy was limited, but the painterly automatism and fluid space of Masson and Matta were particularly influential. What interested the Americans in Surrealism were its processes, its attitudes toward creativity and the unconscious, and its emphasis on content as opposed to form. The myth of creation itself became an important metaphor for artistic creation.

Whether Arshile Gorky was the last of the Surrealists or the first of the Abstract Expressionists has not yet been resolved. The answer is that he was both. The last artist to be accepted by the Surrealists as a member of their group, he was the protégé of André Breton, who found Gorky with his poetic temperament a kindred spirit. It was Breton who invented the term "hybrid" to describe Gorky's mysterious, ambiguous images. By means of these biomorphic hybrid images, Gorky was able to reconcile the figurative with the non-figurative. Breton characterized the hybrids as "the resultants provoked in an observer contemplating a natural spectacle and a flux of childhood *and other memories. . . .*"[3]

Although his contact with the Surrealists allowed Gorky to realize himself—by providing him with the technique of automatism through

168

which he could externalize his rich inner world of fantasy—Gorky had also served a long apprenticeship with teachers he never knew. Unlike previous American artists who identified tradition with older art, Gorky accepted the tradition of the modern masters, especially Cézanne, Picasso, and Miró, and the early Kandinsky. He studied and imitated their works as assiduously as Raphael's disciples had copied their master. Meyer Schapiro remembers Gorky in "museums and galleries, fixed in rapt contemplation of pictures with that grave, searching look which was one of the beauties of his face. . . ."[4]

Gorky identified Cubism as the modern tradition, from which one could draw as from the old masters. A number of Gorky's Cubist paintings of the thirties derive specifically from Picasso's 1927–28 studio interiors, in which hard rod-like black lines connect geometric shapes and act as a foil to the shapes. These paintings, such as *Organization* (*Ill. 5-40*), are Gorky's closest approximation to geometric abstraction; yet they are filled with ideographic eyes and allusions to faces and anatomy. But hard contours and strict rectilinear forms were not to Gorky's taste, and in the late thirties he abandoned them for more loosely painted, irregular organic shapes bounded by flexible, pulsating contours of changing thickness. In these paintings it is already clear that the forms are both elusive and equivocal; a dot may be an eye or a nipple, a curved wedge may suggest a wing or a leaf.

The early forties was the time of Gorky's fulfillment. To assist the war effort, he gave a class in camouflage, which, according to his dealer, Julien Levy, helped him to discover that "if the realistic object can be camouflaged, so can the unreal or 'surreal' object be decoded and decamouflaged."[5] In the several versions of *Garden in Sochi* of 1940–42 (*Ill. 6-13*), Gorky allowed his imagination to reconstruct the idyllic

6-14. JOAN MIRÓ,
*Seated Woman II*, 1939.

6-15. ARSHILE GORKY, *Mojave*, ca. 1941–42.

6-16. ARSHILE GORKY,
*Virginia Landscape,* 1943.

orchard known as the "garden of wish fulfillment" on his father's farm. The tapering and bulging biomorphic forms are still close to Miró's *Seated Woman II* (*Ill. 6-14*), which Gorky could have seen at Art of This Century. However, the wish to evoke in abstract terms a specific landscape, with all of its emotional associations, allies this work with Kandinsky's first abstract landscapes. A large dead tree, to which torn strips of clothing were affixed, and a blue rock which village women believed could induce fertility, invoke ancient folk legends in the same manner that Kandinsky's early abstractions evoke the landscape and peasant myths of Russia. Even more Miróesque are the biomorphic motifs of *Mojave* (*Ill. 6-15*).

The six or more works related to the "Sochi" theme mark the beginning of Gorky's use of nature as his principal theme. During a summer at his wife's family's farm in Virginia in 1943, he began a series of drawings (*Ill. 6-16*) in which the forms of nature were generalized

6-17. ARSHILE GORKY,
*The Liver Is the Cock's Comb,*
Study, 1943.

and transformed into universal configurations. By now Gorky had begun to paint thinly, allowing washes of pale tints to spread and run, and separating line from patches of color. This was to be the future direction of his art. According to William Seitz, "The details, delineated with surgical precision, convince us of their actuality: they are real things. Hairline distinctions are established between thoracic projections, fleshly masses, and clusters of fluttering membranes. A single contour can define the swelling of an anatomical bulge, delimit an abstract plane, and initiate a movement."[6] Thus, Gorky's already lush, suggestive imagery became even lusher and denser with conflated meanings.

Normally, it was Gorky's practice to work from carefully prepared drawings. The relationship of the drawings to the paintings may be easily discerned in a comparison of the brilliant *The Liver Is the Cock's Comb* (*Ill. 6-18*) with the drawing that served as its point of departure (*Ill. 6-17*). From the wealth of freely invented forms which sprung without inhibition from his pen, Gorky selected the most telling configurations, rearranging them in a more cohesive order and

6-18. ARSHILE GORKY, *The Liver Is the Cock's Comb*, 1944.

6-19. ARSHILE GORKY,
*Agony,* 1947.

adding spots, patches, haloes, and streams of richly modulated color. In such a process of refinement, the liberating potential of automatism, subjected to the artist's subsequent critical reappraisal, proved a most valuable creative tool.

In his last paintings, the intensity of Gorky's vision caused the forms to be almost unbearably attenuated, tortured, and drawn-out. Tendril-like forms become teeth or claws; and menacing, ominous or eviscerated forms predominate. The nature pictures were followed by a series of "interiors" influenced by Matta, in which furniture, utensils, and anatomical parts were fused. The autobiographical nature of these more intimate last works, done while Gorky suffered a series of

6-20. JACKSON POLLOCK, *Untitled,* ca. 1937.

6-21. JACKSON POLLOCK, *Totem Lesson II, ca.* 1945.

tragedies, including a fire which destroyed many paintings and a grave illness, gives us the picture of a psyche brutalized rather than brutal. The background of these paintings is no longer fluid, but richly brushed and modulated. In his final style, in works like *Agony* (*Ill. 6-19*), Gorky was the first to synthesize abstract painterliness with Surrealist motifs. The apprentice to the modern masters had become one of them.

Like Gorky, Jackson Pollock also was a myth in his own time. Throughout most of his life, Pollock struggled with the problem of figuration, as did de Kooning. In Pollock's celebrated "drip" paintings of 1947–50, however, he used automatism as a means of making totally abstract paintings. In these unique works, Pollock changed the face of American painting by introducing "all-over" composition. He was also the first to arrive at a single characteristic image in the interlaced webs of the drip paintings.

The facts of Pollock's biography lend themselves easily to myth-making. Born in Wyoming and raised in California, an admirer of Ryder and American Indian art, Pollock was the natural candidate for all-American painter. In addition, the crudeness, intensity, and passion shown in his works were qualities that had come to be identified as characteristically American. These qualities are evident in his convulsive, turbulent seascapes of the thirties (*Ill. 6-20*), in the ritual themes of the forties, like *Totem Lesson II* (*Ill. 6-21*), and in the later drip paintings. If Gorky and de Kooning fought to free their art from the binding strictures of Cubism through the agent of emotional expression, Pollock's task was to find a means of ordering raw feeling. Gorky's and de Kooning's triumphs were in the ultimate release of

6-22. JACKSON POLLOCK, *Mural*, 1943.

6-23.
JACKSON POLLOCK,
*Pasiphaë*, 1943.

hidden energy; Pollock's lay in wresting a transcendent order from primordial chaos.

Before he had any direct contact with the Surrealists, Pollock had been involved with certain aspects of Surrealism, such as mythical themes of primeval genealogy. This direct contact came in 1943, when Pollock became affiliated with Art of This Century. Through his friend Robert Motherwell, Pollock learned the technique of automatic creation during the winter of 1941–42. Within a few months, Pollock was producing automatic works, drawings and water colors, culminating in the great, nearly twenty-foot *Mural* (*Ill. 6-22*) (now at The University of Iowa), which Peggy Guggenheim commissioned in 1943 for her entrance hall. This was the first mural-scale painting by an artist of Pollock's generation. Already, in this frieze-like work, line

6-24. JACKSON POLLOCK,
*Eyes in the Heat*, 1946.

6-25. JACKSON POLLOCK, *Mural on Indian Red Ground*, 1950.

has become identified with gesture, and shapes and closed forms have disappeared. The dance-like movement of figures rhythmically intertwined suggests Matisse's *The Dance*. But where the movement in Matisse's composition is rotary, Pollock's frontal disposition of the figures is parallel to the picture surface. His figures interpenetrate and partake of one another like the letters of the Kufic alphabet.

From this point on, Pollock painted an astonishing series of pictures, in which anatomical fragments, heads, ideographic signs, ancient cabalistic symbols, and free arabesques are described by the same electrically charged, nervous meandering line. In some, like *Pasiphaë* (*Ill. 6-23*), totemic figures flank the central portion, which is characteristically organized as the long rectangle of a frieze. In 1946, in such works as *Eyes in the Heat* (*Ill. 6-24*), short, curving brushstrokes cross and recross, dissolving their meteoric brilliance in a swirling, churning continuum. These dense, thickly impastoed works were followed in 1947 by Pollock's first drip masterpieces. These works constitute a

6-26. JACKSON POLLOCK, *Number 27,* 1951.

genuine break-through in the recent formal innovations of American painting; they are moreover the only paintings that can be accurately described as both abstract and Expressionist to the same degree. In such a painting as *Mural on Indian Red Ground (Ill. 6-25)*, the maelstrom has given way to the lyrical beauty of the open, transparent nets and skeins of paint cast over one another. The eye attempts the impossible task of unraveling the dizzying, labyrinthine complexity of these works, finally accepting the total unity and indissolubility of the created image. That this image does not depend on shape or form in the conventional sense, but rather on line and movement, makes it that much more difficult to comprehend. Because the eye must constantly travel the convoluted paths, the sense of movement is preserved even in the static framework of a painting. Since there is no longer any distinction between figure and ground, or any attempt to model forms sculpturally by using line as contour, a new kind of pictorial space is achieved.

This space has been called purely "optical," in contrast to pictorial space composed of a series of planes receding behind the picture plane, which allow the eye to move forward and backward. Since Cubist space, no matter how shallow and how insistent on the integrity of the surface plane, still permits in and out fluctuations in depth, one may interpret Pollock's drip paintings as the first significant change in pictorial space since Cubism. Thus, the drip paintings offered a new kind of "optical" pictorial space as well as a new kind of "all-over" pictorial organization. In this, they became the central point of departure for the abstractions of the fifties and sixties.[7]

Not even Pollock, however, could maintain the volatile synthesis of the contradictory elements of the abstract and the expressionistic represented by the drip paintings. In 1951, he reintroduced figurative elements into paintings such as *Number 27* (*Ill. 6-26*), which were now mainly executed in black Duco enamel on raw canvas. Some of the paintings of the fifties, however, combine the drip technique with impastoed passages for a new richness of surface effects. Pollock did not return again to the free-swinging arcs and hemicycles, the openness and transparency of the drip paintings. Instead, his late works often recapitulate earlier themes, such as the wild turbulence of the flickering seascapes, and the totemic figures of the ritual themes.

It is important to know that Pollock worked on the floor, not on the wall. He did not prime his canvas, but poured or dripped the paint directly onto the raw canvas, which tended to absorb the first layers of paint. Perhaps because he was able to attack the canvas from all sides, he could give each part of the painting equal emphasis and ignore the need to orient or balance the composition in any single direction. Although his method of composition was radical, it allowed for modifications on the basis of subsequent critical re-evaluations. One of the last decisions to be made was the painting's final dimensions; in the final step the painting was cut out and mounted on a stretcher. Because Pollock's art was so emotional and deeply felt, the tendency to dismiss his paintings as spontaneous outpourings has worked against an understanding of them as the result of conscious ordering, technical control, and critical evaluation.

An artist who was also transformed by contact with Surrealism, Robert Motherwell was as beset by opposing impulses as Pollock, if not more so. A student of aesthetics, he brought to painting a keen awareness of its historical situation. But, distrustful of intellectualiza-

6-27. ROBERT MOTHERWELL,
*Pancho Villa,
Dead and Alive,* 1943.

6-28. ROBERT MOTHERWELL,
*Western Air,* 1946–47.

tion, he sought to illuminate consciousness through probing the unconscious. Attracted to the sun-drenched sensuality of Mediterranean cultures, Motherwell valued painting as a source of pleasure, a value it had seldom, if ever, been assigned in America. Yet the need to rationalize sensation, to provide it with some kind of ordered framework which would make it intelligible, forced him to return time and again to the problem of structure.

Because of his erudition, Motherwell was able to take a large view, to see "the history of modern art . . . as the history of modern freedom." Understanding the radical, critical spirit of the European avantgarde, he helped to transmit its values to his own generation. Although he saw automatism as a means of mediating between the conscious and the unconscious, he also believed that this technique had a broader significance:

6-29. ROBERT MOTHERWELL,
*At Five in the Afternoon,* 1949.

6-30. ROBERT MOTHERWELL, *Irish Elegy*, 1965.

The fundamental criticism of automatism is that the unconscious cannot be *directed,* that it presents none of the possible choices which, when taken, constitute any expression's form. To give oneself over completely to the unconscious is to become a slave. But here it must be asserted at once that plastic automatism though perhaps not verbal automatism—as employed by the modern masters, like Masson, Miró and Picasso, is actually very little a question of the unconscious. It is much more a plastic weapon with which to invent new forms. As such it is one of the twentieth century's greatest formal inventions.[8]

Motherwell speaks also of automatism as a kind of doodling or scribbling that is like the original process in children's art. Like Klee, the American artists whom Motherwell introduced to automatism sought to preserve the freshness of the naive eye of the child.

The reconciliation of opposites, one of the characteristics of Abstract Expressionism, is perhaps most dramatically diagrammed in Motherwell's work. The struggle to strike a balance between contradictory elements—the conscious and the unconscious, feeling and intellect, structure and openness, freedom and necessity—is, in fact, the heart of Motherwell's effort. Perhaps because he was as concerned with the destructive effects of culture (in so far as it inhibited sensuality) as he was dedicated to its preservation, Motherwell was more attracted to the Freudian than the Jungian aspects of Surrealist iconography. Thus, he was concerned with the discontents of civilization, the discomfort and anxiety of contemporary Western man in his present situation, rather than with the evocation of prehistoric archetypes or myths. In one of his earliest works, *Pancho Villa, Dead and Alive* (*Ill. 6-27*), a painting done with collage for a collage exhibition Peggy Guggenheim held in 1943, one can find the genesis of Motherwell's major themes. The random drips and spatters testify that he had already adopted the Surrealist attitude that chance and accident enhance spontaneity. On the other hand, the insistence on a logical and coherent structure, in which the picture is divided into quasi-geometrical compartments, exerts some control over accident. Here for the first time Motherwell announces the theme of life versus death, the opposition of Eros and Thanatos that occupied Freud in his late works. Pancho Villa "alive" is distinguished from his dead, blood-drenched mirror image by the presence of genitals, which the "dead" man does not possess. The theme of the Spanish hero (in Pancho Villa's case, Mexican) will find its final form in the phallic configurations of the series of elegies to the Spanish Republic. But in opposition to the somber tragic Spanish themes of death, there will be the life-affirming paintings based on French themes, like the "je t'aime" series of the late forties.

The necessity of maintaining the integrity of the picture plane was clear to Motherwell; his dilemma was how to maintain it in an open painterly style. The problem was to integrate the structure of the more rigid Picassoid works, such as *Western Air* (*Ill. 6-28*), with the freedom and spontaneity of the automatic collages. Having rejected the more formal, hard-edged solution of the earlier "wall paintings," around 1950 he eliminated color in the elegies, restricting himself to black and white. Where background white makes incursions into the foreground black, or vice versa, Motherwell allows painted edge to overlap painted edge so that the two are locked together in a single plane. Thus he is able to reconcile the contrary demands of pictorial structure with those of painterly expressiveness dependent on the play

6-31. ROBERT MOTHERWELL, *Jour la Maison, Nuit la Rue,* 1957.

of the brush and the individuality of the artist's personal mark. In the theme of the Spanish elegies, with their few dominant Stonehenge-like shapes (which nonetheless have freely brushed edges), Motherwell found a subject and a composition in which he could unite both drives. The subject has occupied him since 1949, when he painted the prototype of the elegy motif, *At Five in the Afternoon (Ill. 6-29)*. The most recent of the elegies, *Irish Elegy (Ill. 6-30)*, commemorates the tragedy of Irish nationalism.

Motherwell's paintings of the fifties occupy a point midway between gestural and chromatic abstraction. Although painterly improvisation is important, gesture—as the path of a nervous line—is not. Clarity is not lost in a welter of charged strokes. Shapes tend to be simple, large, and easily distinguishable, with the improvisation kept to the irregularly brushed edges. In *Jour la Maison, Nuit la Rue (Ill. 6-31)*, the handwriting is a painterly reformulation of Cubist lettering, but unlike Cubist lettering, it serves to blur distinctions between figure and ground by demonstrating that both are part of a subtly modulated atmospheric space. In the sixties, landscape is Motherwell's most frequent motif; the harsh monochromatic tones of the Spanish landscape are often replaced by the more brilliant blues and greens of the Mediterranean coast.

6-32. WILLEM DE KOONING,
*Queen of Hearts,* 1943–46.

6-33. WILLEM DE KOONING,
*Woman,* 1948.

Gorky had no direct heir among the Abstract Expressionists, but certain aspects of his work, particularly his free interpretation of Cubism and his delicate, disembodied line, had parallels in the work of Willem de Kooning. But de Kooning, who had shared a studio with Gorky in the late thirties, had no interest in Surrealism. He resembled Gorky mainly in his respect for the old masters. His subjects

6-34. WILLEM DE KOONING,
*Woman, I,* 1950–52.

6-35. WILLEM DE KOONING, *Sailcloth, ca.* 1949.

were not the remote evocations of poetic fantasy, but the most tangible realities of the human figure and the urban environment. This preoccupation with the tangible and the immediate experience characterizes de Kooning's tougher, more brutal, sensibility.

During the thirties, de Kooning painted in several manners. His sketch for the Williamsburg Federal Housing Project, done during the year he spent working on the Federal Art Project, is close to Gorky's interpretations of Picasso. But more important to his development were the series of muted abstractions of a few simple biomorphic or loose geometric shapes and the sensitive portraits of himself and his friends. The grayed tints of these works and the transparent painting add to the ghostly quality of the figures, which seem to merge with their diaphanous backgrounds.

Of the major artists of his generation, de Kooning was the only one to choose the human figure, first male, then female, as his principal theme. From the late thirties on into the present, he has developed variations on the "woman" that quickly came to be identified as his characteristic image. From the more gentle and lyrical *Queen of Hearts* (*Ill. 6-32*) of the early forties to the scarred and scumbled *Woman* (*Ill. 6-33*) of the middle forties to the culminating fragmented and violated women of the early fifties (*Ill. 6-34*), one can trace both a pictorial and psychological development of the theme.

De Kooning's pictorial dilemma is spatial. Contours are opened to allow flesh and environment to flow into one another, and anatomical forms themselves have been fragmented; hence there is no clear statement as to where the figure is actually located in space. This ambiguous space de Kooning has referred to as the "no-environment," a metaphor for the dislocated space in which the flux of modern life takes place. Tension then arises out of the difficulty in determining where the figure is placed as it emerges from its chaotic environment to assume its own identity. In the paintings of the early fifties there is a new violence, aggressiveness, and brusqueness of attack as the paint is hurled on the canvas in the heat of execution. Such an attack, in which the loaded brush is allowed to drag and sweep across the canvas trailing meteoric splashes and drips, came to be identified as the characteristic means of execution of gestural abstraction or "action painting."

Paralleling the opening up and fragmenting of the "women" paintings in the fifties were the increasingly violent accidents and collisions of de Kooning's painterly abstractions. In *Sailcloth* (*Ill. 6-35*), for example, fragments of anatomy are described by fine-angled lines which also serve to bound planes without closing them off; and planes seem to spill into each other, as if rent open by some dynamic, explosive force. De Kooning's abstract works of the fifties, although simpler and employing larger forms than Gorky's, are related to Gorky in their displacement of humanoid forms into a landscape context. In this spirit, patches of flesh pink recall skin even when no specific anatomical correspondences exist.

De Kooning's "women" of the fifties may be taken as symptomatic of the crisis facing figure painting, or more specifically, of the difficulty of representing the figure without contour or modeling. The impossible transitions, suggested perhaps by de Kooning's practice of ripping up drawings and sticking them back together with the parts slightly askew, suggest jumps in space that are analogous to the manner in which forms dissolve, disappear, and reappear in the paintings. Earlier, such discontinuities were suggested in the elegant figures of the forties, such as *Pink Angels* (*Ill. 6-36*), in which ribbonlike curves

6-36. WILLEM DE KOONING,
*Pink Angels, ca.* 1947.

travel along, weaving in and out of space with roller-coaster speed, ending in amorphous hands and feet. Like the other painters of his generation who wrestled with the problem of figuration, de Kooning left physiognomic and anatomical fragments floating around in an ambiguous ambience, sometimes superimposing them in the heat of revisions and modifications. Taking certain existential concepts as his point of departure, de Kooning, among others, saw each painting as constantly in the state of being defined. In this sense, the skirmishes and conflicts he pictured reflect a world view that sees man in constant struggle, both with himself and with his environment.

De Kooning's work of the late forties is perhaps his finest. In a remarkable series of works of this period—many executed in black and white—line is allowed to function independently of form; its normal job of describing contour is minimized in the interest of an all-over rhythm of swiftly executed dramatic movement. At this point, de Kooning is closest to automatic procedures, his nervous calligraphy dancing wildly and brilliantly across the canvas surface. These black-

and-white de Koonings, and the collage paintings of Marca-Relli, such as *The Battle* (*Ill. 6-37*), which are based upon them, represent the end of the biomorphic phase of Abstract Expressionism.

In the fifties, the slipping planes and open contours of paintings like *Excavation* (*Ill. 6-38*) gave way to denser, more crowded works, in which charged brushstrokes smash against one another. Rejecting geometric structure, de Kooning announced that "nothing is less clear than geometry." His works, consequently, grew more unstructured. Because of this development toward increased painterliness, by the late fifties, line had become merely a residual element. The wild strokes, which seem to describe the broad planes of landscape, collide with each other with the brutal force of tidal waves.

Tracing the development of Gorky, Pollock, Motherwell, and de Kooning, we have seen how Abstract Expressionism in the late forties, having rejected "abstraction" or formalism per se, ultimately turned its back on Surrealism to find its own identity. During this period, other aspects of American art of the late thirties began to reassert themselves. For example, whether or not it was intentional, a distinctly American character began to emerge in the new painting. It involved an unconditional pragmatic approach toward materials and techniques, which allowed greater freedom and more dramatic gestures. This, in turn, led to the appropriation of the house painter's brushes and paints. The easel, on the other hand, gave way to the painting wall. Artists saw the possibility of mural-scale art which, by virtue of its sheer size,

6-37. CONRAD MARCA-RELLI, *The Battle,* 1956.

6-38. WILLEM DE KOONING, *Excavation,* 1950.

would encompass the spectator and become his total environment, thus forcing him into a more direct confrontation with the work of art. By the end of the forties, the mythic symbols and biomorphic forms of Surrealism were replaced, on one hand, by rapidly executed, sweeping gestures, and on the other, by large fields of resonant color. In this manner, by 1950 the "first generation" of Abstract Expressionists had distilled the characteristic images by which they would be known.

The adjective "heroic" has been applied to the first-generation Abstract Expressionists. Certainly their aim was to restore to painting the heroic dimension, in a time when men had shown themselves at their least heroic and often at their most bestial. This contradiction—between contemporary reality and the intention of art—must be seen as adding to the difficulty of creating works which assumed that modern man remained the spiritual heir to the entire complex of Western culture. The ideals of the ancient classical and Judeo-Christian tradition were often invoked by artists as disparate as de Kooning, Motherwell, Newman, and Rothko, when describing their own aspirations. Although little is said of the relationship of Abstract Expressionism to World

War II, surely some of the tensions in the works arose out of the attempt to maintain humanistic values—to present a heroic image—during a time of world holocaust. The Messianic, heroic, and humanistic aspects of Abstract Expressionism, however, must be seen in the general context of American art, which so often in the twentieth century tried to transcend the merely aesthetic.

To complicate matters further, the Abstract Expressionists wished to maintain only the humanistic values of classical art, not its forms. They knew that an authentic American art could only express itself in terms of the American experience. This presented yet another contradiction, since the very qualities that define the American experience—dynamism, flux, violence—may be described as antithetical to the classic spirit.

## Chapter Seven

# The New American Painting

It was with the utmost reluctance that I found the figure could not serve my purposes. . . . But a time came when none of us could use the figure without mutilating it.

        —MARK ROTHKO (quoted by Dore Ashton,
           *The New York Times,* October 31, 1958)

Around 1950, Abstract Expressionism broke into two clearly defined camps, which may be called gestural abstraction or, as Harold Rosenberg termed it, "action painting," and chromatic abstraction. Among the artists for whom gesture was paramount were Pollock, Kline, Guston, and de Kooning; whereas Newman, Rothko, Gottlieb, and Reinhardt became primarily interested in focusing a single, central image in terms of large, barely inflected fields of color. The work of Motherwell, Still, and Tomlin can be seen as occupying a position somewhere between the two extremes. By the early fifties each of the leading Abstract Expressionists had achieved a highly individualized style, a kind of personal imprimatur that was more closely identified with the painter's ego than style had previously been.

The "action painters," with the exception of Pollock, remained closer to late Cubist structure and space; the "color field" painters, originally more deeply involved with Surrealism, eventually distilled simple, unified, abstract images from the richness of their Surrealist experience, but maintained the atmospheric space of Surrealism. The former, in their emphasis on surface effects created by a loaded brush cutting a wide swath across the canvas, achieved an unprecedented degree of looseness and painterliness. By means of gesture, the artist made of his personal "handwriting" or calligraphy an individualized personal stamp. The movement of the wrist and the arm came into play, displacing the previous emphasis on the hand and making possible a new

7-1. MARK TOBEY, *New Life (Resurrection)*, 1957.

breadth and speed of execution. De Kooning, whose success in transforming his draftsman's line into painterly gesture made him the central figure among the action painters, acknowledged that Pollock "broke the ice" for the others. Indeed, although Gorky's late paintings of 1947 exhibited a new fluidity, openness, and freedom, they still combined drawing with painting in a relatively conventional manner. On the other hand, Pollock's series of "drip" paintings begun in 1947 provided the key to a broader, bolder way of working. Hofmann had

7-2. BARNETT NEWMAN,
*The Euclidean Abyss*, 1946–47.

7-3. BARNETT NEWMAN, *Tundra*, 1950.

hinted at this way in his paintings of the middle forties, which combined painting with drawing as gesture. Pollock resolved any conflict between the two extremes of linearity and painterliness by uniting them in a single process.

The term "all-over" has been used to describe the composition of the drip paintings. Although Pollock was the first to realize fully the implications of all-over paintings, he was not the first to treat the canvas surface in such a way that there was no central focus. Monet, in his late water-lily paintings, had eliminated sharp value contrasts, treating the entire canvas surface as a densely packed continuum. In these paintings hierarchical distinctions among forms disappeared, and no single element detached itself from the total image. Later, Miró in his "Constellations" had strewn shapes across the entire field of the canvas, and Klee and Tobey had used tangled webs of lines in an atmospheric space. In Pollock's drip paintings, however, these tendencies toward all-over, nonhierarchical compositions without a single climactic focus came to fruition.

7-4. BARNETT NEWMAN,
*Concord*, 1949.

A member of the mystical Baha'i faith, Mark Tobey studied Japanese calligraphy. Inspired by Oriental script, he developed the all-over markings of his delicate "white writing" paintings. Tobey's pale grisaille paintings like *New Life (Resurrection)* (*Ill. 7-1*) preserve the intimate scale of European cabinet painting. Pollock's drip paintings, on the other hand, in their vast scale, dramatic contrasts, and unconventional technique, mark a more genuine break with the European tradition.

During the crucial years of the late forties, while de Kooning and Pollock explored the possibilities of gestural abstraction, Clyfford Still, Barnett Newman, and Mark Rothko were working toward a more static, reductive abstraction, emphasizing the power of large areas of pure color to provide dramatic impact.

Although Still, Newman, and Rothko were the first to work toward a simplified art based on color rather than gesture, their approaches were radically different. Beginning in the late forties with such works as *The Euclidean Abyss* (*Ill. 7-2*), Newman grappled with the problem of structuring his compositions without recourse to the internal relationships of forms or to the dry precision of geometric painting. As he put it, "Instead of using outlines, instead of making shapes or setting off spaces, my drawings declare the space. Instead of working with the remnants of space, I work with the whole space."[1] Ultimately, he arrived at the solution hinted at in *The Euclidean Abyss:* that of dividing up the colored field by an irregular, pulsating vertical band or bands. By lining up these bands parallel to the framing edge, Newman made it explicit that the structure of the painting was derived from the canvas support, as in *Tundra* (*Ill. 7-3*) and *Concord* (*Ill. 7-4*). By dividing space into areas by means of bands, he introduced a pictorial structure based on the relationship of the single image to the framing edge. In a sense, the treatment of the canvas as a unified, uniformly articulated field is an extension of Pollock's all-over principle of composition. That is, neither Pollock's skeins nor Newman's fields create shapes in the conventional sense. All-over composition differs from Cubist composition in that it is not based on the repetition of analogous forms or on the relationship of parts, but on the coherence and integrity of a single image that fills the entire space of the canvas. Because it does not depend on hierarchical ordering or on relationships of discrete elements, Newman's method of composing has been called "non-relational."

Clyfford Still was among the first to arrive at a characteristic image by which his work is identifiable. In the late forties, he painted broad fields of impastoed pigment eaten away by flamelike patches. The raw vigor of these paintings was already discernible in Still's crude Surrealist works like *Jamais* (*Ill. 7-5*), which he showed at Art of This Century in 1946. His dark romantic paintings, wrenched open by bolts

7-5. CLYFFORD STILL, *Jamais,* 1944.

of lightning, such as the early abstraction *1943-A* (*Ill. 7-6*), have an affinity with Ryder's romanticism and Pollock's turbulent landscapes. The suggestion of ravines, gorges, crevices, and other natural formations in the paintings of the late forties, such as *1948-D* (*Ill. 7-7*), remains even after Still has expunged any Surrealist metaphors. In the works of the fifties and sixties, the feeling is often that of a romantic landscape cut by canyons and waterfalls, and lit by a strange phosphorescent unnatural light.

Still is known as a pioneer of the mural-scale painting. (William Rubin has suggested that the unique type of wall-size painting created by the Abstract Expressionist generation—neither a mural nor an easel picture—was arrived at more or less simultaneously in 1950 by Pollock, Newman, Still, and Rothko.)[2] In some of his works, the vast, irregular fields of dense color are so heavily loaded with paint that they appear literally ploughed by the knife or brush. Forms seem gouged out of the palpable pigment with the elemental force of ice-age glaciers tearing out lakes and uprooting forests. However, because the flamelike patches bite into the adjoining fields, any conventional figure-ground reading is prevented; the forms are not seen as objects against a background. Like Motherwell, Still is the dramatist who deals in the starkest contrast—wild yellows and sizzling reds against somber blues and sinister blacks; like Newman, he presents color as pure optical sensation by using areas of rich, fully saturated color in open fields. But Still's thick pigment is the opposite of Newman's fluidity. Newman offers a lyrical atmospheric continuum, but Still presents the impervious surface of a wall. Thus the opticality of Still's color is contradicted by the tactile quality of his paint surface. In his

7-6. CLYFFORD STILL, *1943-A.*

7-7. CLYFFORD STILL, *1948-D,* 1948.

emphasis on the texture of the pigment rather than on the texture of
the canvas, Still is closer to the action painters than he is to the chromatic abstractionists like Rothko and Newman.

In his "environmental" paintings, Still achieves an impact that
forces the viewer into a more immediate confrontation with the work
of art. The rawness of the paint quality, the willingness to accept as

aesthetic what might be considered ugly or inartistic in another context, is the mark, not only of Still's powerful abstractions, but also of American avant-garde work in general. Like many of the new American painters, Still turned awkwardness into an asset, extracting from it an impressive originality of color and of format. His direct two- and three-color arrangements, stretched like a taut skin across the canvas surface, eliminate conventional modeling and volume. In them, clawlike forms reach across the canvas to mesh into the larger painted field, rather than passing in front of or behind a series of receding planes. This works to establish the continuity of the unbroken picture plane by bringing the image up forward, nearer the viewer and flush with the surface.

Although Newman was first, in his drawings and paintings of 1947–48, to deduce pictorial structure from the actual structure of the rectangle, Mark Rothko and Ad Reinhardt were also working toward similar modes of composition, but from different points of departure. Like Newman and Still, Rothko distilled his characteristic image of two or three delicately brushed rectangles, which echoed the perimeter of the frame and floated in an atmospheric continuum, from his early paintings by expunging all references to Surrealism. A painting like *Number 24* (*Ill. 7-8*) represents the gradual transition from the Surrealist-inspired landscapes to Rothko's typical arrangement of abstract rectangles, such as *Black, Pink and Yellow over Orange* (*Ill. 7-9*). The resulting centralized image is still in a sense a symbol—of oneness or wholeness or transcendent unity—but of a much more abstract and conceptual nature than the more literal Surrealist symbols.

Rothko's large fields, divided into two or three parallel rectangles which echo the framing edge, are painted in close-valued, luminous colors. The quality of light radiating from some hidden central source within the painting is what distinguishes Rothko's color from that of his contemporaries. This is achieved by means of Rothko's sensitive handling of edges, which are softly brushed into the adjoining field, causing a slight vibration to be set up; and by means of his choice of colors, which tend to augment the gentle vibration. As a result of the close-keyed harmonies and painterly edges, Rothko's images appear to float, the rectangles hovering buoyantly in the resonant space.

The apparent simplicity of Rothko's rectangular motif provides a contrast with the richness and opulence of his color. In his works of the late forties, thin washes of delicately hued paint are allowed to soak into the canvas, indicating the direction his later work will take. Al-

7-8. MARK ROTHKO, *Number 24,* 1949.

though Rothko was one of the most adept draftsmen of his generation, by the late forties he had abandoned the elaborate automatic drawing of his earlier paintings in favor of pure areas of color set side by side, adjacent but not touching. These works suggest tranquil idyllic landscapes, differing greatly from Still's brutal and violent primeval images. The sense of tranquillity and harmony is preserved in the paintings of the fifties. These later works, however, take on the grandeur of objects for contemplation. In a joint statement prepared by Gottlieb, Newman, and Rothko, the three artists speak of the "impact of elemental truth," which favors the "simple expression of the complex thought, and the importance of the large shape because it has the impact of the unequivocal."

The works of the fifties of Rothko, Newman, and Gottlieb, although simple in format, are meant to convey a content as rich as their earlier Surrealist work. Asserting that "there is no such thing as a good painting about nothing," they were equally adamant that "the subject is crucial and only that subject-matter is valid which is tragic and timeless."[3]

Adolph Gottlieb was interested in Matisse's color at a time when most New York painters were involved with Picasso or Miró. After

7-9. MARK ROTHKO, *Black, Pink and Yellow over Orange*, 1951–52.

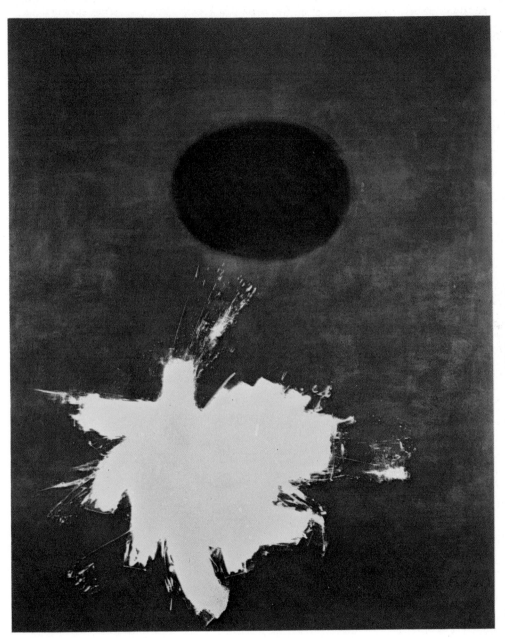

7-10. ADOLPH GOTTLIEB, *Counterpoise*, 1959.

7-11. ADOLPH GOTTLIEB, *The Frozen Sounds, Number 1*, 1951.

leaving the WPA Federal Art Project in 1937, Gottlieb painted for a year in the Arizona desert. The series of still lifes based on cactus forms of the late thirties are a prelude to his "pictographs" of the forties, like *Voyager's Return (Ill. 6-12)*, which were stylized symbolic motifs based on human and natural forms isolated in compartments. The cryptic images of the pictographs, which bring to mind both ancient hieroglyphics and the compartments of Torres-Garcia, were a means of structuring the composition; they also have certain similarities to the decorative signs of the Kwakiutl Indians.

Like his contemporaries, Gottlieb looked for mythic, universal themes. For a while he thought that the myths of the American Indians might be a possible subject, but ultimately he concentrated on ancient mythology. Gradually, the symbols of the pictographs became simpler and less specific, until they were refined into two essential images: a peaceful disc for the sun or moon and an angry exploding ball of undifferentiated matter for the earth. This process of refinement was nearly complete when Gottlieb began his "stratified landscapes" in 1951. By the time he painted *The Frozen Sounds (Ill. 7-11)*, Gottlieb had discarded the confining grid of the compartments and the linear pictographs in favor of zoned compositions divided by a horizon line. Above the horizon hang the celestial symbols; and below, the earth seethes in chaos.

From the early thirties—when his paintings were reminiscent of Avery's interpretation of Matisse—Gottlieb's work has been distinguished by refined technique and subtle color. In the late fifties he began to simplify and center his images. Balancing out areas in terms of their weight as colors, he often achieved startlingly original effects with his use of ice-cream colors and pastel tints. Typical of the imagery of his later paintings is the masterful *Counterpoise* (*Ill. 7-10*), in which the stable brown disc of the "sun" hangs peacefully above the exploding yellow mass of the "earth."

Ad Reinhardt, one of the few New York artists who has been an abstract painter since the thirties, was never drawn to Surrealism, action painting, or figurative art. Instead, he found his inspiration from the first in Oriental, Indian, and Arabic abstract decorative art. In the late forties, his geometric abstractions, such as the *Abstract Painting* of 1947 (*Ill. 7-12*), were shattered into calligraphic strokes disposed in the all-over fashion of Oriental calligraphy and of Tobey's "white writing." Reminiscent of the misty, layered space of classical Chinese landscapes, these works anticipate the dusky twilight atmosphere of Reinhardt's "black" paintings. Around 1950, the fragments of the tracery began to coalesce into larger horizontal and vertical brush-strokes, ultimately becoming a series of interlocking rectangles, as in the 1952 *Red Painting* (*Ill. 7-13*). Since 1953, Reinhardt has confined himself to making only black paintings.

In his search for an absolute, Reinhardt wished to arrive at an indivisible image and a single color; he sought a scheme that was, like the Buddha image in Eastern art, "breathless, timeless, styleless, lifeless, deathless, endless." Finding this image in the trisected "black" canvas,

7-12. AD REINHARDT, *Abstract Painting*, 1947.

7-13. AD REINHARDT,
*Red Painting*, 1952.

he chose low-key greens, browns, and violets, so close in value as to be virtually indistinguishable. Reinhardt's relentless polemicizing for a mystically pure art-for-art's sake (embodied, it would appear, only in his own work) made him a thorn in the side of his contemporaries, who called him the "black monk." However, his insistence on an uncompromising, reductive, minimal art has made him an important source for younger artists, who came to share his views on the rhetorical nature of action painting.

The most influential artist to reject representational art around 1950 was Franz Kline. Celebrating the special dynamism of the urban environment, Kline had much in common, in terms of his sensibility at least, with his friend Reginald Marsh, although Kline's genius was much greater. Kline's feeling for the great looming structures of the metropolis links him with the earlier New York realists, who had also found their inspiration in the forms and colors of the city. In fact, his paintings of the early forties echo Ash Can School themes.

Until the late forties, Kline painted modest but moving urban landscapes; they show his ability to perceive monumentality in the shapes of the railroads and bridges that streak across Manhattan. In the late forties, he began experimenting with brush drawings that were mainly free versions of figures. In 1950, he took the step toward which these drawings pointed; he magnified the brushstrokes into enormous, ab-

7-14. FRANZ KLINE,
*Nijinsky (Petrouchka)*, 1948.

7-15. FRANZ KLINE,
*Nijinsky, ca.* 1950.

stract ideograms which filled the canvas, as the many sketches he had made on telephone books and sheets of newspaper had filled the page. The drawings were done in black enamel, a quick-drying house paint Kline used in his paintings because it was cheap and fluid. His use of this paint caused contrasts in texture and finish that seem essential to the variety of the brushstroke. The two portraits of the dancer Nijinsky (*Ills. 7-14, 7-15*) show the transition of Kline's style from representational to abstract. Although the black shapes in his abstract paintings read as strong silhouettes, Kline, like Motherwell, did not conceive of the white as background in the conventional sense. The white areas in a painting like *Ninth Street* (*Ill. 7-16*) are as much painted figure as the black, and modifications in white paint smudge over or cut into black areas underneath. Kline's attitude toward his work was direct and pragmatic; he did not clothe his methods or motives with metaphysical pretensions. In such powerful black-and-white paintings as *Chief* (*Ill. 7-17*), he did not literally extract his images from the characteristic structures of the city, but invented abstract equivalents—massive trajectories which speed across the canvas field, capturing the energy of the urban experience. Even so, in some cases, the sweeping diagonals and girderlike strokes seem to find analogies in his realistic cityscapes of the forties. In the middle fifties, Kline reintroduced color,

7-16. FRANZ KLINE, *Ninth Street,* 1951.

7-17. FRANZ KLINE, *Chief*, 1950.

as his paintings became denser (like de Kooning's later works), and the energies grew more explosive.

Kline was not the only artist who limited himself to black and white around 1950. A number of others, including Motherwell, de Kooning, Pollock, and Newman, also painted canvases restricted to the dramatic contrast of black and white. Such an opposition was easily interpreted as a Manichaean struggle of the powers of light against the powers of darkness. Its practical advantage was that black enamel was the cheapest paint, and in the late forties, this was still an important consideration, even for an artist like de Kooning. These black-and-white pictures seem especially typical of the New York School. The sooty black has been equated with the grime of downtown New York, and the white has been identified with the white-washed walls of the studio-lofts.

Kline's conversion to abstraction came at the moment when a num-

7-18. PHILIP GUSTON, *Passage,* 1957-58.

ber of other painters were abandoning figurative styles for abstract styles. Around 1950, these included Philip Guston, Jack Tworkov, James Brooks, and Bradley Walker Tomlin. Guston became the master of a subdued gestural style which concentrated on delicately brushed, roughly square patches of cool pastel tints huddled together in the center of the canvas. His vaporous lyrical image and more controlled painterly brushwork became the model for painters like Esteban Vicente, Milton Resnick, and Adja Yunkers who were drawn toward a more intimate kind of "abstract impressionism." In *Passage* (*Ill. 7-18*), sensitively brushed passages evoke a poetic landscape. The flamelike diagonal brushstrokes dancing and flickering across Jack Tworkov's *Watergame* (*Ill. 7-19*), although more restless as an image, are equally controlled and purposeful. Tomlin's statement, on the other hand, represents a more complex and self-conscious resolution of the problem of loosening the hold of the Cubist grid on pictorial structure. His earlier paintings, sensitive Cubist still lifes, were sometimes surprising in their interjection of Surrealist motifs like disembodied eyes. They were transformed into open, calligraphic configurations, apparently under the influence of automatism, to which he was introduced by Motherwell. Tomlin was also influenced by Gottlieb's pictographs, from which he derived his imagery of the late forties. In 1949, in paintings like *Number 20 (Ill. 7-20)*, Tomlin's loose brushstrokes were hardened into simple curves, channeled into place by means of an underlying grid framework. But Tomlin's grids allowed a greater freedom of movement than orthodox Cubist structure.

The years 1947–53 were in many ways the high point of Abstract Expressionism. The intensity of activity and the interchange and dialogue among artists, as well as the quality of performance and richness of innovation, was greatest during these years. However, public recognition did not attend these achievements. In desperation, in 1951 a group of artists who called themselves "the irascible eighteen," including Motherwell, Newman, Kline, Pollock, Baziotes, Hofmann, Rothko, Reinhardt, Gottlieb, and de Kooning, picketed the Metropolitan Museum, demanding that a department of American art be set up. Then, taking matters into their own hands, the artists organized the Ninth Street Show in a store front on East Ninth Street, as a collective statement

7-19. JACK TWORKOV, *Watergame,* 1955.

7-20. BRADLEY WALKER TOMLIN, *Number 20,* 1949.

of their progress and aims. Among those represented were Pollock, Motherwell, de Kooning, Kline, Tworkov, Marca-Relli, and Cavallon, and a number of sculptors, such as James Rosati and Peter Grippe. The show was organized mainly by the members of the Artists' Club, a discussion group that had formed in late fall, 1949. The Club, in turn, had grown out of the need to find a time and place to discuss informally issues of general interest. Earlier, the "Subjects of the Artists" school, organized by Baziotes, Motherwell, Rothko, and David Hare, held open sessions and lectures which many artists attended. (Although Still had helped to formulate plans for the school, he did not teach there; and Newman joined the faculty after the school opened.) After one semester the school closed, but the loft where it was housed was taken over by a group of artists. For two seasons discussion groups continued at "Studio 35." Lectures were delivered by Baziotes, Joseph Cornell, de Kooning, Motherwell, Newman, Rothko, and Reinhardt, and by such European luminaries as Hans Arp and Richard Hulsenbeck. Topics of interest to the avant-garde were discussed, and a generally lively tone prevailed, at least until the mid-fifties, when older members began to lose interest in the Club as the avant-garde became established and accepted.

It is always tempting to identify the end of a creative epoch with the death of its leader. Yet it is impossible not to remark that Gorky's suicide in 1948, Pollock's death in an auto accident in 1956, and Kline's untimely death in 1960 at the age of 51 dramatically close chapters in the history of Abstract Expressionism. By 1948, the Surrealists had returned home to Europe, automatism had spurred Gorky to a new fluidity and painterliness and inspired Pollock to make the breakthrough to the "all-over" drip paintings, which in turn permitted others a new freedom of gesture. By 1956, Surrealist content and morphology had been rejected, and the last of the major Abstract Expressionists—Kline, Guston, and Tomlin—had cleansed their work of representational elements and were painting large-scale gestural abstractions. After Pollock's death, a market for these paintings was found, and the avant-garde had few battles left to fight—mainly with the mass media and the museums.

From 1956 to 1960, American art received international recognition, and a second generation of New York painters emerged. They were, it has been pointed out, the first American artists to have domestic heroes. Some like Alfred Leslie, Michael Goldberg, Grace Hartigan, and Joan Mitchell, to name the most talented, chose to imitate de Kooning; others turned to the potential implicit in Pollock and in chromatic abstraction. Although the work of Newman, Still, and Rothko became the point of departure for the new abstraction of the sixties, during the fifties it took second place to the spectacular pyrotechnics of the action painters, whose more flamboyant personalities were also magnets for attraction. During the late fifties, new artists poured into New York to join the loft Bohemia, which had shifted its center from Eighth Street to East Tenth Street. Here a series of cooperative galleries exhibited a potpourri of works covering the entire range from the figurative to the abstract. Imitating the life style of the first-generation Abstract Expressionists, the second generation often slavishly imitated their pictorial styles as well. At the Five Spot Cafe and the Cedar Bar, "action painting" became a modish phrase and its technique a subject for endless discussion. As the art market was glutted with the works of de Kooning's admirers, the real achievements of de Kooning and his generation were becoming obscured. Soon their art was to undergo re-evaluation by the strongest and most original among their successors.

If the end of an art style may be marked by the moment when no young painters of the first rank choose to work within it, then 1960 constitutes such a date for Abstract Expressionism. The physical destruction of the original neighborhood in which it flourished—the tearing down of Tenth Street, the closing of the original Cedar Bar, and the dissolution of the Club—were only the external events that paralleled a general shift in sensibility within the art world. In the sixties, the remaining members of the first generation would continue their development, and gifted members of the second generation would make significant contributions. However, Abstract Expressionism as a style would not serve as a point of departure, but as an established tradition, as the new Academy—perhaps the first Academy worthy of the name in the history of American art—to be attacked in terms of its own limitations and contradictions.

The internal contradictions implicit in Abstract Expressionism as a style are most visible in the works of de Kooning's followers. They include the conflicts of figuration versus abstraction, the unresolvedness of an ambiguous pictorial space, and the lack of structure of gestural abstraction. These were the basic pictorial problems that younger artists would be considering. Equally important, perhaps, would be their rejection of the rhetoric of action painting—the notion of the artist as existential matador alone in the "arena" of his canvas. To the extent that the world view of Abstract Expressionism was tied to the philosophy of Existentialism, one must understand the new art of the sixties as rejecting that world view and its implications.

## Chapter Eight

## After Abstract Expressionism

Though it may have started toward modernism earlier than the other arts, painting has turned out to have a greater number of *expendable* conventions imbedded in it, or at least a greater number of conventions that are difficult to isolate in order to expend. It seems to be a law of modernism—thus one that applies to almost all art that remains truly alive in our time—that the conventions not essential to the viability of a medium be discarded as soon as they are recognized.

—CLEMENT GREENBERG, " 'American-Type' Painting," *Art and Culture*, 1961

The novelty of our work derives therefore from our having moved away from simply private human concerns towards the world of nature and society of which all of us are part.

. . . object is *fact*, not symbol.

—JOHN CAGE, *Silence*, 1961

For about fifteen years Abstract Expressionism was able to absorb the energy of the indigenous tradition in the context of a high art by making virtues of its characteristics: speed of execution, rawness, and vitality. But when the internal contradictions that marked Abstract Expressionism as a style could no longer be held together in a viable synthesis, the demands for an art tied more directly to the moment and to the realities of the American scene could no longer be denied. These internal contradictions derived mainly from the figurative and Cubist roots of Abstract Expressionism. The lack of clarity or apparent structure of action painting in its most painterly phase of the late fifties was taken by younger artists as a sign of a lack of pictorial or emotional conviction. In reaction, they discarded not only the painterliness, but also the emotional, autobiographical quality of Abstract Expressionism.

Young artists began to question whether or not the marks of struggle and anxiety—the dragged brush and the violent attack—might be as easily simulated as felt. They wondered to what extent the spontaneous splashes and random drips had become mere mannerisms, stylistic effects that could be manufactured at will. By the end of the fifties, the high purpose of the first-generation Abstract Expressionists impressed many of their heirs as mere rhetoric; their drama was considered inflated or bathetic, and the latest phase of the movement chaotic, academic, or mannered. Fortunately, however, the exhaustion of the gestural manner in the hands of de Kooning's and Kline's imitators coincided with the finding of new potential in the works of Pollock and the chromatic abstractionists.

Rejecting the expressionistic basis of Abstract Expressionism, the new generation also renounced the symbolic and the metaphoric, along with the mystical. They questioned whether or not emotional states were indeed communicable and whether communication depended on the use of recognizable objects and images or on formal relationships; they were skeptical regarding the possibility of communicating a subjective content through the means of an abstract art, which Abstract Expressionism held to be not only possible but necessary.

The younger artists came of age at the time when the "New American Painting" (the name of the exhibition that toured Europe in 1958–59) was bringing international recognition to American painting. As is so often the case in the recent history of art, Abstract Expressionism began to lose impetus as a style at the point when it began to win public acclaim. For the most fruitful and revolutionary decade in American art, Abstract Expressionism temporarily wedded the contradictory impulses of Cubism and Surrealism. When such an unstable compound ultimately dissolved, the opposing tendencies once more assumed their divergent paths. By 1960, these two movements were clearly identifiable as pop art and the new abstraction (termed "post-painterly abstraction" by its champion, Clement Greenberg).

In pop art, certain aspects of action painting continue to find expression—for example, the emphasis on tactile surface qualities and the close tie to the environment and urban life, as well as the implicit romanticism. The new abstraction, on the other hand, by insisting on the primacy of color presented in terms of non-relational, all-over composition, carries painting forward in the direction that chromatic abstraction had begun to travel. Both pop art and the new abstraction, however, remain faithful to the scale, impact, and directness of Abstract Expressionism.

8-1. RAYMOND PARKER, *Untitled*, 1959.

The polarization began in the late fifties with the revolt of some second-generation artists, such as Robert Goodnough, Raymond Parker, and Al Held. Reacting against the formlessness of the Tenth Street phase of Abstract Expressionism, they began to order painterly areas into more discrete, legible shapes. In Parker's untitled 1959 abstraction (*Ill. 8-1*), Abstract Expressionist brushwork is disciplined into a more coherent structure.

Both post-painterly abstraction and pop art reacted against Abstract Expressionism in favor of a more impersonal, detached, and clearly articulated art. Because it was the most overtly sensational, pop art was the first of these reactions to claim public notice. It is, however, a mistake to characterize pop art as popular art. Its creators are part of the same artistic milieu as contemporary abstract painters. Intended for the same public as Abstract Expressionism, their works share similar antecedents and, in some cases, the same pictorial conventions as contemporary abstraction. That pop art has been so readily assimilated as artistic novelty rather than as art is attributable to the new appetites of the mass media for material carrying the cachet of culture, which may be digested and spewed back at a mass literate public, more eager for gossip and sensation than for art itself. In an ironic metamorphosis, the American artist, whom John Sloan described as the unwanted cockroach in the kitchen of a frontier society, is now a national hero, the rival of movie stars and TV celebrities for public attention. Now that American art has become a prestigious commodity for export and the "culture boom" has given new status to art, a rapprochement between artist and society is being heralded.

In fact, it could be argued, in more or less the same terms used to vindicate American Scene painting during the thirties, that pop art is the genuinely American expression of the American experience. John Sloan, after all, insisted that Hieronymous Bosch was the first artist to capture the American scene. In any event, it is undeniable that aspects of pop art have antecedents in earlier American art: Stuart Davis' still lifes of soap boxes and cigarette packs, de Kooning's gargantuan breasty Marilyn Monroe, Demuth's ironic titles, Marsh's Broadway marquees. All these represent responses to the bewildering vulgarity of the carnival of American life and the orgiastic fantasy of the American Dream, just as Hopper's lonely filling stations and Wyeth's empty fields reflect its barrenness and lack of fulfillment.

Thus there is no need to search for the source of pop imagery in Dada. To the degree that American pop is distinctly an American art, it partakes of the parochialism that has always shadowed American art. Because Andy Warhol's theatricality has made him an international celebrity, the American avant-garde may presume to have its own Salvador Dalí, a sign both of its maturity and its decadence. Since the line between commercial and fine art has never been finely drawn in this country, pop art is unusual in the context of American art only in that it self-consciously, with an eye to parody, appropriates the techniques and images of commercial illustration and advertising; but it uses them with the sophistication of the fine artist instead of the naïveté of the "buckeye" painter. The billboard images, Ben Day dots, and cartoons are interpreted and transformed in accord with a solid, firmly established pictorial tradition. Not to see this is to miss the irony at the heart of pop art.

Because it is fine art rather than popular art or illustration, pop art differs from earlier movements that sought to gain closer contact with the American public. It resembles them in its nostalgic evocation of

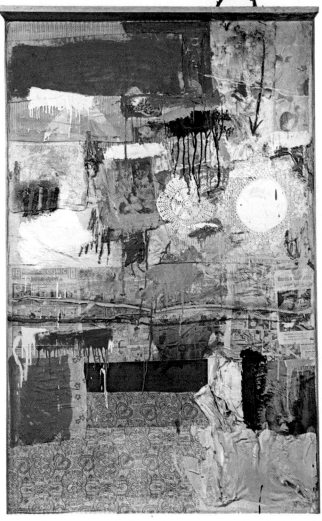

things past—forties' movies, thirties' cars, twenties' underwear. Fraught with irony and ambiguity, pop art allows itself to be characterized as cousin to the comic strip, when in actuality its nearest relatives are Léger, Magritte, Matisse, and de Kooning. Although it has been eagerly embraced by a mass public happy once again to recognize familiar objects and to relax from the strain of attempting to interpret Abstract Expressionism, pop art has been rejected by the most respected critics of the older generation. In general, the amount of publicity it has received, both pro and con, is entirely out of proportion to its importance.

The best pop artists are already moving away from the most blatant aspects of pop imagery. To trace the genealogy of pop art, one must re-create the atmosphere in which it came into being. That atmosphere was generated mainly by the composer John Cage, whose essays and lectures have been instrumental in forming the sensibility of some of the most important young composers, choreographers, painters, and sculptors at work today. Cage's aesthetic, derived in equal parts from Dada and Zen, in many respects served to open a situation that had closed down, much in the manner that Surrealism helped open the door to Abstract Expressionism.

In a series of lectures, beginning with those he gave as an instructor at Black Mountain College in 1952, and continuing with his classes at the New School, Cage, like the Surrealists before him, called on artists to efface the boundary between art and life. An advocate of noise as music, he attacked preconceived notions about the function, meaning, and context of art. He asked such questions as, "Is a truck in a music school more musical than a truck passing by in the street?" Favoring the use of repetition and the elimination of dramatic climax, he denied the existence of an "objective correlative" for subjective experience, damned the audience's demand to be entertained, and urged that each moment be appreciated for its own singular value. Denying the validity of teleological reasoning, Cage proposed instead an association of meanings that resembled collage, which in many ways anticipated Marshall McLuhan's thesis of "everything influencing everything."

Two artists close to Cage who applied his attitude toward painting and, in doing so, attacked Abstract Expressionism at its foundations were Robert Rauschenberg and Jasper Johns. Rauschenberg, who met Cage at Black Mountain where he was studying with Josef Albers, was already sympathetic to Cage's basic attitude that even the banal and the commonplace had an aesthetic potential. Earlier, in 1950–51, Rauschenberg had painted a series of all-white paintings whose only image was the shadow reflected by the viewer. This was followed by a series of all-black paintings in which torn and crushed newspapers, pasted down and coated with black enamel, created a surface as irregular as the crumbling façades of New York's decaying downtown neighborhoods. A series of audacious constructions made from the refuse of the city—rusty nails, rags, pieces of rope—anticipated the "combine" paintings of 1953–55, such as *Satellite* (*Ill. 8-2*). In these predominantly red paintings, Rauschenberg used images for the first time, not painted images but found images: pieces of printed fabric, newspaper photographs, postcards. The title of one of these paintings, *Rebus,* suggests the manner in which the images should be read, not as literal narrative but as a fused metaphor.

The painterly medium Rauschenberg chose resembled Abstract Expressionist brushwork, except that it was denser. Soon he began to affix real three-dimensional objects to the surface of his paintings as a challenge to the ambiguous, illusionistic space of Abstract Expressionism. By allowing the contents of the paintings to spill out into the spectator's space, Rauschenberg literally began to fill the "gap between art and life." In such a use of materials, his work is not far from the literalness of Dove's collages.

In 1953 Rauschenberg erased a de Kooning drawing, an act that has been variously interpreted as paying homage to an admired hero and as wiping out, literally and symbolically, his achievement. That this erased drawing became a valuable commodity was doubly shocking, because such an act attacked not only Abstract Expressionism but also the newly won success of American painting and its aspirations to old-master status. It was an act reminiscent of Duchamp's painting a mustache on the Mona Lisa. Similarly, in *Factum I* and *Factum II,* Rauschenberg meticulously duplicated each splash and drip, thus exposing the myth of Abstract Expressionist spontaneity.

Although Rauschenberg has been dismissed by some as a latter-day Schwitters, and his compositions seen as paraphrases of Cubist collage, it is much more fruitful to consider his work in relation to Abstract Expressionism. By the same token, Jasper Johns has been described as a follower of Duchamp, although nothing in his work implies that he was even aware of Duchamp until after 1960, when certain direct references to the Dada master began to appear. There is, however, no question but that Johns and Duchamp belong to the same "family of mind," which sees art as a speculative activity related to physics or philosophy. Like Duchamp, Johns has devoted himself to challenging some of our most cherished preconceptions about aesthetics and perception. Because of his play with the theme of illusion versus reality, his work is one of the most important sources for pop imagery.

When Johns's 1954–55 flags (*Ill. 8-3*) and targets were seen at his first one-man show in 1958, they created a storm of controversy. Dis-

8-3. JASPER JOHNS, *Flag*, 1954.

missed as Neo-Dada by unsympathetic critics, they were hailed by others as the first viable alternative to Abstract Expressionism. Organizing the all-over pattern of brushwork into coherently structured bands or concentric rings, Johns reduced gesture once again to the small, controlled maneuverings of the hand. In his revival of the ancient technique of encaustic, he was able to call attention to surface texture without resorting to splashy execution. Like Rauschenberg, he attacked the ambiguity of Abstract Expressionist space, not by making a statement about its actual nature, as Rauschenberg had done, but by presenting a more clearly structured alternative in the stripes of the flag and the concentric circles of the targets.

By identifying the image with the field, as he did by painting a replica of a flag instead of a picture of a flag, Johns was able to achieve a new degree of flatness. This flatness, however, was contradicted by the tonal modeling of value contrasts. Thus the complex play of flatness versus illusionism is a formal equivalent for the interplay of painted illusion versus objective reality. The reinforcement of one level of meaning by another gives added authority to each, while it also complicates interpretation.

Although the formal innovations of these paintings were immediately recognized and capitalized on by younger artists, Johns himself chose not to pursue their implications. Beginning in 1960, like Rauschenberg, he turned to a more fluid, broad, painterly style. But unlike Rauschenberg, whose imagery appears to oscillate between the macrocosmic and the microcosmic, Johns has concentrated on a limited number of themes. He has explored his themes with a kind of dogged logic, combining motifs, paraphrasing them, and changing their context, as

8-4. JASPER JOHNS,
*Painted Bronze*, 1960.

if to extract the last drop of meaning from the most banal object. In
the later works, however, the official public images of the flags and
maps are replaced by the more intimate, personal world of coat-hangers,
coffee cups, and domestic paraphernalia. Often in the recent paintings
the levels of meaning are so numerous that a guide as exhaustive as
the "Green Box," Duchamp's explanatory notes to the *Bride Stripped
Bare by her Bachelors, Even,* is needed to decode even a single aspect.
Like Duchamp's *Large Glass,* Johns's later works offer entire systems
of seeing, while maintaining a running dialogue with the history of art.
At the same time, the lonely, isolated coat-hangers and homely coffee

8-5. CLAES OLDENBURG,
*Hamburger with Pickle
and Tomato Attached,*
1963.

8-6. GEORGE SEGAL,
*Cinema*, 1963.

cups provide a genuine continuity with American still life and genre painting from Peto to Hopper.

Johns's blatantly American imagery, as well as his elevation of the commonplace, as in *Painted Bronze* (*Ill. 8-4*), touched off a flurry of interest in common objects and the banal trivia in the everyday environment. Had a tradition of genre been alive, doubtless such debased

8-7. JAMES ROSENQUIST,
*Early in the Morning*, 1963.

themes would not have seemed so shocking. In the context of Abstract Expressionist heroics, however, they were doubly jarring. But Johns's irony is directed toward art, not toward life, which is meant to be valued in even its pettiest manifestations. In this sense, both Johns's and Rauschenberg's affirmations are distinctly different from those of the Dadaists who were (or so they claimed) anti-art. Pro-art in that they were willing to remove the boundaries separating life from art, these two second-generation artists set the detached tone, at least with regard to value judgments, of the pop artists who took over many of their attitudes.

Independent of one another, the group who became known as the pop artists, Claes Oldenburg, George Segal, Jim Dine, Roy Lichtenstein, Tom Wesselmann, James Rosenquist, Robert Indiana, Marisol, and Andy Warhol, based their work on images from discredited mass culture sources like advertisements, billboards, comic books, movies, and TV. Intent on mining art history and commenting on its development, they were aware that the "museums without walls" and wide-screen movies had changed ways of seeing, and that the abundance of reproductions had turned masterpieces overnight into clichés. Taking Cage's advice to wake up to the life they were living, they painted what they saw around them—seeming in the process to embrace the materialism, spiritual vacuity, and ludicrously sexualized environment of affluent America. But just as Lichtenstein's re-creations of Picasso

8-8.
ROY LICHTENSTEIN,
*Blam,* 1962.

and Mondrian in the idiom of the comic book were double-edged, the pop artists' use of commercial images was equally ambivalent.

Closest to the Abstract Expressionists, Dine and Oldenburg both developed their art in the atmosphere of the "environments" and "happenings," theatrical events that use people as part of living environments. Environments made out of the detritus of the city were originally Allan Kaprow's response to Abstract Expressionist paintings. In 1958 Kaprow wrote, "Pollock left us at the point where we must become preoccupied with and even dazzled by the space and objects of our everyday life. . . . Not satisfied with the suggestion, through paint, of our other senses, we shall utilize the specific substances of sight, sound, movement, people, odors, touch. . . ."[1] As Pollock had incorporated bits of glass and mirrors from the environment into his painting and de Kooning had pasted the smile from a Camel ad onto one of his "women," Kaprow, Dine, Oldenburg, Red Grooms, and Robert Whitman incorporated junk from the city into their environments. Kaprow, who studied composition with Cage, was the first to extend the concept of the environments to the theater as happenings. But Oldenburg's ambition to produce the *Gesamtkunstwerk* has made him the master of the happenings, as it has led him often to conceive of his exhibitions as total environments. His "store," in which plaster repro-

8-9. SAM FRANCIS, *Blue on a Point,* 1958.

8-10. HELEN FRANKENTHALER, *Mountains and Sea*, 1952.

ductions of real objects raised questions about their identity as art objects, was followed by oversized stuffed replicas of food, and more recently by the eccentric "soft" typewriters, electric mixers, and fans. These common objects are made of stuffed cloth or vinyl; the material flops and bulges in such a manner as to invest the objects with human vulnerability. "City nature," as he terms it, is Oldenburg's main theme. The painterly surface of such monumentalized re-created common objects as his *Hamburger with Pickle and Tomato Attached (Ill. 8-5)* recalls Abstract Expressionist paint handling, which is now transferred from the two-dimensional surface to the three-dimensional object. Similarly, George Segal's tableaux of real people in real situations, such as *Cinema (Ill. 8-6)*, represent a kind of environmental genre that recalls American Scene painting.

Unlike Oldenburg and Dine, whose vision remains closer to Abstract Expressionism, Roy Lichtenstein, James Rosenquist, and Tom Wesselmann work as the young abstract painters do, bringing up their images close to the surface in imitation of the movie close-up, using brilliant color, and stressing surface tension. In *Early in the Morning (Ill. 8-7)*,

223

Rosenquist combines fragmented images in a dreamlike billboard Surrealism which marries Magritte's technique to collage space and composition. Lichtenstein's *Blam* (*Ill. 8-8*) is closer to Léger's bold, mechanical Cubism than to the comic strip that inspired it.

As pop art was born of the reaction of second-generation artists such as Rivers, Rauschenberg, and Johns to Abstract Expressionism, post-painterly abstraction also finds its antecedents in the fifties. Not only are the chromatic abstractions of Newman, Rothko, and Reinhardt, with their single images and deductive structures, part of its background, but so are the high color and clear legible shapes of Matisse's large cut-out gouaches, shown in 1961 at the Museum of Modern Art. Josef Albers' simplified square-on-square compositions also provided examples of non-allusive, conceptual paintings.

The series of exhibitions arranged by Clement Greenberg at French & Co. in 1959–60, including major shows by Newman, Gottlieb, Morris Louis, and Kenneth Noland, was important in establishing a climate for the new abstraction. Emphasizing the expressive power of pure color, the new abstraction is characterized by even, non-textured paint application, flat, non-illusionistic space, and suppression of value contrasts in favor of the interaction of adjacent colors.

Foremost among its sources, of course, are Pollock's drip paintings, with their all-over compositions, and his black-and-white paintings of 1951. In the latter, Pollock identified figure with ground by allowing the black Duco enamel to soak directly into the raw canvas, uniting drawing with painting in such a way as to allow greater freedom and fluidity than had been previously possible. Although most of the second generation had chosen de Kooning as a model, a few, like Helen Frankenthaler, Sam Francis, and Friedel Dzubas, rejected de Kooning's ties to Cubist space and composition, and were drawn to Pollock's open, loose painting. Opposed to successive records of brushed gestures that crowded the canvas and threatened to swamp it with muddy overpainting, these painters chose to leave areas of the canvas free to "breathe." They allowed marks, stains, and blots to stand, discarding what was not usable rather than revising the same canvas. In *Blue on a Point* (*Ill. 8-9*), for example, Sam Francis permits islands of brilliant color to float on an open sea of unpainted canvas.

Helen Frankenthaler's gifts as an original colorist and her lyric sensibility equipped her to achieve a unique interpretation of Pollock's methods. With her, the conflict between painting and drawing that had plagued too many Abstract Expressionists did not exist because she

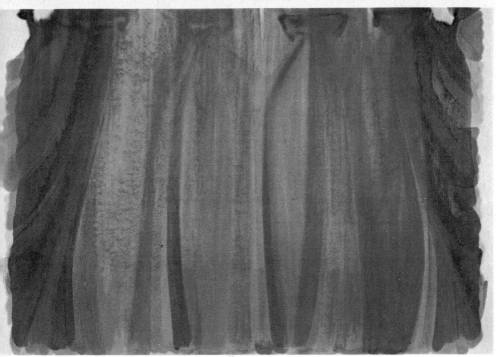

8-11. MORRIS LOUIS, *Saraband*, 1959.

chose to draw in paint. In 1952 she painted a large lyrical abstraction called *Mountains and Sea* (*Ill. 8-10*), which in the fragility of its blues and pinks and the thinness of its soaked paint looked strangely pallid and empty to most of her contemporaries. She was painting then as

8-12.
KENNETH NOLAND,
*Par Transit*, 1966.

Pollock had done, directly into the raw canvas, and working on the floor rather than on the wall. More recently, she has used stronger, although equally original color, presented in clearer, more solid-looking shapes. *Mountains and Sea,* however, attracted the attention, in 1953, of Morris Louis and Kenneth Noland, two painters from Washington, D.C. Soon they were converted to staining paint into raw canvas in an effort to achieve the maximum opticality in their work.

In *Saraband (Ill. 8-11)*, one of the series of "veil" paintings, Louis was able to communicate the sensation of color more directly and nakedly perhaps than had been done before. Because the successive veils of paint sink into the raw canvas and become identified with it, foreground and background are one. These pictures, which appear to materialize like natural phenomena emerging from a mist, seem to defy a reconstruction of the method by which they were created. No self-conscious shapes or hard contours inhibit their mysterious flow; the diaphanous superimposed veils, stained directly into each other, do not harden into the parallel planes of Cubist composition. In his later paintings, the so-called unfurl series, diagonal rivulets of color stream off each canvas toward its edges. In these, Louis presented colors in their purity and did not permit them to interpenetrate or to create an atmospheric haze. His last paintings of parallel bands placed adjacent to one another achieve the most straightforward presentation of pure, saturated colors, which seem burned into the canvas. The structure of these paintings is partly indebted to Noland's use of concentric rings as vehicles for the unhampered presentation of extremely original color combinations.

Noland arrived at this lucid means of structuring color in the late fifties, when he became increasingly concerned about the relationship of the image to the framing edge. Noland's structure does not relate to earlier geometric art, but was extrapolated directly from the chromatic abstraction of Rothko and Newman, as his method of staining directly into the canvas was derived from Pollock. By arriving at such a direct and candid means of presenting color, Noland played an important historical role, offering an alternative in his soft, blurred, and bleeding stained edge to the hardness and dryness of the mechanical precision of geometric paintings. Following his example, the Washington color painters, including Gene Davis, Tom Downing, Howard Mehring, and Paul Reed, arrived at a similar means of structuring pure color. In the sixties, Noland began to allow the shape and proportion of the canvas field to determine the kind of structure it would contain. At first these were centered "bull's-eye" motifs, but more recently they have been symmetrical and asymmetrical chevrons and parallel bands of color.

In the bull's-eye and chevron paintings, areas of raw canvas are left unpainted, allowing the image to "breathe" or expand to achieve greater openness. In recent works, however, like *Par Transit* (*Ill. 8-12*), Noland evenly saturates the entire canvas surface with closely keyed, stained color, causing the eye to focus that much more intensely on the interaction of juxtaposed colors. With characteristic logic, Noland lines up adjacent bands in such a way as to echo the perimeter of the lozenge-shaped support. The space in Noland's paintings is determined by the interaction of contrasting adjacent hues, not by value contrast or drawing. In this sense it is purely "optical" space, which does not evoke the tactile sensation associated with line and value contrast. The opticality of Noland's paintings is further enhanced by his method of staining resonant color directly into the raw canvas, thus locating the image on the surface, rather than behind it as it appears in Cubist pictures.

8-13. JACK YOUNGERMAN, *Anajo*, 1962.

8-14. JULES OLITSKI,
*Prince Patutsky
Command,* 1965.

228

Other leading post-painterly abstractionists include Jules Olitski, Ellsworth Kelly, Jack Youngerman, Al Held, Frank Stella, and Larry Poons. Olitski's first stained paintings, organized around cores, presented large areas of saturated color alternating with areas of bare canvas. The lazy forms and opulence of his palette provide a voluptuous color experience. Recently, abandoning shapes entirely in paintings like *Prince Patutsky Command* (*Ill. 8-14*), Olitski has combined a process of dyeing with spraying that has led to increasingly rich optical effects with great potential for his essentially hedonistic vision. In these paintings the shape of the rectangular canvas field is stamped out with particular vividness. Successive sprayings cause colors to melt into one another, producing a brilliance as dazzling as sunlight and an atmosphere as fluid and buoyant as sky and clouds. Because of his ability to achieve these atmospheric effects, Olitski's work seems in many ways the first fully abstract version of Impressionism, which, like Olitski's mists and hazes, delighted in effects of light, atmosphere, and movement.

Kelly and Youngerman, having served apprenticeships to Constructi-

8-15. ELLSWORTH KELLY, *Red Blue Green,* 1963.

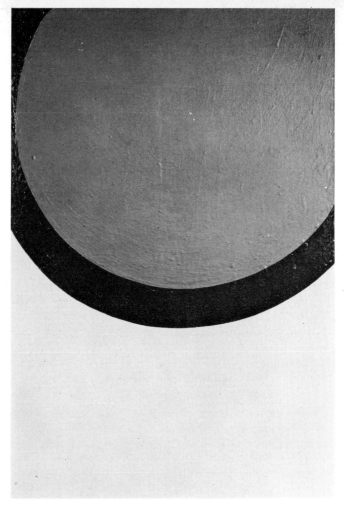

8-16. AL HELD, *Venus Arising,* 1963.

vist painting in Paris, where both worked after the war on the G.I.
Bill, returned to New York in the fifties. Confronting the latest developments of Abstract Expressionism, they modified their clear, flat
images to conform with the scale and power of New York painting.
Kelly allowed his bright, two-dimensional images, isolated on equally
brilliant fields, to be interpreted either as figure or ground; Youngerman, on the other hand, became increasingly concerned with generating new shapes, such as the graceful forms in *Anajo* (*Ill. 8-13*). Kelly's
immaculate surfaces are an outstanding example of "hard-edge"
painting, that aspect of the new abstraction which stresses hard, razor-

sharp contours as opposed to blurred, stained edges. His *Red Blue Green* (*Ill. 8-15*) demonstrates how the principle of all-over composition can be extended to geometric painting.

Al Held's hard-edge paintings are intentionally less precise than Kelly's, since Held was far more intimately involved with Abstract Expressionism. Among the first to react against the unstructured look and ambiguous space of action painting in the late fifties, Held began to tighten his brushwork, ordering it into discrete, legible shapes. In the sixties, his work has assumed the monumental proportions of the mural as his forms have become increasingly bold and dramatic, as in *Venus Arising* (*Ill. 8-16*). Similarly, Nicolas Krushenick chooses to structure bold, essentially Expressionist compositions, such as *Allard Jak* (*Ill. 8-17*), in quasi-geometric forms.

Frank Stella's logical progression through a series of black, aluminum, copper, rainbow, and purple "stripe" paintings has the inevitability of a programmed attack on the problem of pictorial structure. Dividing the canvas into equal parallel bands, he arrived at the method of composition Michael Fried has termed "deductive structure" by allowing the frame to generate the composition within its borders. In 1960, in an effort to make the internal dynamics of the painting conform more absolutely to the framing perimeter, he began to notch the

8-17. NICOLAS KRUSHENICK, *Allard Jak*, 1965.

corners and cut holes in the centers of the aluminum paintings. This reduced illusionism to a minimum and further identified the image with the canvas surface. In the sixties, these shapes became more eccentric and took on an objectlike impassivity in such works as *Ifafa II* (*Ill. 8-18*).

Stella came close to producing absolutely flat paintings in his shaped metallic stripe pictures. He soon realized, however, that, because of the way the human eye perceives pictorial space, it was impossible to produce works without some illusionism if these were to remain paintings rather than become three-dimensional objects, which exist in real rather than illusory space. Consequently, in his most recent paintings, he has used a variety of devices to heighten a complex and often contradictory illusionism. In these, Stella shows himself converted to the primacy of color, and for the first time exhibits considerable gifts as a colorist. Large areas of flat color are laid out in eccentric geometric patterns that set up a play between the actual shape of the canvas support and the shapes depicted on the canvas. Like Darby Bannard, Stella maximizes surface tension by contrasting matte and gloss finishes. In addition, he mixes Dayglo, epoxy, and ordinary house paints in combinations that are both highly arbitrary and original.

The coin-sized dots and ellipses of Larry Poons's *Han-San Cadence* (*Ill. 8-19*), scattered across a brilliant field of contrasting color, induce perceptual effects, such as afterimages and vibrations, which cause the viewer to take a more active role. Poons, whose paintings derive in equal measure from Pollock's all-over paintings, Newman's chromatic fields, and Mondrian's grids, became celebrated as an "optical artist" when the Museum of Modern Art held its exhibition of perceptual abstraction in 1965. Popularized in the press as the successor to Abstract Expressionism, hard-core optical art represents a continuation of Bauhaus design principles, and is a misnomer for the new abstraction. Although painting largely dependent on color for expression will cause an optical flicker or afterimage, these are secondary side effects like the vibration of Rothko's edges or the dark incandescence of Reinhardt's disappearing squares. Whereas these painters, like Poons, deal in feeling, so-called optical art presents experiments in sensation, in which the optical effects are the ends and not simply a means. Optical art also differs from the new abstraction in its reliance on *trompe-l'oeil* illusionism; this disrupts the integrity of the picture plane, which the new abstractionists wish to preserve.

The term "post-painterly," as defined by Greenberg, implies that the traditional opposition of linear to painterly has been superseded by an opposition of tactile to optical. According to this interpretation, tactile painting, which stresses the sculptural qualities of modeling and

8-19. LARRY POONS, *Han-San Cadence*, 1963.

8-20. DARBY BANNARD,
*Green Grip I,* 1965.

value contrasts, is less suited to the present development of painting than optical painting; in stressing the optical sensation of color, post-painterly abstraction is considered more appropriate to the purely visual medium of pictorial art. This argument presumes that the artist working in a particular medium should strive for a more explicit statement of the properties that exclusively belong to that medium, such as the property of opticality, which differentiates painting from sculpture. Furthermore, in the process of self-definition, an art form will tend toward the elimination of all elements that are not in keeping with its essential nature. According to this argument, visual art will be stripped of all extravisual meaning, whether literary or symbolic, and painting will reject all that is not pictorial. This view of modernism has brought about the emergence of a reductive, minimal art, which stresses the literal qualities of the painting—that it is two-dimensional and of a specific shape.

The acceptance of this view is seen in the shaped canvases of Frank Stella, Charles Hinman, Neil Williams, Ron Davis, and others. It also accounts for the renaissance of pure abstraction among such younger artists as Edward Avedisian, Robert Irwin, Larry Zox, Robert Huot, and Darby Bannard. In Bannard's *Green Grip I (Ill. 8-20),* for example, simple geometric motifs are combined with a new coolness and sophistication.

Twentieth-century American painting has offered two possible courses—one which exalts life over art, and another which holds that art derives from art rather than from life. By the middle of the sixties, these views have received extreme formulations. Cage, Rauschenberg, Johns, and the pop artists have insisted that there is no boundary between art and life, that one spills over into the other; furthermore, they also wish to efface the boundaries between the various arts, encouraging hybrid forms such as assemblage and happenings. Greenberg and the post-painterly abstractionists, on the other hand, hold for an art that is increasingly refined, and committed to the pursuit of its unique and irreducible essence.

Both approaches represent the logical conclusions of positions implicit in earlier modern movements. Cage's point of view may be traced to the Dada belief that art is art by virtue of its context and not of its inherent value. Greenberg carries on the Cubists' insistence on the actuality and concreteness of the aesthetic experience, achieved only through limiting art to its essences. These then are the predominant points of departure at a time when American artists, finally equipped with native heroes, a mature tradition, and the necessary technical means, are taking up the flags of some of the unfinished revolutions of

8-21. RICHARD DIEBENKORN, *Girl and Three Coffee Cups,* 1957.

235

8-22. LARRY RIVERS,
*Double Portrait of
Birdie,* 1955.

twentieth-century art. Some of these revolutions are being re-invented. Futurism, Dada, Constructivism, geometric abstraction—ignored if not despised by Abstract Expressionism—are being re-evaluated. Nevertheless, this re-evaluation is being conducted in the shadow of Abstract Expressionism, even as leading Abstract Expressionists continue to enrich the situation with their own recent work.

8-23. JAN MÜLLER,
*Jacob's Ladder,*
1958.

Figure painting also has strong proponents, some like California artists Richard Diebenkorn, David Park, and Elmer Bischoff, working in a painterly manner derived from Abstract Expressionism. Diebenkorn's *Girl and Three Coffee Cups* (*Ill. 8-21*) represents an attempt to organize Abstract Expressionist brushwork into the recognizable forms of representational art. Nathan Oliveira, Larry Rivers, and Jan Müller are other artists who also adapted the freedom of the Abstract Expressionist technique toward figurative ends. In *Double Portrait of Birdie* (*Ill. 8-22*), Rivers, whose representations of money and cigarette advertisements helped to establish pop iconography, simulated movie montage by showing the same figure in two poses. Indebted to the original German Expressionists as well as to the New York School, Jan Müller peopled his fantastic landscapes such as *Jacob's Ladder* (*Ill. 8-23*) with demonic figures. Other realistic artists, such as Wayne Thiebaud, work in a manner related to pop art. Still others, like James McGarrell, Jack Beal, Robert Barnes, and Philip Pearlstein (*Ill. 8-24*), are reviving a tight, controlled realism. And some, like Fairfield Porter, continue to make well-painted pictures that stress structure and pattern rather than modeling.

Because of the speed-up of communications, the American artist faces new pressures as well as new prospects. The avant-garde has inherited not only the modernist tradition of eliminating the inessential, but also the characteristically American drive toward constant innovation and experiment. But despite these pressures and the demands of a society newly awakened to art, the prospects for the future of American art have never been brighter or more open.

8-24. PHILIP PEARLSTEIN,
*Woman Reclining on Couch,*
1966.

# Chapter Nine

# Toward a Sculptural Renaissance

Plastic thought has geometrical possibilities that have not been exhausted by the requirements of Egyptian or Greek or Gothic cathedrals. These thoughts are pressing for expression and have not yet found a place, which is the reason why so much modern sculpture finds its way to museums of art, permanently unplaced, a specimen, not an actor in the life of the day.
—A. S. CALDER, *The American Architect,* December 8, 1920

Twentieth-century American sculpture, like twentieth-century American architecture, is dominated by a single genius. As Frank Lloyd Wright transcends national boundaries in architecture, so David Smith towers above his contemporaries, both American and European, as the sculptor who realized the potential of Gonzalez' and Picasso's welded metal Cubist works. And in the same fashion that Wright's last works point to the current direction in American architecture, the monumental steel pieces Smith executed before his death in an auto accident in 1965 announce the newest developments in American sculpture, developments that, it is hoped, portend a sculptural renaissance.

The last of the American arts to mature, American sculpture in the early part of the century was graced by a few interesting works, mainly based on French examples, which heretofore have been largely ignored. Eakins' reliefs, Davies' charming figures, and the classical works of the eccentric William Rimmer and of A. Stirling Calder, the father of Alexander Calder, represent examples of modeled and cast bronze sculpture that have a vitality and originality absent in the heavy-handed academic statues of the official sculptors, such as Gutzon Borglum, Daniel Chester French, and Anna Hyatt Huntington. Outside of Eakins, Davies, Rimmer, and the elder Calder, however, cast and modeled sculpture in America was, except for the outstanding contribution of the French émigré Gaston Lachaise, a dreary and pedestrian affair until the forties. This was the decade when Reuben Nakian began his mature work, and Jacques Lipchitz, perhaps the greatest bronze worker of the twentieth century, arrived as a refugee to become an example for American sculptors, as the Surrealists were for American painters.

As in painting, the inadequacies of the academic tradition, the lack of a classical or high art, and the provincialism of American culture may be blamed for the poverty of American work in cast metals until the forties. The early twentieth-century genre sculpture of Abastenia St. Leger Eberle and Mahonri Young, tied as it was to Ash Can School imagery, can scarcely be called imaginative. Similarly, the Rodinesque works of the Swedish émigré Charles Haag were not particularly distinguished. And although the portraits done by Mrs. Whitney and her friend Jo Davidson have a certain elegance, they, too, finally must be judged minor efforts.

On the other hand, carving, in stone and wood, fared better. Beginning early in the century with Elie Nadelman's serpentine creatures, and continuing up to the present with Chaim Gross's acrobats and Raoul Hague's monumental abstract torsos, carving from the block of wood has had its high moments in America. Stone carving, in William Zorach's early work and in John B. Flannagan's original pieces, has also achieved a certain level. Again, one must see this activity within the context of the indigenous tradition, which was rich in examples

9-1. ELIE NADELMAN,
*Two Women, ca.* 1934.

9-2. MAX WEBER,
*Spiral Rhythm,* 1915.

of primitive carving, from ships' prows to cigar-store Indians. Thus, sculpture in America remained either provincially immature or tied to academicism long after painters had begun to experiment within the modern idiom. In the decade preceding the Armory Show, only Elie Nadelman had produced modernist sculpture of any consequence. His elegant painted wood figures, in their simplification and reduction to geometric volumes, parallel the treatment of the figure by painters such as Guy Pène du Bois. In such works as the painted terra cotta *Two Women (Ill. 9-1)*, Nadelman shows his skill at treating mass in a summary manner. But charming, original, and sensitive as they are, Nadelman's waltzing couples and witty men in bowlers and bow-ties are limited in their range and ambition.

Similarly, the few isolated efforts made in the direction of abstract sculpture were unrealized promises. *Spiral Rhythm (Ill. 9-2)*, Max Weber's 1915 sculpture, was among the first pieces of Cubist sculpture produced anywhere. And in America, Weber's sculptures were unique efforts. While Picasso, Duchamp-Villon, and Lipchitz translated Cubist planes into sculptural volumes in daring experiments, America could boast little more advanced than Robert Laurent's semi-abstract carvings, such as *The Flame (Ill. 9-3)*. Even though Brancusi's first show

9-3. ROBERT LAURENT,
*The Flame, ca.* 1917.

was held in America, before World War II Laurent was apparently the only American (with the possible exception of Nadelman) to learn anything from the pure flow of Brancusi's reductive volumes.

Perhaps the most original American sculptor working in the teens and twenties was John Storrs, whose abstract architectonic sculptures, such as *Seated Gendarme* (*Ill. 9-4*), though of a remarkable quality, were barely acknowledged. Much more typical were the compromise solutions of Maurice Sterne and William Zorach, who looked to archaic

9-4. JOHN STORRS,
*Seated Gendarme,* 1925.

9-5. WILLIAM ZORACH, *Floating Figure*, 1922.

and primitive art for a way to invigorate the figurative tradition. When Zorach abandoned painting for sculpture in 1917, he chose a far more conservative means of expression than the Cubist vocabulary of his paintings. His early works, like *Floating Figure* (*Ill. 9-5*), exhibited an admirable economy of means. Hailed for carving directly and staying close to the monolithic contours of the stone, Zorach achieved a major reputation in the thirties as his art became more sentimental and less inventive. This was probably so because his solidly built Maillol-like women, involved in domestic situations, and his idealized workers meshed perfectly with the ideology of the thirties. Along with Paul Manship, a less gifted, more academic sculptor, Zorach was one of America's leading official sculptors of the decade.

The single sculptor to realize a major *oeuvre* in America before David Smith was Gaston Lachaise. Because of the erotic content of his work, Lachaise has received a somewhat belated recognition. However,

9-6. GASTON LACHAISE, *Passion*, 1932–34.

9-7. GASTON LACHAISE,
*Standing Woman,*
1912–27.

owing to his skill as a craftsman, he never lacked commissions, and was well known in the twenties for his decorative garden sculpture of gulls, peacocks, and dolphins. But not until the sixties was the American public sufficiently mature to be exposed to Lachaise's most voluptuous earth goddesses, fertility symbols, and intertwined couples. He borrowed the latter motif from Rodin, charging it with an even more explicit sexuality, as in *Passion* (*Ill. 9-6*). Thus, even if not for his genius as a plastic artist, Lachaise would stand apart from his contemporaries because of his frank treatment of unconventional subjects.

Born in Paris, Lachaise came to America in 1906, following the woman he later married who became his lifelong inspiration. After working in Boston for several years, he quite naturally found his way to 291; his interest in the generative forces of nature found parallels with the themes that Dove, O'Keeffe, and Stieglitz were exploring. Lachaise's portraits, which derived from Rodin's tradition of robust modeling, prompted people like John Marin and Marianne Moore to pose for him. During the twenties, Lachaise was supported in part by the portraits he made of the staff of the *Dial,* who also purchased other of his works. Many photographs of his sculpture were published in the *Dial,* and the first issue carried Lachaise's relief *Dusk* as its frontispiece.

Lachaise had been trained in the Paris Beaux-Arts Academy; consequently, when he arrived in the United States, a twenty-four-year-old journeyman-sculptor, he quickly found employment as the assistant to Henry Hudson Kitson, an academic sculptor of Civil War monuments. In 1912 he moved to New York, where he lived until his death in 1935. As the assistant to Paul Manship from 1914 to 1921, he watched Manship's popularity grow, while his own work was decried by official academic sculptors like Daniel Chester French as "an atrocity."

Lachaise's development as a sculptor proceeds from the rather modest curves of the languid early nudes to the vigorous plasticity of the *Standing Woman* (*Ill.* 9-7). This figure was the prototype for many later elaborations Lachaise made on the theme of the full matronly figure that tapered downward, balancing on slender tiptoes which seem hardly adequate to support the substantial form of the body. In his

9-8. PAUL MANSHIP,
*Indian Hunter, ca.* 1926.

9-9. JOHN FLANNAGAN,
*Jonah and the Whale,* 1937.

standing figures of the thirties, Lachaise's forms became more stylized
and ponderous; in his fragmentary female torsos, his forms assumed
an almost abstract geometric quality, without losing their primitive,
explosive sexual charge. Besides the standing and fragmentary female
figures, Lachaise also executed a number of reliefs of female figures, as
well as a series of architectural reliefs for the American Telegraph
Building, the New York Electricity Building at the Chicago World's
Fair (since destroyed), and the Rockefeller Center–RCA International
Building. Toward the end of his life, Lachaise executed smooth, polished quasi-geometric torsos of heroic volumes as well as a number of
extraordinarily forceful, baroque torsos, which embody the violence of
the primitive forces of passion.

Lachaise's death in 1935 left America without a major sculptor.
David Smith and Reuben Nakian were youthful experimenters who
had not yet arrived at their mature styles. Manship and Zorach were

245

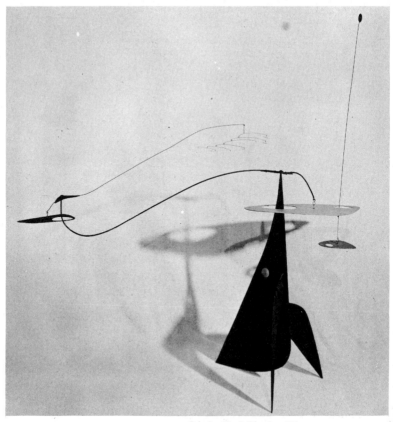

9-10. ALEXANDER CALDER, *Little Red Under Blue*, 1947.

officially praised, but their work was an American version of the international "moderne" of muscular athletes, heroes, and superworkers who sprang up all over Europe and America during the decade. Typical of these stylized figures is Manship's *Indian Hunter* (*Ill. 9-8*). The single sculptor of merit working primarily in the thirties was John Flannagan, whose mystical religious imagery and organic forms relate his work to the painting of Dove and Hartley. Flannagan's free-standing wooden pieces are flattened carving, distorted in the manner of the German Expressionists to approximate archaic and primitive sculpture. His later works in stone reflect Brancusi's loyalty to the monolith and to the sensuous properties of directly carved stone. Animal life provided most of the imagery, although Flannagan began to look for universal abstract symbols. For such works as the low carving of *Jonah and the Whale* (*Ill. 9-9*), Flannagan wished to capture the "remote memory of a stirring impulse from the depth of the unconscious." Like the later work of the Stieglitz group, Flannagan's sculpture was a deeply personal affair.

Outside of America, Alexander Calder was developing a sophisticated sculptural art based on Miró's and Arp's forms. In the late twenties, Calder designed a wire circus which revealed his promise as a sculptor and his unconventional imagination and antic wit. But Calder's great fame is as an abstract sculptor and pioneer of kinetic art. Calder dates his conversion to both abstraction and movement from 1930, when he visited Mondrian's studio. Mondrian's static rectangles caused him to wonder "how fine it would be if everything there moved." Earlier, Calder had experimented with hand-directed movement; now he put his training as an engineer into practice, arriving at the subtle balances of the suspended mobiles. These constructions used flat, free

9-11. ALEXANDER CALDER, *Three Arches*, 1963.

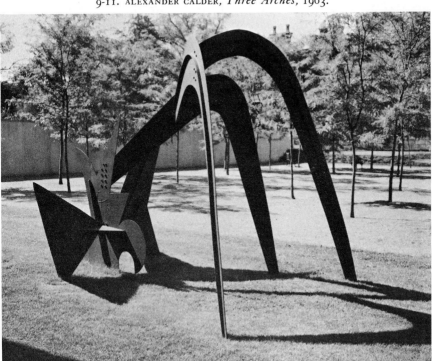

shapes, derived from Miró, and colored balls whose concentric orbits suggested the movement of the universe. The mobiles provided Calder with a form in which both his plastic imagination and his mechanical ingenuity could express themselves. In the late thirties, he began to work on small constructions which did not move. These gradually emerged as the stabiles, earthbound cousins to the mobiles. In works like *Little Red Under Blue* (*Ill. 9-10*), Calder suspended mobiles from static bases. Gradually, as the stabiles became increasingly monumental, Miró's organic shapes gave way to Matisse's decorative plant and leaf motifs. Constructed of thin sheets of painted metal bolted together, the soaring arches, tails, and fins of the stabiles became the prototypes for ambitious monumental sculpture in the fifties and sixties (*Ill. 9-11*). The stabiles showed how sculpture could rest flat on the floor so that bases could be discarded. In their use of painted cut-out metal sheets, they inspired an artist like Ellsworth Kelly to produce simple geometric sculpture, such as *Gate* (*Ill. 9-12*).

Living half the year in Europe and half in Connecticut, Calder has combined in his late work American largesse with European refine-

9-12. ELLSWORTH KELLY,
*Gate*, 1959.

ment. However, outside of scale and directness, his work has little in common with recent developments in American sculpture.

Abstract Expressionism was a style not easily translated into sculptural terms. The sculptors of David Smith's generation, contemporaries of the first-generation Abstract Expressionists, were subject to the same influences as the painters—the exhaustion of the Cubist aesthetic, the promise of Surrealist content and attitudes, and the need to find new forms and a new style.

The descendant of a pioneer blacksmith who settled in Decatur, Indiana, David Smith had worked in factories assembling metal parts before he applied the technique of welding to sculpture. At the Art Students League, Smith studied painting with the Czech Cubist Jan Matulka, who taught him the rudiments of Cubism and Constructivism. Part of the small New York group of advanced artists in the thirties, Smith was exposed to abstract art through his friendships with Stuart Davis, Jean Xceron, and, especially, John Graham. Although he thought of himself primarily as a painter, in 1933 Smith was inspired to borrow welding tools after seeing reproductions of Gonzalez' and Picasso's welded iron sculpture in *Cahiers d'Art*. Like Matisse, Picasso, and the other great sculptors of the twentieth century, Smith drew his inspiration from painting. He explained his transition from painting to sculpture, which occurred in 1930–33, thus:

My student period was involved with painting. The painting developed into raised levels from the canvas. Gradually the canvas was the base and the painting was a sculpture. . . . My student days, W.P.A. days, Romany Marie and McSorley days were with painters. . . . In these early days it was Cubist talk. Theirs I supposed was the Cubist canvas, and my reference image was the Cubist construction. The lines then had not been drawn by the pedants—in Cubist talk. Mondrian and Kandinsky were included.[1]

From 1937 to 1940 Smith produced the "medals for dishonor," bronze plaques whose expressionistic images were a searing moral indictment of the hypocrisies and injustices of contemporary society. Throughout his career, this moral force illuminates Smith's work and raises it above the level of the merely decorative.

During the war, Smith's sculptural output was curtailed because of his job as a welder in a defense plant, but in the late forties he began once again to make sculpture. Some of his works, which he called "interiors," seem directly based on Giacometti's *The Palace at 4 A.M.* On the other hand, his open welded steel constructions of the forties were often organized around a central core from which branchlike twisted rods and projections curved and intertwined. His masterpiece of 1950, *Blackburn—Song of an Irish Blacksmith* (*Ill. 9-13*), a steel and bronze sculpture, combines these rodlike forms with quasi-geometric planes and fanciful plantlike forms in a complex interplay. In the early fifties, Smith's constructions grew more linear and calligraphic, and solids gave way to the free play of "drawing-in-space," as in *Hudson River*

9-13. DAVID SMITH, *Blackburn—Song of an Irish Blacksmith*, 1950.

9-14. DAVID SMITH, *Hudson River Landscape, 1951.*

*Landscape* (*Ill. 9-14*). Arriving at rhythmic silhouettes with transparent interiors, Smith's "drawing-in-space" in its spontaneous ability to generate new forms, appears akin to Surrealist automatism. In the fifties, Smith began to conceive his images in related series, the two major series of this period being "Agricola" and "Tank Totem." These works were based on the relationships of the human figure (Smith continued throughout his career to make figure drawings). In these sculptures, solids and transparencies alternated with shieldlike discs and rods. Many incorporated "found" objects, which had figured in his work since his collage-constructions of the early thirties. These had no associational value, but were usually standard industrial units which could be recombined within a series in different ways. Toward the end of the fifties, Smith's forms became more straight-edged, upright, and geometric, and less organic and fanciful. In the years before his death, his work came to fullest flowering in three major series, "Voltri-

Bolton," "Zig," and "Cubi." The "Voltri-Bolton" series, begun in Spoleto, Italy, in 1962, touched off a period of sustained creative production which Smith maintained until his death. This series is the last based on the human figure. Combining found objects like tools with flat metal sheets cut into geometric patterns, Smith used the same basic set of shapes in a variety of basically planar relationships.

The new direction in Smith's work of the sixties, toward a more rigorously geometric, less fanciful style, parallels the changed direction of painting. The painted metal *Zig VII* (*Ill. 9-15*), for example, finds many analogies in the new abstraction, particularly in the chevrons and circles of Kenneth Noland. In fact, Smith once described himself as "a sculptor who painted his images." Because some of these works are designed to be seen only from a frontal view, they are even more pictorial in their insistence on silhouettes and planes. However, in the monumental stainless steel "Cubi" series (*Ill. 9-16*), Smith gives full play to three-dimensional volume, basing the relationships and epic scale on architecture rather than on the human figure. The series of cubes are balanced majestically yet dynamically above cylinders which thrust the mass of the sculpture above the viewer's head. The scored surface of the cubes causes their dense volumes to be dissolved in dazzling spangles of light. The brilliance of the metallic surface, polished to reflect sunlight (Smith wanted his sculpture to be seen

9-15. DAVID SMITH, *Zig VII,* 1963.

9-16. DAVID SMITH, *Cubi XIX*, 1964; *Cubi XVII*, 1963; *Cubi XVIII*, 1964.

out of doors), counterbalances the heaviness of the forms, providing a contradictory sense of buoyancy. The last works of the "Cubi" series, the architectonic gates, which combine openness with three-dimensional volume, represent a brilliant synthesis of Smith's main concerns. Thoroughly abstract, they point to the path Smith was about to pursue when his career was tragically cut short.

Smith's use of geometry as a flexible means of ordering rather than as a restrictive canon is characteristic of the manner in which American artists have used geometry. It bears certain analogies to Wright's free interpretation of geometry in his plans, forms, and ornaments, and supports the view that the typical American style is romantic. Like the Precisionist painters, Smith was able to see the abstract value of concrete forms. The coincidence of the symbol and the structure links him to the aesthetic of the Abstract Expressionist painters who were his friends. Discussing his use of machine parts, Smith said, "When one chooses a couple of old iron rings from the hub of a wagon, they

9-17. IBRAM LASSAW,
*Procession,* 1955–56.

are circles, they are suns; they all have the same radius; they all perform the same Euclidean relationship."[2]

Like Wright, Smith was at ease in the twentieth century and felt no spiritual conflicts with the Machine Age. He did not feel obliged either to romanticize or to combat the machine. Machinery, he said, has "never been an alien element, it has been in my nature." His ambition was to turn his studio into a factory, where he could produce sculpture whose forms were as impressive, monumental, and contemporary as the locomotive. He preferred to work in iron or steel because it "possesses little art history. What associations it possesses are those of this century: power, structure, movement, progress, suspension, destruction, brutality."[3] Assessing Smith's work, Hilton Kramer concluded that his achievement lay "in submitting the rhetoric of the School of Paris to the vernacular of the American machine shop."[4]

In the forties, a number of other sculptors of Smith's generation began to work in welded metal. Like Smith, Seymour Lipton, Herbert Ferber, David Hare, and Ibram Lassaw adopted many of the attitudes of Abstract Expressionist painting, and were closely tied to its dynamic aesthetic.

One of the few Americans accepted by the Surrealists into their

254

9-18. DAVID HARE,
*Juggler,* 1950–51.

9-19. SEYMOUR LIPTON,
*Sorcerer,* 1958.

circle, David Hare incorporated Surrealist motifs in works such as the elegantly posed *Juggler* (*Ill. 9-18*). Ibram Lassaw's early gridlike structures were reminiscent of Mondrian's works, but he turned to freer structures in his more ornate, elaborate, later works, such as *Procession* (*Ill. 9-17*).

9-20. HERBERT FERBER,
*Spherical Sculpture,* 1954–62.

9-21. RICHARD LIPPOLD,
*Primordial Figure,* 1947–48.

9-22. THEODORE ROSZAK,
*Sea Sentinel,* 1956.

A carver of social realist themes in the late thirties, Seymour Lipton abandoned the human figure in 1942 and began casting horns and skeletal pelvic forms. Lipton, like Hare and Ferber, became involved with the mythic themes of the Surrealists in the forties: the universal cycle of birth and death, primordial shapes, celestial and chthonian imagery. He outlined the "main genesis of artistic substance" as "the bud, the core, the spring, the darkness of earth, the deep animal fountainhead of man's forces."[5] He was especially attached to spiky, aggressive forms, which continue to appear even in his late work. Declaring that "everyone had used solid forms, pierced forms, prefabricated forms, etc.," Lipton said that he began to "feel the rightness of curved convoluted forms." Although his later works, such as *Sorcerer* (*Ill. 9-19*), are less convoluted, they still maintain the dramatic and lyrical tensions of his earlier forms.

In his work, Herbert Ferber has attempted to retain the energies of a restrained barbarism. Outside of Smith, he is virtually the only sculptor of his generation who sought to capture the energy of the gesture in the durable medium of metal. Turning away from representation in 1945, Ferber experimented in a number of materials, and made several cast bronzes of an aggressively Expressionist imagery. In the interest of working in open, welded sculpture, he refined this imagery in the fifties and early sixties into a series of large curves, folded like giant leaves or leaping around an open core, like arms grasping or attacking each other, as in *Spherical Sculpture* (*Ill. 9-20*). Arriving at a more monumental form of expression in the sixties, Ferber began enclosing these violent, aggressive forms in "cages" or environments; these giant enlargements of the leaping, writhing, baroque forms on a superhuman scale seemed to encompass the viewer as the "environmental" canvases of Pollock, Newman, Still, and Rothko had done.

9-23. REUBEN NAKIAN, *Olympia*, 1960–62.

9-24. ISAMU NOGUCHI,
*Kouros,* 1944–45.

Although Archipenko, one of the leading Cubist sculptors, had re-sided in the United States since 1923, his presence had little influence on American sculpture. Similarly, the arrival of Gabo and Lipchitz as refugees during World War II did not spur sculpture to the degree that the painters-in-exile transformed painting. However, Richard Lippold's string constructions, such as *Primordial Figure (Ill. 9-21),* may have been inspired by Gabo's example; and Theodore Roszak, who had been making geometric sculpture in a Constructivist vein, may have been influenced to work in bronze by Lipchitz' work. Reuben Nakian, on the other hand, seems to have developed inde-pendently of any European precedent. Roszak, in the fifties and sixties, developed a powerful imagery based mainly on insect or plant motifs, as in *Sea Sentinel (Ill. 9-22).* Nakian, like Ferber and Lipton, was more involved with the baroque fullness of Abstract Expression-ism, and, like the painters, often tried to express the pathos of ancient tragedy in abstract works. In the fifties, Nakian used flat planes of curved metal mounted on an armature, although more recently he has used draped and billowing forms, as in *Olympia (Ill. 9-23).*

Sculptors who worked primarily in wood in the forties and fifties are Isamu Noguchi, Raoul Hague, Louise Nevelson, and Gabriel Kohn. Noguchi, an American of Japanese descent, has never relinquished a tie to natural forms. Like Calder, Noguchi has his roots deep within the French tradition. As Brancusi's assistant, he learned to love the purity of simple, closed forms and polished surfaces; his respect for materials may have come partly from his Japanese heritage. Adapting his forms from the organic shapes of the Surrealists, Noguchi purged them of much of their mythic content, using them instead as a point of departure for highly sophisticated and refined works, such as *Kouros* (*Ill. 9-24*).

Raoul Hague has used the technique of direct carving to produce smooth, supple, monolithic forms of an impressive volume and robust-

9-25. RAOUL HAGUE,
*Walnut—1949,* 1949.

9-26. GABRIEL KOHN, *Acrotere,* 1960.

ness. While suggesting the human torso, the volumes are sufficiently generalized to remain convincing as abstract forms, as in *Walnut-1949* (*Ill. 9-25*). The most original wood sculptor in America, Gabriel Kohn, has adapted the techniques of carpentry, joinery, and ship-building to the art of sculpture. The tension and drama of the clean, quasi-geometrical shape of Kohn's *Acrotere* (*Ill. 9-26*) reside entirely in the inventiveness of the single unified form. Kohn's rejection of the base has led him to devise ingenious ways of balancing the blocky volumes. These balances are achieved by a series of thrusts and counter-thrusts, engineered toward producing maximum grace and elegance.

9-27. LOUISE NEVELSON, *Black Majesty*, 1955.

Kohn's natural wood surfaces provide a changing patchwork of light and dark, where various sections of wood have been laminated together; but they are unified by being part of a continuous plane or a single pure curve.

9-28. MARK DI SUVERO, *Hank Champion*, 1960.

9-29. JOHN CHAMBERLAIN, *Mr. Press,* 1961.

Louise Nevelson's constructions are made up of compartments and boxes fitted together, sometimes in sections large enough to constitute an environment; they are painted a single color—usually black, white, or gold—in order to give them unity. In her earlier wooden pieces, such as *Black Majesty* (*Ill.* 9-27), Nevelson used simple, organic shapes, but in the boxes of the late fifties and sixties, found objects and more complex forms are incorporated. Unlike her earlier works, which were to be viewed as sculpture-in-the-round, the more recent compartments and "walls" are to be seen frontally like reliefs.

The sculptors who emerged along with the second generation of Abstract Expressionists were interested, like them, in the effect of isolating and freezing movement. Mark di Suvero's beams in *Hank Champion* (*Ill. 9-28*) are connected with Kline's imagery; Chamberlain's crushed automobile parts in *Mr. Press* (*Ill. 9-29*) are related to de Kooning's colliding waves of paint; and David Weinrib's organic forms are related to Gorky's formal vocabulary. George Sugarman's *The Shape of Change* (*Ill. 9-30*), in its winding and curving, brightly colored forms, appears to share Al Held's "hard-edge" repertoire of

9-30. GEORGE SUGARMAN, *The Shape of Change*, 1964.

9-31. PETER AGOSTINI,
*Christmas Package,* 1963.

forms; whereas Peter Agostini's plaster casts of balloons, egg cartons, pillows, etc., such as *Christmas Package* (*Ill. 9-31*), anticipate pop imagery. Following Nakian's precedent of casting the casual folds of material draped over an armature, Agostini recently has been casting simpler, more volumetric forms such as tires. In the late fifties, junk sculpture (sculpture made of assembled found objects) was popular with artists such as Jean Follett and Richard Stankiewicz, whose witty *Kabuki Dancer* (*Ill. 9-32*) divorces junk from its usual associations. Similarly, Lee Bontecou has made elegant abstract works, using laundry bags stretched and sewn over a wire armature (*Ill. 9-33*).

In the fifties and sixties, "assemblage" has emerged as a distinctly American form of sculpture. Like Surrealist objects, a lineal descendant of collage, assemblage—the art of joining unlikely objects or images together in a single context—has as ancestors Duchamp's 1913 *Bicycle Wheel* and Picasso's 1914 *Absinthe Glass with Spoon.* Because it uses material from the environment and lends itself to eccentric experiments, assemblage seems especially suited to the American tempera-

9-32. RICHARD STANKIEWICZ,
*Kabuki Dancer*, 1956.

ment. At least three Americans have made significant works of assemblage; they are Joseph Cornell, H. C. Westermann, and Edward Kienholz. As early as 1936, Julien Levy, the celebrated Surrealist dealer, called Cornell "one of the few Americans . . . who understands

9-33. LEE BONTECOU,
*Untitled*, 1962.

9-34. JOSEPH CORNELL, *Chocolat Menier*, 1950.

the Surrealist point of view." Like Schwitters, Cornell is able to distill poetry and drama from ordinary fragments. But Cornell is not attracted to "merz" or garbage but to precious fragments—crystal goblets, bits of sparkle, etc. His "boxes" are actually three-dimensional collages, star-maps of a private universe. In fact, astronomical imagery is important to Cornell's iconography. Like Surrealist objects, Cornell's boxes present irrational juxtapositions, as in *Chocolat Menier* (*Ill. 9-34*), with its tattered labels and worn surfaces. His objects in their new context take on new meanings akin to poetic metaphor.

The brutal sensibility of Kienholz could not be more at odds with Cornell's gentleness. The creator of monstrous brothels and images of death and decay, Kienholz is, above all, the moralist who sees disorder and decadence in contemporary society. Like Bruce Conner and a number of other creators of assemblage, Kienholz reverts to the seamy Surrealism and sordidness of Magic Realists like Ivan Albright. In a sense, his revolting images like *The Birthday* (*Ill. 9-35*) are related to international Dada and Surrealism; but even more, they seem a specifically American reaction—a kind of negative puritanism and extreme form of local eccentricity—to the American scene. And in general, the recrudescence of Dada activity of the sixties may be attributed to the bizarreness and ironies of contemporary American experience.

The present moment is one of intense activity in sculpture. In the thirties and forties, according to Smith, many of the most promising American sculptors could not afford to build their planned works; however, Smith was able to overcome this difficulty and to transform his Bolton Landing studio into a fully equipped machine shop and factory for sculpture. This is the situation in which the most ambitious American sculptors would like to work today. For a number of years, artists like Ellsworth Kelly, Alexander Liberman, and José de Rivera have had their pure, geometric conceptions industrially manufactured. The clean lines of works like Rivera's *Construction #85* (*Ill. 9-36*) are admired by a number of younger American sculptors, who have grown dissatisfied with the tradition of open, welded sculpture, as it was articulated by Picasso and Gonzalez and codified by Smith. These

9-35. EDWARD KIENHOLZ, *The Birthday*, 1964.

9-36. JOSÉ DE RIVERA, *Construction #85*, 1964.

younger sculptors are turning to elementary volumes, such as Robert Morris' untitled work (*Ill. 9-37*), and redundant three-dimensional reliefs like Donald Judd's row of aluminum boxes (*Ill. 9-38*). These are meant to be seen, like the images of the new abstraction, as integral *Gestalts*. Rather than organizing a series of parts related in the familiar way of form echoing analogous form, these blunt, clumsy structures eliminate parts in favor of the whole.

A number of young artists, such as Judd, Morris, Ronald Bladen, and Larry Bell, began as painters and rejected painting on the ground that it lacked concreteness. Thus their work often has less in common with traditional sculpture than with painting and architecture. Working mainly in industrial materials like sheet steel, aluminum, fiberglass, and molded plastics, these young sculptors have brought new vitality and interest to sculpture, which for many years has been the stepchild of American art, lagging behind painting in invention and daring. Recently, the mammoth plywood constructions of architect Tony Smith have raised the possibility of the creation of a monumental sculpture based on volume rather than plane, the basis for Cubist-derived sculpture. (Like Smith's, Judd's, and Morris' bulky structures, Claes Oldenburg's "soft" sculptures, made of stuffed and sewn canvas or vinyl, present a single image rather than a series of related parts. But unlike the makers of "primary structures," as the

9-37. ROBERT MORRIS, *Untitled,* 1965.

simple, redundant object sculpture has been termed, who place primary importance on shape and color, Oldenburg remains interested in the traditional tactile values of sculpture.) The problem now is to insure that the best American sculptors of the sixties are able to build their works. With the renewed interest of architects and industry in becoming the patrons of sculpture, it is possible that sculpture as an art in America will flower as never before.

9-38. DONALD JUDD, *Untitled,* 1965.

## Chapter Ten

# Toward an American Architecture

In the better aspects of eclecticism and taste, that is to say, in those aspects which reveal a certain depth of artistic feeling and a physical sense of materials, rather than mere scene-painting or archaeology, however clever, there is to be discovered a hope and a forecast. For it is within the range of possibilities, one may even go so far as to say probabilities, that out of the very richness and multiplicity of the architectural phenomena called "styles" there may arise within the architectural mind a perception growing slowly, perhaps suddenly, into clearness, that architecture in its material nature and in its animating essence is a *plastic art.*
—Louis Sullivan, *The Autobiography of an Idea,* 1922

In 1891, the distinguished critic Montgomery Schuyler agreed with his friend the architect Leopold Eidlitz that "American architecture was the art of covering one thing with another thing to imitate a third thing, which, if genuine, would not be desirable."[1] Wishing to draw attention to the weakness of eclecticism with its haphazard imitation and combination of historical styles, Schuyler perhaps overstated his case. In fact, he found much to praise in the organic functionalism of the Chicago School, led by Louis Sullivan and Frank Lloyd Wright. Schuyler recognized that "such designers as Mr. Sullivan and Mr. Wright have the root of the matter, and that their works are of good hope, in contrast with the rehandling and rehashing of admired historical forms in which there is no future nor any possibility of progress."[2]

But Schuyler's early appreciation of the Chicago School was as easily forgotten as the work itself. During the academic reaction, the "interregnum" as Lewis Mumford termed it, that followed the highly successful Chicago World's Fair of 1893, the Neoclassical ensemble that housed the Fair's exhibits became the model of architectural excellence. The pursuit of a princely Renaissance image fit for a newly powerful imperial America eradicated much of the progress made by Richardson and his successors toward the development of a modern style. Clearly, the humbleness of a utilitarian style, suited for commercial use, would not suffice as an expression of an Age of Elegance.

The eclipse of the Chicago School, under the impact of the Beaux-Arts revival, reintroduced many retarded practices, such as the reliance on historical prototypes and the "estrangement between architecture and building" against which Schuyler had preached. Hence, the revival of the Neoclassical aesthetic of the conservative French Ecole des Beaux-Arts—where a generation of American architects, including Sullivan, had received its training—displaced a progressive and rational style, which was free of historicism and consistent with the needs and ideals of the modern age. That this contemporary achievement could so easily have been rejected in favor of the outworn patterns of the past is another testimony to the ambivalence with which Americans greeted the Machine Age. By the time Machine Age architecture was acceptable to the majority, it would, ironically, have to be reimported from Europe.

In the meantime, various compromise formulas and reprises from times past would lend a spurious dignity to American architecture. The tragedy was that at the turn of the century, architecture was by far the most advanced and original of the plastic arts in America; one can only guess what might have been accomplished had it followed a straight line of development.

The collapse of the Chicago School, however, was not so much a failure of nerve on the part of architects as a failure of taste on the part of clients. The fantasies of luxury and grandeur of the newly rich led them to imitate the style of the great princes in their homes and summer palaces. The need to supply symbols of power and stability, indicating a continuity with the great ages of Western civilization, impelled businesses, churches, and schools to re-create the entire history of art on native ground. As the twentieth century opened, it appeared that Americans were not yet capable of appreciating the present moment. Wealthy patrons still looked to the past to validate the present. Before the present could have value in itself, America's feelings of cultural inferiority remained to be assuaged.

The turning point for the Chicago School—if one can point to a single event—may have been the death of John Wellborn Root in January, 1891, during the planning stages of the Chicago Fair. Together with his partner D. H. Burnham, Root had been responsible for a number of the most daring and original feats of architecture in Chicago, including the massive, undulating façade of the Monadnock

10-1. FRANK LLOYD WRIGHT, Robie House, Chicago, 1909.

Building, and the prophetically transparent glass and steel cage of the Reliance Building. When Burnham and Root became the main consultants for the World's Columbian Exposition, it was presumed that the Chicago School had gained an international showcase. However, with the death of Root—always the more progressive member of the firm—Burnham came under the sway of the powerful New York firms that had been invited to participate. Impressed with the grandeur of the Renaissance palaces of the New York firm of McKim, Mead, and White and the elegance of the Gothic Fifth Avenue chateaux of Richard Morris Hunt, Burnham saw the error of Chicago's "originality" and became converted to New York's "pure ideal of the ancients." Thus, when in 1893, Jackson Park was tranformed into the White City, only Henry Ives Cobb's Fisheries Building and Adler and Sullivan's Transportation Building deviated from the norm of resurrected domes, orders, aedicules, and colonnades. Again, Schuyler was one of the few to speak out against the folly of nostalgically invoking the past: "Arcadian architecture is one thing and American architecture another. Men bring not back the mastodons nor we those

272

times."[3] Sullivan, on the other hand, his Irish temper lending fire to his sense of outrage, predicted direly: "The damage wrought by the World's Fair will last for half a century from its date, if not longer. It has penetrated deep into the constitution of the American mind, effecting there lesions significant of dementia."[4]

Sullivan had cause for bitterness, as had Wright. Though both received commissions during the first quarter of the century, neither fared well. Sullivan's last major commission, the Schlesinger and Mayer Store (now Carson Pirie Scott) in Chicago's Loop, was completed in 1904. During the remaining twenty years before his death in a lonely Chicago hotel room, Sullivan constructed a series of small banks in Indiana, Iowa, Ohio, Wisconsin, and Minnesota; the best of these were in his favored combination of brick enlivened with terracotta ornament.

As his master sank into obscurity, Wright's reputation grew. During the first decade of the century, Wright attracted increasing attention with his low-slung, ground-hugging prairie houses in Chicago and its suburbs. Typical of these domestic works are the 1902 Ward Willits house, the 1909 Robie house (*Ill. 10-1*), and the country villa designed in 1908 for Avery Coonley. Wright's 1904 Administration Building (since destroyed) for the Larkin Company in Buffalo was a gravely monumental solution to the problem of the modern office building; his Unity Church in Oak Park, Illinois, was a poured-concrete structure of uncompromisingly modern design.

Although, with the few exceptions by Wright, the first quarter of the century produced little architecture to compete with what was done in Chicago in the preceding decades, the picture was not entirely dark. Some architects continued to design and build organic, functional architecture, free of historicism. From Wright's office came Barry Byrne, while Sullivan's disciples—William Gray Purcell and George Grant Elmslie—carried on the master's tradition. In addition, Dwight H. Perkins, George W. Maher, and Walter Burley Griffin also produced some notable buildings, again mainly in the Midwest, where preconceptions with the "grand manner" and prejudice against native expression did not predominate.

Although the architecture of the twenties and thirties was generally more modest and less given to fantastic extravagance than that of the early years of the century, there was little improvement in design. Unfortunately, the Age of Elegance was not brought to an end by an upgrading of taste, but by a series of legislative acts. The graduated

273

income tax of 1913, although it scarcely demolished the great American fortunes, did put a damper on wild spending. The immigration acts of 1921 and 1924 meant the end both of cheap labor and of European craftsmanship, which changed the conditions and character of American building.

Throughout these decades, Wright continued to be the single dominant figure in American architecture. A self-proclaimed genius able to withstand all critical onslaughts, Wright began his career at an early age. When he was eighteen, he quit the engineering program at the University of Wisconsin to join the firm of Adler and Sullivan as a draftsman. He remained with the firm for six years until 1893, when he opened his own office in Chicago. From Sullivan, the young Wright had learned much about structural integrity, organic design, and the place of ornament in architecture. He never forgot those lessons, even when others had turned their backs on Chicago School principles. For Wright, European architecture had less to offer than Japanese architecture, from which he derived much of the inspiration for his organic buildings. His low, horizontal houses, with their fluid interior space, their porches and patios, established a rapport with the natural environment. Visualizing walls as screens instead of barriers, Wright began to divide interior space in an unorthodox manner, freeing the ground plan from the rigidity of the box. "Democracy needed some-

10-2. FRANK LLOYD WRIGHT, Kaufmann House ("Falling Water"), Bear Run, Pennsylvania, 1936.

10-3. FRANK LLOYD WRIGHT, The Solomon R. Guggenheim Museum, New York, 1959.

thing basically better than the box," he declared. Irregular plans, eccentric projections, and interpenetrating rooms, which flowed into one another, became characteristic of Wright's houses. And as the inner structure became increasingly coherent, unfolding from within outward, the contours of the ground plan exhibited an increasing regularity. Finally, in Wright's later houses, the rooms radiate from around the hearth, as life in ancient dwellings centered around the fireside.

Frequently, Wright was most daring in designing houses for his own use. Rebuilt in the mid-twenties after several fires, Taliesin East in Spring Green, Wisconsin, served Wright as a headquarters where he could gather around him a fellowship of younger architects. Taliesin West, in the Arizona desert near Phoenix, was first laid out in 1938. Here Wright set up an informal training ground for his disciples. Both houses are examples of Wright's peerless ability to integrate building and landscape, and they demonstrate his use of local building materials, such as the desert stone of which Taliesin West is built. In 1936, Wright created a tour-de-force marriage of building to site in his "Falling Water" house for the executive E. J. Kaufmann in Bear Run, Pennsylvania (*Ill. 10-2*). Here, great

10-4. FRANK LLOYD WRIGHT, Midway Gardens, Chicago, 1913.

white concrete slabs, actually extensions of the interior parapets, are dramatically cantilevered over the mountain stream that runs below.

Like Sullivan, Wright suffered many setbacks. Some people denied his genius, others resented his arrogant willfulness in denying the place of any other kind of art in architecture. Many feel that his last monument, the Guggenheim Museum (*Ill. 10-3*), completed in 1959, is one of Wright's greatest buildings. However, it has been widely criticized as a museum on the grounds that the pictures are forced to take second place to the architecture that houses them.

Throughout his long life, Wright's career was a stormy one. During the twenties, he had to be saved from bankruptcy by friends. His largest commission of the period, the Imperial Hotel in Tokyo, kept him occupied outside of this country from 1916 to 1922. Small domestic commissions during the twenties, however, prevented him from being idle. Unfortunately, one of his most original creations, the 1913 Midway Gardens (*Ill. 10-4*), a Chicago recreational building, was destroyed during Prohibition because it had been a drinking parlor. Here Wright had applied ornament, in Sullivan's manner, as a complement to structure; the originality of his decoration was a strong contrast to the belated Art Nouveau and cheap thirties "moderne" ornament that became popular. In 1927–28, Wright published a series of articles in the *Architectural Record* that brought him new prominence. Reacting against the European deification of the machine as the model for architecture, Wright warned against the standardization of the machine style; he urged that the machine be used creatively as a tool, but not as a model for design. He argued that the "logic of the plan" and the form of the building develop from the personality of the designer, the materials, the site, and the structure, rather than from any external, *a priori* set of ideas. He also discussed the possibilities of new architectural materials—glass, concrete, and sheet metal —finding them full of promise. In 1929, his project for a giant skyscraper, the St. Mark's in the Bouwerie Tower, was considered too advanced for its time; not until 1955 was a similar project, the Price Tower in Bartlesville, Oklahoma, actually constructed (*Ill. 10-5*).

More important commissions came to Wright in the thirties. In the interior of the 1939 Administration Building for the Johnson Wax Company in Racine, Wisconsin, Wright planted spreading lily-pad

10-5. FRANK LLOYD WRIGHT, Price Tower, Bartlesville, Oklahoma, 1955.

10-6. FRANK LLOYD WRIGHT, Johnson Wax Administration Building (interior), Racine, Wisconsin, 1939.

10-7. FRANK LLOYD WRIGHT, Johnson Wax Administration Building (exterior), Racine, Wisconsin, 1939.

columns, over which light filters from the pyrex skylight (*Ill. 10-6*). The exterior (*Ill. 10-7*) is a wrap-around brick and tubular glass skin; the sculpturesque quality of brick turrets looks forward to the emphatically sculptural late works, such as the Guggenheim Museum in New York and the Humphreys Theater in Dallas, Texas. Wright's buildings of the postwar period extended his nearly limitless range of solutions. They included the 1949 V. C. Morris Store in San Francisco, with its blind façade, all-over pattern of brick work, and arched doorway, recalling Sullivan's late work; the 1950 Research Center of the Johnson Wax Company; and one of Wright's most ambitious commissions, the Florida Southern College at Lakeland, Florida. The first of sixteen campus buildings to be completed was the Pfeiffer Chapel of 1940; this was followed by the Roux Library of 1942, the Administration Building of 1948, and the Industrial Arts Building of 1952.

No commercial structure built in America in the twenties or thirties compares with Wright's Johnson Wax Administration Building in originality or excellence. In fact, the best buildings, according to Lewis Mumford, were often anonymous constructions such as grain elevators, warehouses, and factories, which interested European visitors more than the official architecture of the period. At least one prominent American architect, however, was engaged in designing such utilitarian structures. By 1929, Albert Kahn, chief architect for Detroit's giant automotive companies, was conducting a business doing about $500,000 of building a week. He built the first reinforced concrete structure in the United States, the Packard Motor Car Company in 1905, and was the inventor of the "daylight factory," such as the Dodge Half-Ton Truck Plant (*Ill. 10-8*), which he constructed in 1938. In its use of extensive fenestration and simple, unified geometric volumes, his work resembled that of many of the European pioneers of the modern movement, such as Peter Behrens. In his 1917 Ford plant at River Rouge, Michigan, Kahn integrated production facilities, furnaces, mills, and assembly lines in such an impressive and coherent manner that Charles Sheeler and Margaret Bourke-White made the ensemble a subject for numerous photographic studies. But even Albert Kahn, as adept as he was in solving industrial problems in a straightforward, direct fashion, clung to the notion that plainness was appropriate for industry but not for public monuments. Thus, when he came to design the Clements Library of the University of Michigan, he clothed it in Neoclassic disguise. He confessed that real architects designed capitols

10-8. ALBERT KAHN,
Dodge Half-Ton
Truck Plant,
Detroit, 1938.

and monuments, whereas "the office boy was considered good enough for factories." Fortunately, he considered himself "still that office boy designing factories" who had "no dignity to be impaired."

Of the commercial structures of the twenties and thirties, the multi-storied office building, despite its illustrious Chicago birth, fared the worst. Because the skyscraper was a symbol of prestige, as well as a necessity due to rising land costs, it did not, like the humble factory and warehouse, escape the return to eclecticism. Rejecting the monumental simplicity of the early skyscrapers, architects disguised new office buildings as giant classical columns, with base, shaft, and capital, or as medieval towers, replete with pinnacles and gargoyles. However, changes took place as a result of increased economic pressure to construct cheaply and quickly, and the new zoning law (adopted by New York in 1916), which called for the top stories to be set back from the base (supposedly in order to allow light to filter down into the street), changed some of the ways in which architects worked. Thus, the epoch that opened with the forced Gothicism of Cass Gilbert's 1913 Woolworth Building (*Ill. 10-9*) ended in the stripped anonymity of Shreve, Lamb and Harmon's Empire State Building—leaving critics hard pressed to say which was the lesser of the two evils.

From draped cube to thinned slab to glass box, the skyscraper has undergone a radical transformation during this century. In 1857, the first practical passenger elevator was installed in the cast-iron Haughwout Building in New York. As new processes for manufacturing steel made practical curtain walls hung on a steel skeleton, which could do the work formerly done by load-bearing masonry, it became clear that the tall office building would assume a paramount role in American construction. Beginning in Chicago with William Le Baron Jenney's 1885 Home Insurance Company Building and Holabird and Roche's 1886 riveted skeleton Tacoma Building, steel-cage building became one of the most challenging problems facing American architects. By the end of the nineteenth century, however, most of the formal possibilities of steel-cage architecture had been explored. Sullivan's Wainwright Building in St. Louis and Guaranty Building in Buffalo foretold the verticality of the soaring office tower. Burnham and Root had erected their prophetic massive slab, the Monadnock Building, and their nearly transparent Reliance Building in Chicago.

The period of experiment was followed, as often is the case, by a conservative reaction. The concentration of the population in urban centers increased the need for tall buildings, but the complacency of a prosperous period dulled any urges toward innovation. The loss of contact with Europe brought about by World War I decreased possibilities for a stimulating exchange with European modernists. Although the twenties and thirties saw many advances in construction and technology, such as new systems of heating and air conditioning, greater standardization of parts, and new techniques for painting, spraying, and welding, design did not keep pace with these developments.

10-9. CASS GILBERT, Woolworth Building, New York, 1913.

10-10. HOOD AND HOWELLS,
Chicago Tribune Building,
1923–25.

The outcome of the major architectural competition of the twenties, the 1922 contest for the Chicago Tribune Building (*Ill. 10-10*), is an example of how retarded taste kept advanced concepts from penetrating American architecture. Although entries were received from the illustrious German firm Gropius and Meyer and from the Finn Eliel Saarinen, the prize was awarded to Raymond Hood and John Mead Howells; their cathedral tower, erected in 1923–25, with its flying buttresses and pseudo-Gothic detail, was but a more sophisticated recasting of the Woolworth Building formula. In awarding the second prize to Eliel Saarinen, the judges touched off a major controversy. Sullivan, for one, wanted to reverse the decision; he stated, "The Finnish master's edifice is not a lonely cry in the wilderness, it is a voice, resonant and rich, ringing amidst the wealth and joy of life." Ultimately, Saarinen was invited to head Cranbrook Academy in Detroit, where his son Eero and the designer Charles Eames received their training.

By the late twenties, however, such revivalist solutions as the Chicago Tribune Building had been abandoned for reasons probably more practical than aesthetic. Under the provisions of the new zoning law, the setback silhouette (called "ziggurat" by Frank Lloyd Wright in derision) soon came to dominate the skyline. The surfaces of these stepped, cubistic blocks were unbroken except by window openings, which offered the only relief from the monotonous wall surfaces; since the setbacks took care of horizontal divisions, belt courses were abandoned and piers were flattened to become broad vertical bands. Typical buildings in the new fashion were Holabird and Root's two 1928 skyscrapers, the Palmolive Building in Chicago and the Daily News Building in New York, and Ely Jacques Kahn's 120 Wall Street Building in New York.

Thus, when Raymond Hood came to design the new McGraw-Hill Building in 1930 (*Ill. 10-11*), he abandoned the Gothic formula of the Chicago Tribune Tower in favor of the massive, unadorned, streamlined style with its succession of setbacks. In its cleanness and bareness, the McGraw-Hill Building had certain superficial similarities to the work of the modernists in Europe. Its continuous planes, alternating the opacity of the wall with the transparency of broad horizontal windows further accentuated the building's streamlined modern look.

From layered ziggurat to lean slab was the next step in the skyscraper's changing silhouette. The Rockefeller Center complex, on which Reinhard and Hofmeister; Corbett, Harrison and MacMurray; and Hood and Fouilhoux collaborated, was the most discussed architectural grouping in America in the thirties (*Ill. 10-12*). It was the

10-11. RAYMOND HOOD, McGraw-Hill Building, New York, 1930–31.

10-12. REINHARD & HOFMEISTER; CORBETT, HARRISON & MACMURRAY; HOOD & FOUILHOUX, Rockefeller Center, New York, 1931–40.

first significant attempt made in America to deal with the problem of planning urban space, of integrating a group of related buildings as a functional unit. Second, it represented a return to the slab-type of building, presaged by the Monadnock Building.

Except for a few isolated examples, again mainly by Wright, American architecture of the thirties was scarcely more distinguished than that of the twenties. Although the New Deal housing legislation placed new stress on community planning and urban development, little was accomplished practically. American architects were generally remiss in considering the social function of architecture, so basic a concern of the modern movement in Europe. However, pioneers in community planning, such as Clarence Stein and Henry Wright, made some progress in prescribing remedies, and in designing projects for towns, villages, and garden cities. But very few of the projects were executed.

Even so, American awareness of the achievements of the progressive Dutch architects of de Stijl and the German members of the Bauhaus was growing. But there was little notice of the most revolutionary conceptions of the twenties: Mies van der Rohe's 1921 glass tower project, Gropius' 1925 Bauhaus at Dessau, J. J. P. Oud's Café de Unie, Le Corbusier's 1929 house at Poissy, and Wright's 1929 project for the St. Mark's in the Bouwerie Tower. Despite the retarded practice of American architecture in the twenties, however, the "interregnum" was over. In 1932, the new Museum of Modern Art held as one of its first exhibitions a tribute to the modern movement, featuring the work of Oud, Mies, Gropius, and Le Corbusier—the pioneers of the "International Style." In a historic survey of the International Style, published in 1932, Philip Johnson and Henry-Russell Hitchcock included only one American, Frank Lloyd Wright, as a member of the pantheon of modernists.

Johnson and Hitchcock were optimistic in describing the new style:

> The idea of style, which began to degenerate when the revivals destroyed the disciplines of the Baroque, has become real and fertile again. Today a single new style has come into existence. The aesthetic conceptions on which its disciplines are based derive from the experimentation of the individualists. They and not the revivalists were the immediate masters of those who have created the new style. This contemporary style, which exists throughout the world, is unified and inclusive, not fragmentary and contradictory like so much of the production of the first generation of modern architects. In the last decade it has produced sufficient monuments of distinction to display its validity and vitality. It may be fairly compared in significance with the styles of the past. In the handling of the problem of structure it is related to the Gothic, in the handling of the problem of design it is more akin to the Classical. In the preeminence given to the handling of function it is distinguished from both.[5]

Although the ideas of the International Style were presented in exhibitions and publications, buildings in this style were not constructed in America until the late thirties, when some of the masters themselves, fleeing Hitler, arrived in the United States. Their work, however, was not immediately welcomed in all quarters. The official reaction is best exemplified by a statement made in 1936 by a leading academic architect, Ralph Adams Cram. According to Cram, the new architecture was "a betrayal of trust, a vicious though unintentional

10-13. IRVING GILL,
Ellen Scripps House,
La Jolla, California,
1917.

assault on the basic principles of a sane and wholesome society." The theories of the French architect Le Corbusier, particularly, came in for abuse. Many agreed with H. L. Mencken's denunciation: "If I were building a house tomorrow it would certainly not follow the lines of a dynamo or a steam shovel." Thus, the theories of the International Style reached America, followed by some of the leading European architects, who built examples of their work. However, architectural practice generally did not become more progressive until the refugee architects joined the educational system, and were able to transform the leading architectural schools by introducing the principles of the Bauhaus.

Many members of the original Bauhaus faculty, of course, were responsible for this transformation. Gropius, founder of the Bauhaus, joined the faculty of the Harvard School of Design, where he remained from 1937 to 1952. He later organized The Architects Collaborative (TAC), based on the idea of group practice. Marcel Breuer, a former Bauhaus colleague, joined Gropius at Harvard until 1940, when he withdrew to practice on his own. In 1939 Mies van der Rohe came to direct the architectural school of Chicago's Armour Institute (later the Illinois Institute of Technology); and Laszlo Moholy-Nagy established the New Bauhaus at the University of Chicago, where Georgy Kepes soon became a faculty member. The models and methods of instruction of the Bauhaus architects indelibly stamped modernism in America with the mark of the International Style. These architects introduced the rigorous training of the Bauhaus curriculum as a new academic discipline, offering a firm grounding in the principles of structure and design which was as rational and useful as the Beaux-Arts discipline had been for Richardson and Sullivan.

Before the Bauhaus ideas gained currency in America, only a handful of architects had accepted the strict rectangularity of compositions based on the intersection of planes, ultimately derived from Cubism. Among the earliest examples of modernist domestic architecture were Irving Gill's spare cubic house of 1917 for Miss Ellen Scripps, in La Jolla, California (*Ill. 10-13*), and the houses designed by R. M. Schindler in the twenties, such as the 1928 C. H. Wolfe residence on Catalina Island, California. Commercial buildings, prophetic of the new steel and glass machine aesthetic that was to take hold, included the glass-curtain façade of Willis Jefferson Polk's 1918 Halladie Building in San Francisco and the 1932 Philadelphia Saving Fund Society Building by Howe and Lescaze (*Ill. 10-14*), which accepted many of the Bauhaus principles of functionalism and rational construction.

In the years that followed the migration of the Bauhaus architects to America, buildings by Gropius, Mies, Breuer, and their followers began to transform the American landscape. Gropius' 1950 Harvard Graduate Center and Breuer's 1951 Vassar College Cooperative Dormitory and 1966 Whitney Museum provide examples of their strict geometric style. Mies van der Rohe, the most prolific and ultimately the most influential of these architects, has executed a number of important commissions in the United States, including the campus of the Illinois Institute of Technology (1942–50) and a number of private homes and apartment houses. In fact, the apex of the influence of the International Style in America coincides with the construction of Mies's masterpiece, designed with Philip Johnson, the 1958 Seagram Building

10-14. HOWE & LESCAZE, Philadelphia Saving Fund Society Building, 1932.

10-15. LUDWIG MIES VAN DER ROHE AND PHILIP JOHNSON, Seagram Building, New York, 1958.

10-16. SKIDMORE, OWINGS & MERRILL, Lever House, New York, 1952.

(*Ill. 10-15*), whose unbroken boxlike strictness and fragile glass façade have spawned so many inferior versions as neighbors. Among the most successful buildings in the Miesian manner is the 1952 Lever House (*Ill. 10-16*), designed by Gordon Bunshaft of Skidmore, Owings & Merrill; this, in turn, has provided a formula for opening up the ground level as a pedestrian plaza, above which floats the vertical slab of the skyscraper itself.

A new chapter in skyscraper architecture is presently being written. The abandonment of the glittering glass-box transparency of the International Style for a more solid and massive façade, often largely stone or precast concrete, is part of the general reaction against Bauhaus aesthetics that has characterized the post-Seagram Building period. Although Eero Saarinen's 1951 General Motors Research Center, near Detroit, is a classic of the purist glass-box style, before his untimely death in 1961, he designed the dark, aggressive piers of the CBS Building in New York, erected in 1965. Saarinen was one of the first American architects to offer alternative solutions to the geometric severity of the Bauhaus style. In the fluid, sculptural TWA Terminal at Kennedy Airport (*Ill. 10-17*), the curved roofs of the Ingalls Hockey Rink at Yale, and the John Foster Dulles Airport terminal, Saarinen looked to the inspiration of engineering and sculpture, turning away from the pictorial spatial effects of the Bauhaus geometricians. Here, precisely, is the point at which many of the most daring American architects find themselves today.

Domestic architecture perhaps was not so transformed by the International Style as was commercial and institutional architecture. During the thirties, strides were made in the direction of more modern housing, but these efforts generally remained in the model stage. In 1926, Lawrence Kocher and Albert Frey designed a model "aluminaire" house, a construction hung on six aluminum columns, which Wallace K. Harrison eventually purchased and moved near his home at Hungtington, New York. In 1933, the year in which Hitler dissolved the Bauhaus, Chicago's Century of Progress exposition included a number of prefabricated houses. Far more revolutionary, however, was Buckminster Fuller's Dimaxion house, with its molded fixtures and single-unit bathroom facilities, which, although the materials called for were available, never reached the production stage.

10-17. EERO SAARINEN, TWA Terminal, John F. Kennedy International Airport, New York, 1956–62.

With the arrival of the émigré architects in the late thirties, the situation improved, although domestic building was necessarily curtailed during the war years. The three houses built by Gropius and Breuer in 1938–39 in Lincoln, Massachusetts (one for each of the architects and another for Harvard Professor James Ford), incorporated New England's characteristic white wooden siding into a strict geometric design that appeared both modern and American. In many ways, however, the classic example of International Style housing in the United States is the glass house that Philip Johnson built for himself in New Canaan, Connecticut, in 1949 (*Ill. 10-18*). A single interior space enclosed by glass walls, it is divided only by furniture and a glazed brick-clad cylinder containing the bathroom. In 1951, Mies himself provided an example of his finely proportioned, rational style in the glass-curtain–walled apartment house at 860 Lake Shore Drive in Chicago.

When the reaction against the International Style set in, attention turned toward the work of California architects, who had been consistently more independent of European sources, maintaining ties with such original local architects as Bernard Maybeck and the brothers Greene. Romantic and eccentric, Maybeck married such diverse styles as Tudor and Chinese in his 1912 First Church of Christ Scientist in Berkeley, with results that were strangely unified, picturesque, and inventive. Designing for California's warm climate, Charles Sumner Greene and his brother Henry Mather Greene popularized the bungalow style, a traditional housing type in California since the Spaniards had arrived there. The success of the California architects in using local materials, such as redwood, and in integrating structure and landscape ranked them among the most progressive architects in

10-18. PHILIP JOHNSON, Glass House, New Canaan, Connecticut, 1949.

America. Offering an alternative to the casual picturesque tradition was the cool geometric formalism of Irving Gill, a pioneer modernist who believed that "the straight line, the arch, the cube, and the circle" were the basis of architecture. Another modernist was the Viennese architect Richard Neutra, who arrived in Los Angeles in 1925. A student of Adolf Loos, Neutra had also worked for Eric Mendelsohn, eventually another emigrant to the United States. In Chicago, Neutra spent time in the office of Holabird and Roche; later—in the late twenties—he also worked with Wright at Taliesin East. But in his earliest California houses, such as the 1929 Lowell house in Los Angeles, Neutra's purist roots are obvious—as they continue to be in his most recent works.

Among the first to criticize the International Style, California architects have preached a respect for textures and site. R. M. Schindler was most articulate in his hostility to machine aesthetics. He felt that "funtionalism, with its white stucco, stainless steel, glass, and poster color schemes" was even more out of place in semitropical California than elsewhere in the United States. In his criticism of the standardization and impersonality of the International Style, Schindler voiced a growing dissatisfaction among American architects: "The classical mode of set forms for columns, architraves, and cornices is replaced by a stereotyped vocabulary of steel columns, horizontal parapets, and corner windows, to be used . . . both in the jungles and on the glaciers."[6]

The question was, and remains, what should replace the cold functionalism of the International Style. After a point it was no longer considered sufficient for a building merely to express its function. In recent years, the characteristics of the International Style have come to be replaced by their opposites. Thus, in place of impersonality and anonymity, individual expression and personal style are stressed; spareness and economy (in accord with Mies's famous dictum "less is more") are now often superseded by richness and elaboration. Similarly, flat, planar compositions have given way to fluid sculptural forms; and the divisive floor plan, in which a single space is divided into units, has given way to an additive plan, in which individual, strongly articulated elements are rhythmically grouped together. Some of these qualities are to be found in Wright's work; others exist in Le Corbusier's later works, such as the chapel at Ronchamp, France. Certain features of the new architecture—such as its insistence on the strong, the direct, and the monumental—derive directly from the Chicago School, which has re-emerged as a major source of inspiration for contemporary American architects.

In general, the current reaction has been against the extremes of transparency and lightness—the pictorial qualities that belie the Cubist roots of the International Style—in favor of a new solidity, massiveness, and forcefulness. At present, three main lines of development, at times overlapping, may be observed: first, neotraditionalism, which asserts the freedom of the architect to be eclectic and to mine art history for inspiration without embarrassment; second, a freer, more primitive style often related to sculpture in its forms; and third, a more emphatic and robustly monumental style, which in its blunt articulation of individual elements and boldness of design has been described as "the new brutalism." Stylistically these three distinct modes of expression can be characterized as an art-for-art's-sake eclecticism stressing richness and elegance; a baroque, exuberant style of fluid contours and bulging volumes; and finally, a ponderous, severe style whose grave masses evoke an archaic monumentality. The new architecture often prefers reinforced concrete, stone, and rock to glass and steel.

Ease of travel and availability of photographs of exotic models have given impetus to the new eclectics. Often the neotraditionalists have been formed by the International Style, so that their work, in many cases, represents merely a revision of Miesian forms, overlaid with rich materials. It is not unusual, for example, to see Moorish screens embellishing the pure frontality of standard rectangles, or the delicate arches of a Gothic narthex decorating the entrance to a conventional theater. Not surprisingly, such eclectic structures have been found particularly suitable to house cultural enterprises; examples include Edward Stone's Gallery of Modern Art in New York, his project for the John F. Kennedy Center of the Performing Arts in Washington, D.C., and Harrison and Abramovitz' Lincoln Center buildings in New York and Dartmouth College Hopkins Center.

But the quest for richness and elegance is not the search which occupies today's most progressive American architects. Louis Kahn, pioneer of a direct and uncompromising formalist architecture, and Gropius' pupils, I. M. Pei and Paul Rudolph, have successfully dealt with problems of mass and scale in contemporary terms. Younger architects such as Robert Venturi and Charles Moore are searching through art history in order to reconstruct the expressive power of a vital style like the Baroque.

With architectural schools offering training as sound, thorough, and up-to-date as any in the world, young American architects today are in an enviable position. But the problem, as always, is one of taste as well as of education. Because the architect cannot subsidize his work merely by lowering his living standard, architecture, more than the other arts, is closely tied to patronage, to the taste of the client. In America, some thoughtful businessmen have been most receptive to progressive ideas. On the other hand, official taste—the taste of the U.S. Congress, and of state governments—has been notoriously laggard, continuing to choose a moribund, academic Neoclassicism for monuments and public buildings. Until recently, the taste of religious and educational institutions, with few exceptions, has been conservative and undistinguished. Since the fifties, however, progressive institutions have been responsible for commissioning many of the best buildings built in America. Examples include Harvard's 1960 Fine Arts Building (Le Corbusier's single commission in the United States) and Paul Rudolph's 1957 Wellesley College Art Center. The new Yale campus buildings—Rudolph's Art and Architecture building (*Ill 10-19*), Louis Kahn's art gallery, and Eero Saarinen's new colleges and hockey rink—represent a distinguished university complex. Kahn's

10-19. PAUL RUDOLPH, Yale School of Art and Architecture, Yale University, New Haven, Connecticut, 1961–63.

10-20. LOUIS KAHN, Richards Medical Research Building, University of Pennsylvania, Philadelphia, 1957–61.

Richards Medical Research Building at the University of Pennsylvania (*Ill. 10-20*) is a high mark in contemporary architecture. Outstanding contemporary churches and synagogues also have been designed by Wright, Saarinen, Kahn, and others.

As the second half of the twentieth century unfolds, one may expect a greater emphasis to be placed on matters which formerly concerned only visionary architects like Wright, Le Corbusier, Frederick Kiesler, and Buckminster Fuller and utopian critics, such as Lewis Mumford, Colin Rowe, Vincent Scully, and Reyner Banham. Primary issues confronting today's architects are community planning, urban decongestion, the humanizing of both domestic and commercial architecture, the use of standardized mass production for greater efficiency and economy, the enlistment of the machine as a tool rather than a model. The present may be viewed as the beginning of an epoch in which the promise of the technological revolution at last will be realized. For, when we have mastered, as cyberneticist Norbert Wiener put it, "the human use of human beings," the machine will no longer be a god or devil but the tool and servant of man.

# Notes

## CHAPTER ONE

[1] As quoted in Lloyd Goodrich, *Thomas Eakins, His Life and Work* (New York: Whitney Museum of American Art, 1933), p. 139.

[2] Everett Shinn, "Recollections of The Eight," in *The Eight* (Brooklyn: Brooklyn Institute of Arts and Sciences, 1943), p. 11. Catalogue of the Brooklyn Museum Exhibition, November 24, 1943–January 16, 1944.

[3] Robert Henri, *The Art Spirit*, comp. Margery A. Reyerson (Philadelphia: J. B. Lippincott, 1960), p. 71.

[4] John Sloan, *Gist of Art* (New York: American Artists Group, 1939), p. 38.

## CHAPTER TWO

[1] Alfred Stieglitz, "Six Happenings," *Twice a Year*, Nos. 14–15 (1946–47), p. 117.

[2] Paul Haviland in *291*, No. 1 (March, 1915), unpaginated.

[3] Oscar Bluemner, "What Is 291?" *Camera Work*, No. 47 (July, 1914), p. 53.

[4] Max Weber, "Chinese Dolls and Modern Colorists," *Camera Work*, No. 31 (July, 1910), p. 51.

[5] *Ibid.*

[6] Abraham Walkowitz, in a statement for the Archives of American Art, *Art in America*, LIII, No. 4 (August–September, 1965), 76.

[7] Georgia O'Keeffe, Catalogue statement for an exhibition at the Anderson Gallery, January, 1923; quoted in Daniel Catton Rich, *Georgia O'Keeffe* (Chicago: Art Institute of Chicago, 1943), p. 22. Exhibition Catalogue.

[8] John Marin, *Selected Writings of John Marin*, ed. Dorothy Norman (New York: Pellegrini and Cudahy, 1949), p. 197.

[9] Lewis Mumford, "The Metropolitan Milieu," in *America and Alfred Stieglitz*, eds. W. Frank, L. Mumford, D. Norman, P. Rosenfeld, H. Rugg (New York: Doubleday, Doran & Co., 1934), p. 46.

[10] Paul Rosenfeld, "The Boy in the Dark Room," in *ibid.*, p. 86.

[11] *Ibid.*

[12] John Marin, "A Few Notes," *Twice a Year*, No. 2 (1939), p. 177.

[13] Marsden Hartley, "Art—and the Personal Life," *Creative Art*, II (June, 1928), xxxii.

[14] Arthur Dove, as quoted in Frederick S. Wight, *Arthur G. Dove* (Berkeley: University of California Press, 1958), p. 37.

[15] *Ibid.*, p. 64.

[16] Elizabeth McCausland, Alfred Maurer Exhibition Catalogue, Buchholz Gallery, 1943.

[17] Gertrude Stein, *The Autobiography of Alice B. Toklas* (New York: Modern Library, 1933), p. 11.

[18] Sherwood Anderson, broadside reproduced by Elizabeth McCausland in *A. H. Maurer* (New York: A. A. Wyn, 1951), p. 156.

[19] Marsden Hartley, "291—and the Brass Bowl," in *America and Alfred Stieglitz*, p. 239.

## CHAPTER THREE

[1] Walt Kuhn, in a letter to his wife, December 12, 1911, published in *Art in America*, LIII, No. 4 (August–September, 1965), 71.

[2] As quoted in Milton Brown, *The Story of the Armory Show* (New York: Joseph H. Hirshhorn Foundation, 1963), p. 39.

3 Walt Kuhn, as quoted in Brown, *ibid.*, p. 56.

4 As quoted in Brown, *ibid.*, p. 26.

5 Frank J. Mather, Jr., "Newest Tendencies in Art," *The Independent*, LXXIV (March, 1913), 512.

6 Jerome Myers, *An Artist in Manhattan* (New York: American Artists Group, 1940), p. 37.

7 *Ibid.*, p. 36.

8 Quoted in Brown, *op. cit.*, p. 63.

9 Milton Brown, *American Painting from the Armory Show to the Depression* (Princeton, N.J.: Princeton University Press, 1955), p. 52.

10 Ben Benn, in the Catalogue of the Forum Exhibition (New York: Hugh Kennerly, 1916), explanatory notes.

11 W. H. de B. Nelson, in *ibid.*, p. 34.

## CHAPTER FOUR

1 Henry McBride, "A Hero Worshipped," *The Dial*, LXIX (July–December, 1920), 91.

2 Andrew Dasburg, "Cubism—Its Rise and Influence," *The Arts*, IV (November, 1923), 280.

3 Lee Simonson, "No Embargos," *Creative Art*, VIII (April, 1931), 255.

4 *Ibid.*

5 As quoted in William C. Agee, *Synchromism and Color Principles in American Painting* (New York: M. Knoedler & Co., Inc., 1965), p. 19.

6 *Ibid.*, p. 36.

7 *Ibid.*

8 Henri Pierre Roché, statement on Patrick Henry Bruce, in the Catalogue of the Société Anonyme (New Haven, Conn.: Yale University Art Gallery, 1950), p. 144.

9 *Ibid.*, p. 143.

10 Charles Burchfield, "On the Middle Border," *Creative Art*, III (September, 1928), xxix.

11 Charles Sheeler, as quoted in Lillian Dochterman, *The Quest of Charles Sheeler* (Iowa City: State University of Iowa Press, 1963), p. 11.

12 Joseph Stella, "The Brooklyn Bridge (A Page of My Life)," *transition*, Nos. 16–17 (June, 1929), p. 87.

13 Sheeler, as quoted in Dochterman, *op. cit.*, p. 13.

14 Christian Brinton, *Modern Art at the Sesqui-Centennial Exhibition* (New York: Société Anonyme, 1926), unpaginated.

## CHAPTER FIVE

1 John Sloan, *Gist of Art*, p. 3.

2 Arthur Dove, as quoted in Frederick S. Wight, *Arthur G. Dove*, p. 62.

3 Stuart Davis, as quoted in H. H. Arnason, *Stuart Davis* (Washington, D.C.: National Collection of Fine Arts, 1965), p. 42.

4 As quoted in Thomas Craven, *Thomas Hart Benton* (New York: Associated American Artists, 1939), p. 11.

5 Thomas Hart Benton, *An Artist in America* (New York: Robert M. McBride & Co., 1937), p. 48.

6 *Ibid.*, p. 319.

7 Edward Hopper, "Charles Burchfield, American," *The Arts*, XIV (July, 1928), 7.

8 Lewis Mumford, as quoted in Oliver Larkin, *Art and Life in America* (New York: Holt, Rinehart and Winston, 1964), p. 430.

9 Peter Blume, in *Painters on Painting*, ed. Eric Protter (New York: Grossett & Dunlap, 1963), p. 244.

10 George L. K. Morris, "Art Chronicle," *Partisan Review* (1943).

[11] Stuart Davis, as quoted in E. C. Goossen, *Stuart Davis* (New York: George Braziller, 1959), p. 13.

[12] *Ibid.*, p. 11.

[13] As quoted in J. J. Sweeney, *Stuart Davis* (New York: Museum of Modern Art, 1945), p. 16.

[14] As quoted in Goossen, *op. cit.*, p. 28.

[15] Stuart Davis, statement on his painting *The Paris Bit*, in Lloyd Goodrich, "Rebirth of a National Collection," *Art in America*, LIII, No. 3 (June, 1965), 89.

[16] Arshile Gorky, "Stuart Davis," *Creative Art*, IX (September, 1931), 213.

[17] *Ibid.*

[18] Clement Greenberg, "The Late Thirties in New York," in *Art and Culture* (Boston: Beacon Press, 1961), p. 232.

[19] William Seitz, *Hans Hofmann* (New York: Museum of Modern Art, 1963), p. 56.

[20] *Ibid.*, p. 39.

[21] Reported by Gorky's wife in a letter to Patricia Passloff, in *The 30's: Painting in New York* (New York: Poindexter Gallery, 1957). Exhibition Catalogue.

### CHAPTER SIX

[1] Peggy Guggenheim, *Confessions of an Art Addict* (New York: The Macmillan Co., 1960), p. 101.

[2] Peggy Guggenheim, introduction to *The Peggy Guggenheim Collection* (London: British Arts Council, 1964), p. 10. Exhibition at the Tate Gallery, December 31, 1964–March 7, 1965.

[3] André Breton, broadside for Gorky's exhibition at the Julien Levy Gallery, 1945. Museum of Modern Art Archives.

[4] Meyer Schapiro, "Gorky: The Creative Influence," *Art News* (September, 1957), p. 29.

[5] Julien Levy, foreword to William Seitz, *Arshile Gorky* (New York: Museum of Modern Art, 1962), p. 8.

[6] Seitz, *op. cit.*, p. 30.

[7] This discussion of Pollock's space and drawing is based on Michael Fried, *Three American Painters* (Cambridge, Mass.: Fogg Art Museum, 1965), pp. 10–23.

[8] Robert Motherwell, "The Modern Painter's World," *Dyn* (1944), p. 13.

### CHAPTER SEVEN

[1] Barnett Newman, statement in the Catalogue of the VIII São Paulo Biennial (Washington, D.C.: National Collection of Fine Arts, 1966), p. 9.

[2] The nature and chronology of this issue are discussed by Rubin in "Jackson Pollock and the Modern Tradition," Parts I and II, *Artforum*, February and March, 1967.

[3] Mark Rothko and Adolph Gottlieb, letter to *The New York Times*, June 13, 1943, Sec. 2, p. 9.

### CHAPTER EIGHT

[1] Allan Kaprow, "The Legacy of Jackson Pollock," *Art News* (October, 1958), p. 24.

### CHAPTER NINE

[1] David Smith, "Notes on My Work," *Arts*, XXXIV (February, 1960), p. 44.

[2] David Smith, "The Secret Letter," an interview by Thomas B. Hess in *David Smith* (New York: Marlborough-Gerson Gallery, 1964), unpaginated. Exhibition Catalogue.

[3] *Ibid.*

[4] Hilton Kramer, *David Smith* (Los Angeles, Calif.: Los Angeles County Museum of Art, November 3, 1965–January 30, 1966), p. 4. Memorial Exhibition.

[5] As quoted in Sam Hunter, *Modern American Painting and Sculpture* (New York: Dell Publishing Co., 1959), p. 178.

## CHAPTER TEN

[1] Montgomery Schuyler, "The Point of View," in *American Architecture and Other Writings* (New York: Atheneum Publishers, 1964), p. 57.

[2] Montgomery Schuyler, "An Architectural Pioneer: Review of the Portfolios Containing the Works of Frank Lloyd Wright," in *ibid.*, p. 316.

[3] Montgomery Schuyler, "The Beaux-Arts Reaction," in *ibid.*, p. 292.

[4] Louis H. Sullivan, *The Autobiography of an Idea* (New York: American Institute of Architects, 1924), p. 325.

[5] Henry-Russell Hitchcock and Philip Johnson, *The International Style: Architecture Since 1922* (New York: W. W. Norton, 1932), p. 19.

[6] R. M. Schindler, as quoted in Wayne Andrews, *Architecture, Ambition and Americans* (New York: The Free Press of Glencoe, 1964), p. 276.

# Selected Bibliography

*Those works cited in the Chapter Notes are not included in the Bibliography.*

GENERAL

*Art in America.* LIII, No. 4 (August–September, 1965). Archives of American Art issue.

GELDZAHLER, HENRY. *American Painting in the Twentieth Century.* New York: Metropolitan Museum of Art, 1965.

HUNTER, SAM. *Modern American Painting and Sculpture.* New York: Dell Publishing Co., 1959.

LARKIN, OLIVER W. *Art and Life in America.* Rev. ed. New York: Holt, Rinehart and Winston, 1964.

McCAUSLAND, ELIZABETH. "A Selected Bibliography on American Painting and Sculpture," in *Who's Who in American Art*, IV, 611–53. Washington, D.C.: American Federation of Arts, 1947. Originally appeared in the *Magazine of Art*, XXXIX (November, 1946), 329–49.

CHAPTER ONE

GLACKENS, IRA. *William Glackens and the Ashcan Group.* New York: Grosset & Dunlap, 1957.

*New York Realists, 1900–1914.* New York: Whitney Museum of American Art, 1937.

PERLMAN, BENNARD P. *The Immortal Eight: American Painting from Eakins to the Armory Show.* New York: Exposition Press, 1962.

CHAPTER TWO

*Camera Work,* 1902–17.

McCAUSLAND, ELIZABETH. *Marsden Hartley.* Minneapolis, Minn.: University of Minnesota Press, 1952.

MELLQUIST, JEROME. *The Emergence of an American Art.* New York: Scribner's, 1942.

Rosenfeld, Paul. *Port of New York: Essays on Fourteen American Moderns.* New York: Harcourt, Brace, 1924.

*291.* Ed. Alfred Stieglitz. Nos. 1–12 (1915–16).

Williams, W. C., Phillips, D., and Norman, D. *John Marin.* Los Angeles, Calif.: University of California Press, 1955. Memorial Exhibition.

CHAPTER THREE

Catalogue of the Forum Exhibition, Anderson Galleries. New York: Hugh Kennerly, 1916.

Collection of the Société Anonyme. New Haven, Conn.: Yale University Art Gallery, 1950.

Schapiro, Meyer. "Rebellion in Art," in *America in Crisis.* Ed. Daniel Aaron. New York: Alfred A. Knopf, 1952.

Wright, Willard H. "The Aesthetic Struggle in America," *Forum,* LV (January–June, 1916).

CHAPTER FOUR

Baur, John I. H. "The Machine and the Subconscious: Dada in America," *Magazine of Art,* XLIV (October, 1951).

Breeskin, Adelyn. *Roots of Abstract in America, 1910–1950.* Washington, D.C.: National Collection of Fine Arts, 1965.

Friedman, Martin. *The Precisionist View in American Art.* Minneapolis, Minn.: Walker Art Center, 1960.

Ritchie, Andrew C. *Abstract Painting and Sculpture in America.* New York: Museum of Modern Art, 1951.

CHAPTER FIVE

American Abstract Artists. Annual Exhibition Catalogue and checklist from 1937.

Greenberg, Clement. "New York Painting Only Yesterday," *Art News* (Summer, 1957).

Kootz, Samuel. *Modern American Painters.* New York: Brewer and Warren, 1930.

Miller, Dorothy C. (ed.). *American Realists and Magic Realists.* New York: Museum of Modern Art, 1943.

O'Connor, Francis V. *Federal Art Patronage, 1933–1943.* College Park, Md.: University of Maryland Press, 1966.

Schapiro, Meyer. "Populist Realism," *Partisan Review,* IV (December, 1937–May, 1938). Review of Thomas Hart Benton autobiography.

CHAPTER SIX

Janis, Sidney. *Abstract and Surrealist Art in America.* New York: Reynal & Hitchcock, 1944.

Rubin, William. "Arshile Gorky, Surrealism and the New American Painting," *Art International,* VII, No. 2 (February 25, 1963).

———. *Jackson Pollock and the Modern Tradition.* New York: Harry N. Abrams, 1967.

*Tiger's Eye.* Nos. 1–9 (1947–49). Eds. R. and J. Stephan.

CHAPTER SEVEN

Arnason, H. H. *Abstract Expressionists and Imagists.* New York: Solomon R. Guggenheim Museum, 1961.

*Artforum* (Summer, 1965). A special number devoted to Abstract Expressionism.

Ashton, Dore. *The Unknown Shore: A View of Contemporary Art.* Boston: Little, Brown and Co., 1962.

Catalogues of the annual exhibitions: Art Institute of Chicago; Whitney Museum; Corcoran Gallery; University of Illinois Biennial; "Americans" exhibitions, Museum of Modern Art, selected by Dorothy Miller.

*Clyfford Still, Paintings in the Albright-Knox Art Gallery.* Buffalo, N.Y.: Buffalo Fine Arts Academy, 1966.

Goossen, E. C. "The Big Canvas," *Art International,* II, No. 8 (November, 1958).

Hess, Thomas B. *Abstract Painting: Background and American Phase.* New York: Viking Press, 1951.

————. *Willem de Kooning*. New York: George Braziller, 1959.

KOZLOFF, MAX. "The Impact of De Kooning," *Arts Yearbook*, No. 7 (1964).

MOTHERWELL, ROBERT, and REINHARDT, AD (eds.). *Modern Artists in America*. First Series. New York: Wittenborn, Schultz, 1951.

*The New American Painting*. New York: Museum of Modern Art, 1959.

*New York School*. Los Angeles, Calif.: Los Angeles County Museum of Art, 1965. Baziotes, De Kooning, Gorky, Gottlieb, Guston, Hofmann, Motherwell, Newman, Pollock, Pousette-Dart, Reinhardt, Rothko, Still, Tomlin.

O'HARA, FRANK. *Robert Motherwell*. With selections from the artist's writings. New York: Museum of Modern Art, 1966.

ROSENBLUM, ROBERT. "Abstract Sublime," *Art News* (February, 1961).

SCHAPIRO, MEYER. "The Liberating Quality of Abstract Art," *Art News* (Summer, 1957).

CHAPTER EIGHT

ALLOWAY, LAWRENCE. *Systemic Painting*. New York: Solomon R. Guggenheim Museum, 1966.

Exhibition catalogues, Venice and São Paulo biennials.

GREENBERG, CLEMENT. "After Abstract Expressionism," *Art International*, VI, No. 8 (October 25, 1962).

————."Louis and Noland," *Art International*, IV, No. 4 (May 25, 1960).

————. "Post Painterly Abstraction," *Art International*, VIII, Nos. 5–6 (Summer, 1964).

KIRBY, MICHAEL. *Happenings*. New York: E. P. Dutton, 1965.

LIPPARD, LUCY R. *Pop Art*. New York: Frederick A. Praeger, 1966.

*New Abstraction, Das Kunstwerk*. XVIII, Nos. 10–12 (April–June, 1965).

RUBIN, WILLIAM. "Younger American Painters," *Art International*, IV, No. 1 (January, 1960).

SEITZ, WILLIAM C. *The Responsive Eye*. New York: Museum of Modern Art, 1964.

STEINBERG, LEO. *Jasper Johns*. New York: George Wittenborn, 1963.

TILLIM, SIDNEY. "The New Avant-Garde," *Arts*, XXXVIII (February, 1964).

CHAPTER NINE

*Artforum* (Summer, 1967). Special issue on American sculpture.

Catalogues of the Whitney Annual. (Sculpture and painting in alternate years.)

CONE, JANE HARRISON. *David Smith*. Cambridge, Mass.: Fogg Art Museum, 1965.

*Contemporary Sculpture*. Introduction by William C. Seitz. *Arts Yearbook*, No. 8 (1965).

GOODALL, DONALD. "Gaston Lachaise, 1882–1935," *Massachusetts Review* (Summer, 1960).

GREENBERG, CLEMENT. "Cross-breeding of Modern Sculpture," *Art News* (Summer, 1952).

GRIFFEN, HOWARD. "Auriga, Andromeda, Cameoleoparalis," *Art News* (December, 1957). On Joseph Cornell.

"The Ides of Art: 14 Sculptors Write," *Tiger's Eye*, No. 4 (June, 1948).

MCSHINE, KYNASTON. *Primary Structures*. New York: Jewish Museum, 1966.

O'HARA, FRANK. *Nakian*. New York: Museum of Modern Art, 1966.

*Sculpture in America Today*. Los Angeles, Calif.: Los Angeles County Museum, 1967.

SEITZ, WILLIAM C. *The Art of Assemblage*. New York: Museum of Modern Art, 1961.

SWEENEY, JAMES J. *Alexander Calder*. New York: Solomon R. Guggenheim Museum, 1964.

CHAPTER TEN

BURCHARD, JOHN, and BUSH-BROWN, ALBERT. *The Architecture of America*. Boston: Little, Brown and Co., 1961.

CONDIT, CARL W. *The Chicago School of Architecture*. Chicago: University of Chicago Press, 1964.

HITCHCOCK, HENRY-RUSSELL, and DREXLER, ARTHUR (eds.). *Built in USA: Post-War Architecture*. New York: Museum of Modern Art, 1952.

MUMFORD, LEWIS. *Roots of Contemporary American Architecture*. New York: Grove Press, 1959.

SCULLY, VINCENT J. *Frank Lloyd Wright*. New York: George Braziller, 1960.

# List of Illustrations

Artists are listed in alphabetical order. All works are oil on canvas unless otherwise noted. Numbers opposite titles indicate Chapter and Plate No.

AGOSTINI, Peter (1913– )
*Christmas Package*, 1963     **9-31**
Plaster, 23½" h.
Courtesy Stephen Radich Gallery, New York

ALBERS, Josef (1888– )
*Homage to the Square: Frislan*, 1955     **6-3**
Oil on board, 32" x 32"
Collection Nathalie Rahv, Boston
Courtesy Sidney Janis Gallery, New York

ALBRIGHT, Ivan (1897– )
*That Which I Should Have Done I Did Not Do*, 1931–41     **5-15**
97" x 36"
Courtesy The Art Institute of Chicago

AULT, George (1891–1941)
*Sullivan Street Abstraction*, 1928     **4-25**
24" x 30"
Courtesy Zabriskie Gallery, New York
Photograph John D. Schiff

AVERY, Milton (1893–1964)
*Baby Avery*, 1932     **5-23**
36" x 28"
Collection Mrs. Milton Avery, New York
Courtesy Grace Borgenicht Gallery, New York

*Mother and Child*, 1944     **5-24**
40" x 30"
Courtesy Grace Borgenicht Gallery, New York

BANNARD, Darby (1931– )
*Green Grip I*, 1965     **8-20**
Alkyd resin on canvas, 67" x 63"
Courtesy Tibor de Nagy Gallery, New York
Photograph Eric Pollitzer

BAZIOTES, William (1912–1963)
*Congo*, 1954     **6-9**
71¼" x 59¾"
Collection Los Angeles County Museum of Art, Gift of Mrs. Leonard Sperry, through the Contemporary Art Council

BELLOWS, George (1882–1925)
*Stag at Sharkey's*, 1907     **3-13**
36¼" x 48¼"
The Cleveland Museum of Art, Hinman B. Hurlbut Collection

*The Circus*, 1912     **3-5**
34" x 44"
Addison Gallery of American Art, Phillips Academy, Andover, Mass.

*Dempsey and Firpo*, 1924     **3-14**
51" x 63¼"
Collection Whitney Museum of American Art, New York

BENTON, Thomas Hart (1889– )
*City Scenes*, 1930     **5-6**
Oil on board, 77½" x 145½"
New School for Social Research, New York

BIDDLE, George (1885– )
*Sweatshop, ca.* 1935     **5-11**
Study for fresco, fifth floor stairwell, Justice Department Building, Washington, D.C.
Tempera on masonite, 40¾" x 31⅞"
Collection University of Maryland, College Park, Md.

BISHOP, Isabel (1902– )
*Nude*, 1934     **5-4**
Oil on composition board, 33" x 40"
Collection Whitney Museum of American Art, New York

BLUEMNER, Oscar (1867–1938)
*Old Canal Port*, 1914        **2-1**
30¼" x 40¼"
Collection Whitney Museum of American Art, New York

BLUME, Peter (1906–    )
*South of Scranton*, 1931      **5-16**
56" x 66"
The Metropolitan Museum of Art, New York, George A. Hearn Fund

BOLOTOWSKY, Ilya (1907–    )
*White Abstraction*, 1934–35    **5-37**
36¾" x 19"
Courtesy Grace Borgenicht Gallery, New York

BONTECOU, Lee (1931–    )
*Untitled*, 1962             **9-33**
Welded steel with canvas, 75" x 83" x 28"
Courtesy Leo Castelli Gallery, New York

BRAQUE, Georges (1882–1963)
*L'Affiche de Kubelick (Le Violon)*,
1912                      **3-9**
18" x 24"
Collection Andreas L. Speiser, Basel, Switzerland

BRUCE, Patrick Henry (1881–1937)
*Still Life*, ca. 1929–30       **4-10**
23¼" x 36"
Collection Benjamin Garber, New York

BURCHFIELD, Charles (1893–1967)
*Noontide in Late May*, 1917    **5-8**
Water color and gouache, 21⅜" x 17⅜"
Collection Whitney Museum of American Art, New York

CALDER, Alexander, (1898–    )
*Little Red Under Blue*, 1947    **9-10**
Iron-like construction, 58" x ca. 82"
Courtesy Fogg Art Museum, Harvard University, Cambridge, Mass.

*Three Arches*, 1963          **9-11**
Painted metal, 108" x 112½" x 145"
Munson-Williams-Proctor Institute, Utica, N.Y.

CARLES, Arthur B. (1882–1952)
*L'Eglise*, ca. 1910         **2-2**
31" x 39"

The Metropolitan Museum of Art, New York, Arthur H. Hearn Fund, 1962

*Abstraction*, 1939–41         **5-43**
40" x 58"
Courtesy The Graham Gallery, New York

CAVALLON, Giorgio (1904–    )
*Untitled*, 1938–39           **5-36**
17" x 14"
Collection the artist, New York

CÉZANNE, Paul (1839–1906)
*Poorhouse on the Hill*, ca. 1895  **3-10**
32" x 25⅝"
The Metropolitan Museum of Art, New York, Wolfe Fund, 1913

CHAMBERLAIN, John (1927–    )
*Mr. Press*, 1961            **9-29**
Metal relief, 95" x 90" x 50"
Collection Henry Geldzahler, New York
Courtesy Leo Castelli Gallery, New York

CHASE, William Merritt (1849–1916)
*An English Cod*, 1904         **1-2**
36¼" x 40¼"
Collection The Corcoran Gallery of Art, Washington, D.C.

CORNELL, Joseph (1903–    )
*Chocolat Menier*, 1950        **9-34**
Wood with collage, 17" x 12" x 4¾"
Courtesy Tibor de Nagy Gallery, New York
Photograph Eric Pollitzer

COVERT, John (1882–1960)
*Vocalization*, 1919          **4-14**
Oil and wooden dowels nailed to composition board, 23¾" x 26½"
Yale University Art Gallery, New Haven, Conn., Collection Société Anonyme, Gift of the artist

CRAWFORD, Ralston (1906–    )
*Grain Elevators from the Bridge*,
1942                     **4-26**
50" x 40"
Collection Whitney Museum of American Art, New York, Gift of the Friends of the Whitney Museum of American Art

DAVIES, Arthur B. (1862–1928)
*Unicorns*, 1906             **1-14**
18¼" x 40¼"

The Metropolitan Museum of Art, New York, Bequest of Lizzie P. Bliss, 1931

*Intermezzo, ca.* 1913      **3-17**
Oil on panel, 28″ x 14″
Courtesy The Graham Gallery, New York
Photograph Rudolph Burckhardt

DAVIS, Stuart (1894–1964)
*The President,* 1917      **5-26**
36″ x 26¼″
Munson-Williams-Proctor Institute, Utica, N.Y.

*Lucky Strike,* 1921      **5-27**
33¼″ x 18″
Collection The Museum of Modern Art, New York, Gift of The American Tobacco Company, Inc.

*Egg Beater, Number 2,* 1927      **5-28**
29⅛″ x 36″
Collection Whitney Museum of American Art, New York
Photograph Geoffrey Clements

*Hot Still-Scape for Six Colors,*
1940      **5-29**
36″ x 45″
Collection Mrs. Edith Gregor Halpert, New York
Courtesy The Downtown Gallery
Photograph Geoffrey Clements

*The Paris Bit,* 1959      **5-30**
46″ x 60″
Collection Whitney Museum of American Art, New York, Gift of the Friends of the Whitney Museum of American Art

DE KOONING, Willem (1904–   )
*Untitled,* 1937      **5-38**
Oil on board, 8″ x 13½″
Collection Mr. and Mrs. Stephen D. Paine, Boston
Photograph Barney Burstein

*Queen of Hearts,* 1943–46      **6-32**
Oil on board, 46″ x 27½″
Collection Joseph H. Hirshhorn, New York

*Pink Angels, ca.* 1947      **6-36**
52″ x 40″
Collection Mr. and Mrs. Frederick R. Weisman, Beverly Hills, Calif.

*Woman,* 1948      **6-33**
44½″ x 53½″
The Joseph H. Hirshhorn Foundation, New York

*Sailcloth, ca.* 1949      **6-35**
27″ x 32″
Courtesy Sidney Janis Gallery, New York

*Excavation,* 1950      **6-38**
80⅛″ x 100⅛″
Courtesy The Art Institute of Chicago

*Woman, I,* 1950–52      **6-34**
75⅞″ x 58″
Collection The Museum of Modern Art, New York

DEMUTH, Charles (1883–1935)
*Trees and Barns, Bermuda,* 1917      **4-20**
Water color, 9½″ x 13½″
Williams College Museum of Art, Williamstown, Mass.

*Machinery,* 1920      **4-21**
Tempera and pencil on cardboard, 24″ x 19⅞″
The Metropolitan Museum of Art, New York, Alfred Stieglitz Collection, 1949

*Incense of a New Church,* 1921      **4-24**
25½″ x 19¾″
Howard Collection, Columbus Gallery of Fine Arts, Columbus, Ohio

*My Egypt,* 1927      **4-32**
Oil on composition board, 35¾″ x 30″
Collection Whitney Museum of American Art, New York

DE RIVERA, José (1904–   )
*Construction #85,* 1964      **9-36**
Bronze, 8″ x 10″ x 10″
Collection Mr. and Mrs. Herbert Beenhouwer, Scarsdale, N.Y.
Courtesy Grace Borgenicht Gallery, New York

DICKINSON, Edwin (1891–   )
*The Fossil Hunters,* 1926–28      **5-20**
96½″ x 73¾″
Collection Whitney Museum of American Art, New York

DICKINSON, Preston (1891–1930)
*Industry, II, ca.* 1924      **4-2**
24¾″ x 30″

Collection Whitney Museum of American Art, New York, Gift of Mr. and Mrs. Alan H. Temple
Photograph Oliver Baker Associates

DIEBENKORN, Richard (1922–    )
*Girl and Three Coffee Cups,* 1957    **8-21**
59″ x 54″
Collection Richard Brown Baker, New York

DILLER, Burgoyne (1906–65)
*First Theme,* 1955–60    **6-4**
Collection Mrs. Burgoyne Diller, Atlantic Highlands, N.J.
Courtesy Galerie Chalette, New York

DI SUVERO, Mark (1933–    )
*Hank Champion,* 1960    **9-28**
Wood and chain, 84″ x 120″
Collection Mr. and Mrs. Robert C. Scull, New York
Courtesy Park Place Gallery, New York

DOVE, Arthur (1880–1946)
*Nature Symbolized, No. 2,* 1914    **2-23**
Pastel on paper, 18″ x 21⅜″
The Art Institute of Chicago, Alfred Stieglitz Collection

*Sentimental Music,* 1917    **2-24**
Pastel, 21¼″ x 17⅞″
The Metropolitan Museum of Art, New York, Alfred Stieglitz Collection, 1949

*Portrait of Ralph Dusenberry,* 1924    **4-13**
Oil on canvas with applied wood and paper, 22″ x 18″
The Metropolitan Museum of Art, New York, Alfred Stieglitz Collection, 1949

*Fog Horns,* 1929    **2-25**
18″ x 26″
Colorado Springs Fine Arts Center, Gift of Oliver B. James

*High Noon,* 1944    **2-26**
Oil on composition board, 27″ x 36″
Wichita Art Museum, Wichita, Kan.
Roland P. Murdock Collection

DUCHAMP, Marcel (1887–    )
*Nude Descending a Staircase, No. 2,* 1912    **3-8**
58″ x 35″
Philadelphia Museum of Art, Louise and Walter Arensberg Collection

*Chocolate Grinder, No. 2,* 1914    **4-16**

Oil, thread, and pencil on canvas, 25½″ x 21¼″
Philadelphia Museum of Art, Louise and Walter Arensberg Collection

EVERGOOD, Philip (1901–    )
*The New Lazarus,* 1927–54    **5-18**
48″ x 83¼″
Collection Whitney Museum of American Art, New York, Gift of Joseph H. Hirshhorn

FEININGER, Lyonel (1871–1956)
*Gelmeroda, VIII,* 1921    **6-1**
39¼″ x 31¼″
Collection Whitney Museum of American Art, New York

FERBER, Herbert (1906–    )
*Spherical Sculpture,* 1954–62    **9-20**
Bronze, 36½″ x 25″
Courtesy André Emmerich Gallery, New York

FERREN, John (1905–    )
*Multiplicity,* 1937    **5-32**
44¾″ x 57½″
The Solomon R. Guggenheim Museum, New York

FLANNAGAN, John (1895–1942)
*Jonah and the Whale,* 1937    **9-9**
Bronze, 29½″ x 11″ x 3″
The Minneapolis Institute of Arts

FRANCIS, Sam (1923–    )
*Blue on a Point,* 1958    **8-9**
72″ x 96″
Collection Mrs. Harry Doniger, Rye, N.Y.
Courtesy Martha Jackson Gallery, New York

FRANKENTHALER, Helen (1928–    )
*Mountains and Sea,* 1952    **8-10**
86⅜″ x 117¼″
Collection the artist, New York
Courtesy The Smithsonian Institution, Washington, D.C.

FROST, Arthur B. (1851–1928)
*Colored Forms,* 1917    **4-9**
Present whereabouts unknown
Photograph Geoffrey Clements

GILBERT, Cass (1858–1934)
Woolworth Building, New York, 1913    **10-9**

GILL, Irving (1870–1936)
Ellen Scripps House, La Jolla, Calif.,
1917                                    10-13

GLACKENS, William (1870–1938)
*Chez Mouquin,* 1905                   1-3
48⅜" x 36¼"
Courtesy The Art Institute of Chicago,
Friends of American Art Collection

*The Shoppers,* 1908                   1-5
60" x 60"
Collection Walter P. Chrysler, Jr., New
York

*Nude with Apple,* 1910               1-15
40" x 57"
The Brooklyn Museum, New York

*Family Group,* 1911                   3-3
72" x 84"
Collection Mr. and Mrs. Ira Glackens,
Washington, D.C.

GLARNER, Fritz (1899–    )
*Relational Painting: Tondo #43,*
1956                                   6-5
Oil on panel, 16" diam.
Collection Lucie Glarner, Huntington,
N.Y.

GORKY, Arshile (1905–48)
*The Artist and His Mother,*
1926–29                                5-42
60" x 50"
Collection Whitney Museum of American Art, New York, Gift of Julien
Levy for Maro and Natasha Gorky in
memory of their father

*Organization,* 1932                   5-40
49¾" x 60"
Courtesy Sidney Janis Gallery, New
York
Photograph Eric Pollitzer

*Aviation: Evolution of Forms Under
Aerodynamic Limitations, ca.*
1936                                   5-13
Study for mural, Administration Build-
ing, Newark Airport, Newark, N.J.
Gouache on paper, 13⅝" x 29⅞"
On extended loan to The Museum of
Modern Art, New York, from the
United States WPA Art Program

*Garden in Sochi,* 1941                6-13
44¼" x 62¼"

Collection The Museum of Modern Art,
New York, Purchase Fund and Gift
of Wolfgang S. Schwabacher

*Mojave, ca.* 1941–42                  6-15
28¾" x 40½"
Los Angeles County Museum of Art,
Gift of Mr. and Mrs. Burt Kleiner

*Virginia Landscape,* 1943            6-16
Pencil and wax crayon on paper, 20" x
27"
Collection Mr. and Mrs. Stephen D.
Paine, Boston
Photograph Barney Burstein

*The Liver Is the Cock's Comb,* Study,
1943                                   6-17
Ink and crayon on paper, 19" x 25"
Collection Mr. and Mrs. Frederick R.
Weisman, Beverly Hills, Calif.

*The Liver Is the Cock's Comb,*
1944                                   6-18
72" x 98"
Albright-Knox Art Gallery, Buffalo,
N.Y., Gift of Seymour H. Knox

*Agony,* 1947                          6-19
40" x 50½"
Collection The Museum of Modern Art,
New York, A. Conger Goodyear Fund

GOTTLIEB, Adolph (1903–    )
*Sun Deck,* 1936                       5-22
WPA Federal Art Project
24" x 36"
Collection University of Maryland, Col-
lege Park, Md.

*Voyager's Return,* 1946              6-12
37⅞" x 29⅞"
Collection The Museum of Modern Art,
New York, Gift of Mr. and Mrs. Roy
R. Neuberger

*The Frozen Sounds, Number 1,*
1951                                   7-11
36" x 48"
Collection Whitney Museum of American Art, New York, Gift of Mr. and
Mrs. Samuel M. Kootz

*Counterpoise,* 1959                   7-10
108" x 90"
Courtesy Marlborough-Gerson Gallery,
Inc., New York

GRAHAM, John (1881–1961)
*Anschluss,* 1932                      5-31
25" x 35"

Collection Anton Rovinsky, New York

GRAVES, Morris (1910– )
*Bird in the Spirit,* 1940–41     **5-21**
Gouache, 21½″ x 42″
Collection Whitney Museum of American Art, New York, Gift of the Friends of the Whitney Museum of American Art
Photograph Geoffrey Clements

GREENE, Stephen (1918– )
*The Burial,* 1947     **5-19**
42″ x 55″
Collection Whitney Museum of American Art, New York

GROPPER, William (1897– )
*Suburban Post in Winter,*
1934–36     **5-12**
36″ x 14″
Collection University of Maryland, College Park, Md.

GUSTON, Philip (1913– )
*Passage,* 1957–58     **7-18**
65″ x 74″
Collection Mr. and Mrs. David E. Bright, Beverly Hills, Calif.
Courtesy Los Angeles County Museum of Art

HAGUE, Raoul (1904– )
*Walnut—1949,* 1949     **9-25**
Walnut, 45″ x 26″ x 14″
Collection Mr. and Mrs. Roy R. Neuberger, New York

HALPERT, Samuel (1884–1930)
*Brooklyn Bridge,* 1913     **2-4**
34″ x 42″
Collection Whitney Museum of American Art, New York, Gift of Mr. and Mrs. Benjamin Halpert

HARE, David (1917– )
*Juggler,* 1950–51     **9-18**
Steel, 80¼″ h.
Collection Whitney Museum of American Art, New York

HARTLEY, Marsden (1877–1943)
*Mountain Lake, Autumn, ca.*
1908     **2-18**
Oil on academy board, 12″ x 12″
The Phillips Collection, Washington, D.C.

*Forms Abstracted,* 1913     **2-19**
39½″ x 31¾″
Collection Whitney Museum of American Art, New York, Gift of Mr. and Mrs. Hudson D. Walker (and exchange)

*Painting, Number 5,* 1914–15     **2-20**
39½″ x 31¾″
Collection Whitney Museum of American Art, New York, Anonymous gift

*Movement #2,* 1916     **4-5**
Oil on composition board, 24″ x 20″
Courtesy Wadsworth Atheneum, Hartford, Conn.

*New Mexico Recollections, No. 11,*
1922–23     **2-21**
30″ x 40″
Courtesy Babcock Galleries, New York

*Fishermen's Last Supper—Nova Scotia,*
1940–41     **2-22**
29⅞″ x 41″
Collection Mr. and Mrs. Roy R. Neuberger, New York
Photograph Geoffrey Clements

HELD, Al (1928– )
*Venus Arising,* 1963     **8-16**
Acrylic on canvas, 71″ x 49″
Courtesy André Emmerich Gallery, New York

HENRI, Robert (1865–1929)
*Laughing Boy,* 1907     **1-6**
24¼″ x 19⅛″
Collection Whitney Museum of American Art, New York

*The Masquerade Dress: Portrait of Mrs. Robert Henri,* 1911     **1-19**
76½″ x 36¼″
The Metropolitan Museum of Art, New York, Arthur H. Hearn Fund, 1958

HOFMANN, Hans (1880–1966)
*Effervescence,* 1944     **6-6**
54⅛″ x 35½″
University Art Museum, University of California, Berkeley

*Cathedral,* 1959     **6-7**
74″ x 48″
Collection Professor William Rubin, New York

HOLTY, Carl (1900–  )
*Of War*, 1942                    **5-34**
Oil and tempera on masonite, 45" x 36"
Courtesy The Graham Gallery, New
York

HOOD, Raymond (1881–1934)
McGraw-Hill Building, New York,
1930–31                           **10-11**

HOOD, Raymond (1881–1934), and
HOWELLS, John Mead (1868–1959)
Chicago Tribune Building,
1923–25                           **10-10**

HOPPER, Edward (1882–1967)
*Early Sunday Morning*, 1930       **5-9**
35" x 60"
Collection Whitney Museum of American Art, New York

*Second-Story Sunlight*, 1960      **5-10**
40" x 50"
Collection Whitney Museum of Ameri-
can Art, New York, Gift of the
Friends of the Whitney Museum of
American Art
Photograph Geoffrey Clements

HOWE & LESCAZE
Philadelphia Saving Fund Society Build-
ing, 1932                         **10-14**
Courtesy Howe & Lescaze

JOHNS, Jasper (1930–  )
*Flag*, 1954                       **8-3**
Encaustic on canvas, 42" x 60"
Collection Philip Johnson, New York
Courtesy Leo Castelli Gallery, New York

*Painted Bronze*, 1960             **8-4**
Bronze, 5½" x 8" x 4¾"
Collection Mr. and Mrs. Robert C. Scull,
New York
Courtesy Leo Castelli Gallery, New York

JOHNSON, Philip (1906–  )
Glass House, New Canaan, Conn.,
1949                              **10-18**
Courtesy Philip Johnson, New York
Photograph Alexandre Georges

JUDD, Donald (1928–  )
*Untitled*, 1965                   **9-38**
Galvanized iron and aluminum, 33" x
141" x 30"
Collection Philip Johnson, New York
Courtesy Leo Castelli Gallery, New York

KAHN, Albert (1869–1942)
Dodge Half-Ton Truck Plant, Detroit,
1938                              **10-8**

KAHN, Louis I. (1901–  )
Richards Medical Research Building,
University of Pennsylvania, Philadel-
phia, 1957–61                     **10-20**

KANDINSKY, Wassily (1866–1944)
*Improvisation No. 27*, 1912       **3-11**
47⅜" x 55¼"
The Metropolitan Museum of Art, New
York, Alfred Stieglitz Collection, 1949

KELLY, Ellsworth (1923–  )
*Gate*, 1959                       **9-12**
Painted aluminum, 67" x 63" x 17"
Collection Don Factor, Los Angeles
Courtesy the artist, New York

*Red Blue Green*, 1963             **8-15**
84" x 136"
Courtesy Sidney Janis Gallery, New
York

KIENHOLZ, Edward (1927–  )
*The Birthday*, 1964               **9-35**
Mixed media tableau, 84" x 120" x 60"
Collection Mr. and Mrs. Frederick R.
Weisman, Beverly Hills, Calif.
Courtesy Dwan Gallery, New York and
Los Angeles

KLINE, Franz (1910–62)
*Nijinsky (Petrouchka)*, 1948      **7-14**
33" x 28"
Collection Mr. and Mrs. David Orr,
New York

*Nijinsky, ca.* 1950               **7-15**
46" x 35½"
Collection Mrs. Muriel Newman, Chicago

*Chief*, 1950                      **7-17**
58⅜" x 73½"
Collection The Museum of Modern Art,
New York, Gift of Mr. and Mrs.
David M. Solinger

*Ninth Street*, 1951               **7-16**
60½" x 78½"
Collection Mr. and Mrs. Ben Heller,
New York

KNATHS, Karl (1891–  )
*Maritime*, 1931                   **5-33**
40" x 32"

The Phillips Collection, Washington, D.C.

KOHN, Gabriel (1910–   )
*Acrotere*, 1960   **9-26**
Laminated wood, 35½" x 32" x 25⅝"
Collection The Museum of Modern Art, New York

KRASNER, Lee (1911–   )
*Untitled*, 1939   **5-39**
Collection the artist, East Hampton, N.Y.

KRUSHENICK, Nicolas (1929–   )
*Allard Jak*, 1965   **8-17**
Acrylic on canvas, 84" x 70"
Courtesy Fischbach Gallery, New York
Photograph Eric Pollitzer

KUHN, Walt (1880–1949)
*Dressing Room*, 1926   **3-12**
44¹⁵⁄₁₆" x 33¼"
Courtesy Brooklyn Museum

KUNIYOSHI, Yasuo (1893–1953)
*I'm Tired*, 1938   **5-5**
40¼" x 31"
Collection Whitney Museum of American Art, New York

LACHAISE, Gaston (1882–1935)
*Standing Woman*, 1912–27   **9-7**
Bronze, 70" h.
Collection Whitney Museum of American Art, New York

*Passion*, 1932–34   **9-6**
Bronze, 25¾" x 12⅛" x 9"
Courtesy Lachaise Foundation
Photograph Schoelkopf Gallery, New York

LASSAW, Ibram (1913–   )
*Procession*, 1955–56   **9-17**
Wire, copper, bronze, and silver, 32" x 40"
Collection Whitney Museum of American Art, New York
Photograph Geoffrey Clements

LAURENT, Robert (1890–   )
*The Flame*, ca. 1917   **9-3**
Wood, 18" h.
Collection Whitney Museum of American Art, New York, Gift of Bartlett Arkell

LAWSON, Ernest (1873–1939)
*Winter on the River*, 1907   **1-7**
33" x 40"
Collection Whitney Museum of American Art, New York
Photograph Geoffrey Clements

LEVINE, Jack (1915–   )
*Gangster Funeral*, 1952–53   **5-25**
63" x 72"
Collection Whitney Museum of American Art, New York
Photograph Geoffrey Clements

LICHTENSTEIN, Roy (1923–   )
*Blam*, 1962   **8-8**
68" x 80"
Collection Richard Brown Baker, New York
Courtesy Leo Castelli Gallery, New York

LIPPOLD, Richard (1915–   )
*Primordial Figure*, 1947–48   **9-21**
Brass and copper wire, 96" x 18½"
Collection Whitney Museum of American Art, New York, Gift of the Friends of the Whitney Museum of American Art, Charles Simon, and purchase

LIPTON, Seymour (1903–   )
*Sorcerer*, 1958   **9-19**
Nickel-silver on monel metal, 60¾" h.
Collection Whitney Museum of American Art, New York, Gift of the Friends of the Whitney Museum of American Art

LOUIS, Morris (1912–62)
*Saraband*, 1959   **8-11**
Acrylic on canvas, 100½" x 149"
The Solomon R. Guggenheim Museum, New York

LUKS, George (1867–1933)
*The Wrestlers*, 1905   **1-1**
48¼" x 66¼"
Courtesy Museum of Fine Arts, Boston

*Woman with Goose*, 1907   **1-8**
Oil on wood, 20" x 16"
Collection Whitney Museum of American Art, New York

*Roundhouses at Highbridge*,
1909–10   **1-13**

30⅜″ x 36⅛″
Munson-Williams-Proctor Institute,
Utica, N. Y.

MACDONALD-WRIGHT, Stanton
   (1890–   )
*"Oriental." Synchromy in Blue-Green,*
  1918                  **4-8**
36″ x 50″
Collection Whitney Museum of American Art, New York

McNEIL, George (1908–   )
*Green Forms Dominant,* 1938–39  **5-35**
Tempera on gesso panel, 24″ x 20″
Collection the artist, Brooklyn

MANET, Edouard (1832–83)
*Woman with a Parrot,* 1866    **1-18**
72⅞″ x 50⅝″
The Metropolitan Museum of Art, New
  York, Gift of Erwin Davis, 1889

MANSHIP, Paul (1885–1966)
*Indian Hunter, ca.* 1926     **9-8**
Bronze, 13⅜″ x 10¼″ x 8¼″
The Metropolitan Museum of Art, New
  York
Bequest of George D. Pratt, 1935

MARCA-RELLI, Conrad (1913–   )
*The Battle,* 1956         **6-37**
Oilcloth, toned canvas, enamel and
  oil paint on canvas, 70½″ x 103″
The Metropolitan Museum of Art, New
  York, Arthur H. Hearn Fund, 1956

MARIN, John (1870–1953)
*Brooklyn Bridge,* 1910     **2-14**
Water color, 18½″ x 15½″
The Metropolitan Museum of Art, New
  York, Alfred Stieglitz Collection, 1949

*Tree Forms, Stonington, Maine,*
  1919                  **2-15**
Water color, 16½″ x 13⅜″
The Metropolitan Museum of Art, New
  York, Alfred Stieglitz Collection, 1949

*Maine Islands,* 1922      **2-17**
Water color, 16¾″ x 20″
The Phillips Collection, Washington,
  D.C.

*Region of Brooklyn Bridge Fantasy,*
  1932                  **2-16**
Water color, 18¾″ x 22¼″

Collection Whitney Museum of American Art, New York

MARSH, Reginald (1898–1954)
*Bowery and Pell Street—Looking North,*
  1944                  **5-3**
Chinese ink on paper, 40″ x 27″
Collection Senator William Benton, New
  York

MATISSE, Henri (1869–1954)
*The Red Studio,* 1911     **3-6**
71¼″ x 86¼″
Collection The Museum of Modern Art,
  New York, Mrs. Simon Guggenheim
  Fund

MAURER, Alfred (1868–1932)
*Evening at the Club, ca.* 1904  **2-27**
29″ x 36″
Addison Gallery of American Art,
  Phillips Academy, Andover, Mass.

*Autumn, ca.* 1912       **3-1**
18″ x 15″
Collection Mr. and Mrs. Ira Glackens,
  Washington, D.C.
Photograph Oliver Baker Associates

*Green Striped Bowl,* 1927–28  **2-28**
Oil on gesso panel, 22″ x 18″
Courtesy Bertha Schaefer Gallery, New
  York

*Still Life with Doily, ca.* 1930  **4-15**
Oil on composition panel,
  17¾″ x 21½″
The Phillips Collection, Washington, D.C.

*Twin Heads, ca.* 1930     **2-29**
26⅜″ x 18″
Collection Whitney Museum of American Art, New York, Gift of Mr. and
  Mrs. Hudson D. Walker (and exchange)

MIES VAN DER ROHE, Ludwig
  (1886–   ), and JOHNSON,
  Philip (1906–   )
Seagram Building, New York,
  1958               **10-15**

MILLER, Kenneth Hayes (1876–1952)
*The Shopper,* 1928      **5-1**
41″ x 33″
Collection Whitney Museum of American Art, New York

MIRÓ, Joan (1893–    )
*Seated Woman II*, 1939          **6-14**
63½" x 51"
Collection Peggy Guggenheim, Venice

MONDRIAN, Piet (1872–1944)
*Broadway Boogie Woogie,*
1942–43                          **6-2**
50" x 50"
Collection The Museum of Modern Art,
New York

MORRIS, Robert (1931–    )
*Untitled*, 1965                 **9-37**
Fiberglass with light, 24" x 96"
Courtesy Leo Castelli Gallery, New York

MOTHERWELL, Robert (1915–    )
*Pancho Villa, Dead and Alive,*
1943                             **6-27**
Gouache and oil with collage on card-
board, 28" x 35⅞"
Collection The Museum of Modern Art,
New York

*Western Air*, 1946–47           **6-28**
72" x 54"
Collection The Museum of Modern Art,
New York

*At Five in the Afternoon*, 1949  **6-29**
Casein on cardboard, 15" x 20"
Collection the artist, New York
Courtesy The Museum of Modern Art,
New York

*Jour la Maison, Nuit la Rue*, 1957 **6-31**
69¾" x 89½"
Collection Mr. and Mrs. William C.
Janss, Palm Desert, Calif.
Courtesy Los Angeles County Museum
of Art

*Irish Elegy*, 1965              **6-30**
Acrylic on canvas, 69½" x 84"
Courtesy Marlborough-Gerson Gallery,
Inc., New York

MÜLLER, Jan (1922–58)
*Jacob's Ladder*, 1958           **8-23**
83½" x 115"
The Solomon R. Guggenheim Museum,
New York

MURPHY, Gerald (1888–1964)
*Wasp and Pear*, 1927            **4-33**
36¾" x 38⅛"
Collection The Museum of Modern Art,

New York, Gift of Archibald Mac-
Leish

NADELMAN, Elie (1882–1946)
*Two Women, ca.* 1934           **9-1**
Painted terra cotta, 14" h.
Courtesy Zabriskie Gallery, New York

NAKIAN, Reuben (1897–    )
*Olympia*, 1960–62              **9-23**
Bronze, 72" h.
Collection Whitney Museum of Ameri-
can Art, New York, Gift of the
Friends of the Whitney Museum of
American Art

NEVELSON, Louise (1900–    )
*Black Majesty*, 1955           **9-27**
Painted wood, 65" x 32"
Collection Whitney Museum of Ameri-
can Art, New York, Gift of Mr. and
Mrs. Ben Mildwoff through the
Federation of Modern Painters &
Sculptors

NEWMAN, Barnett (1905–    )
*The Euclidean Abyss*, 1946–47   **7-2**
28" x 22"
Collection Mr. and Mrs. Burton Tre-
maine, Meriden, Conn.

*Concord*, 1949                 **7-4**
89¾" x 53⅜"
Collection Mrs. Betty Parsons, New York

*Tundra*, 1950                  **7-3**
72" x 89"
Collection Mr. and Mrs. Robert C. Scull,
New York

NOGUCHI, Isamu (1904–    )
*Kouros*, 1944–45               **9-24**
Pink Georgia marble, slate base, 117" x
34⅛" x 42"
The Metropolitan Museum of Art, New
York, Fletcher Fund, 1953

NOLAND, Kenneth (1924–    )
*Par Transit*, 1966             **8-12**
Acrylic on canvas, 114" x 240"
Courtesy André Emmerich Gallery, New
York

O'KEEFFE, Georgia (1887–    )
*Portrait W, No. II*, 1917      **2-11**
Water color, 12" x 9"

Collection Mr. and Mrs. James W. Alsdorf, Winnetka, Ill.
Courtesy The Downtown Gallery, New York

*Black Spot, No. 2,* 1919    **2-10**
24″ x 16″
Collection Mr. and Mrs. Irving Levick, Buffalo, N.Y.

*Red Hills and the Sun,* 1927    **2-12**
27″ x 32″
The Phillips Collection, Washington, D.C.

*New York Night,* 1928–29    **4-31**
40⅛″ x 19⅛″
Nebraska Art Association, Sheldon Gallery, Lincoln, Neb.

*Patio with Cloud,* 1956    **2-13**
36″ x 30″
Milwaukee Art Center, Gift of Mrs. Edward R. Wehr

OLDENBURG, Claes (1929–   )
*Hamburger with Pickle and Tomato Attached,* 1963    **8-5**
Plaster, cloth, metal, and enamel, 72″ x 72″ x 72″
Collection Carroll Janis, New York
Photograph Geoffrey Clements

OLITSKI, Jules (1922–   )
*Prince Patutsky Command,* 1965  **8-14**
164½″ x 70½″
Courtesy André Emmerich Gallery, New York

PARKER, Raymond (1922–   )
*Untitled,* 1959    **8-1**
68½″ x 69″
Albright-Knox Art Gallery, Buffalo, N.Y., Gift of Seymour H. Knox

PEARLSTEIN, Philip (1924–   )
*Woman Reclining on Couch,* 1966 **8-24**
54″ x 71¾″
Courtesy Allan Frumkin Gallery, New York

PÈNE DU BOIS, Guy (1884–1958)
*Woman with Cigarette,* 1929    **3-15**
36¼″ x 28¾″
Collection Whitney Museum of American Art, New York

PICABIA, Francis (1878–1953)
*Dances at the Spring,* 1912    **3-7**

47½″ x 47½″
Philadelphia Museum of Art, Louise and Walter Arensberg Collection

PICASSO, Pablo (1881–   )
*The Studio,* 1927–28    **5-41**
59″ x 91″
Collection The Museum of Modern Art, New York, Gift of Walter P. Chrysler, Jr.

POLLOCK, Jackson (1912–56)
*Untitled,* ca. 1937    **6-20**
15″ x 20″
Courtesy Marlborough Fine Art, Ltd., London

*Mural,* 1943    **6-22**
95½″ x 228″
The University of Iowa, Iowa City

*Pasiphaë,* 1943    **6-23**
56⅛″ x 96″
Courtesy Marlborough-Gerson Gallery, Inc., New York

*Totem Lesson II,* ca. 1945    **6-21**
70⅛″ x 60″
Collection Mrs. Lee Krasner Pollock
Courtesy Marlborough-Gerson Gallery, Inc., New York

*Eyes in the Heat,* 1946    **6-24**
54″ x 43″
Collection Peggy Guggenheim, Venice

*Mural on Indian Red Ground,* 1950    **6-25**
6′ x 8′
Collection Professor William Rubin, New York

*Number 27,* 1951    **6-26**
Duco on canvas, 53¾″ x 74″
Courtesy Marlborough-Gerson Gallery, Inc., New York

POONS, Larry (1937–   )
*Han-San Cadence,* 1963    **8-19**
Acrylic and fabric dye on canvas, 72″ x 144″
Collection Edwin Janss, Thousand Oaks, Calif.
Courtesy Leo Castelli Gallery, New York

POUSETTE-DART, Richard (1916–   )
*Desert,* 1940    **6-8**
42″ x 72¼″

Collection the artist, Suffern, N.Y.

PRENDERGAST, Maurice (1859–1924)
*Piazza di San Marco, ca.* 1898    **1-16**
Water color on paper, 16⅛″ x 15″
The Metropolitan Museum of Art, New York, Gift of the Estate of Mrs. Edward Robinson, 1952

*The Promenade,* 1913    **1-17**
30″ x 34″
Collection Whitney Museum of American Art, New York, Bequest of Alexander M. Bing

RAUSCHENBERG, Robert (1925– )
*Satellite,* 1955    **8-2**
Combine painting, 80″ x 42½″
Collection Mrs. Claire Zeisler, Chicago
Courtesy Leo Castelli Gallery, New York

RAY, Man (1890– )
*The Rope Dancer Accompanies Herself with Her Shadows,* 1916    **4-6**
52″ x 73⅜″
Collection The Museum of Modern Art, New York, Gift of G. David Thompson

REINHARD & HOFMEISTER; CORBETT, HARRISON & MacMURRAY; HOOD & FOUILHOUX   ·
Rockefeller Center, New York, 1931–40    **10-12**
Courtesy Rockefeller Center, Inc.

REINHARDT, Ad (1913– )
*Abstract Painting,* 1947    **7-12**
60″ x 40″
Collection the artist, New York

*Red Painting,* 1952    **7-13**
144″ x 76″
Collection the artist, New York
Courtesy The Graham Gallery, New York

RIVERS, Larry (1923– )
*Double Portrait of Birdie,* 1955    **8-22**
70¾″ x 82½″
Collection Whitney Museum of American Art, New York

ROSENQUIST, James (1933– )
*Early in the Morning,* 1963    **8-7**
95″ x 56″
Collection Mr. and Mrs. Robert C. Scull, New York

Photograph Eric Pollitzer
Courtesy Leo Castelli Gallery, New York

ROSZAK, Theodore (1907– )
*Sea Sentinel,* 1956    **9-22**
Steel and bronze, 105″ h.
Collection Whitney Museum of American Art, New York, Gift of the artist

ROTHKO, Mark (1903– )
*Prehistoric Memories,* 1946    **6-11**
Water color on paper, 26″ x 19¼″
Courtesy Betty Parsons Gallery, New York

*Number 24,* 1949    **7-8**
88½″ x 57½″
Collection Joseph H. Hirshhorn, New York
Photograph Eric Pollitzer

*Black, Pink and Yellow over Orange,* 1951–52    **7-9**
116″ x 92″
Collection Professor William Rubin, New York

RUDOLPH, Paul (1918– )
Yale School of Art and Architecture, Yale University, New Haven, Connecticut, 1961-63    **10-19**

RUSSELL, Morgan (1886–1953)
*Synchromy,* 1914–15    **4-7**
13″ x 13¾″
Collection Benjamin Garber, New York

SAARINEN, Eero (1910–61)
TWA Terminal, John F. Kennedy International Airport, New York, 1956–62    **10-17**

SCHAMBERG, Morton (1882–1918)
*Machine,* 1916    **4-17**
30½″ x 22¾″
Yale University Art Gallery, New Haven, Conn., Collection Société Anonyme

*God, ca.* 1918    **4-11**
Assemblage (miter-box and plumbing trap), 10½″ h.
Philadelphia Museum of Art, Louise and Walter Arensberg Collection

SEGAL, George (1924– )
*Cinema,* 1963    **8-6**

Plaster, illuminated Plexiglas, and metal sign, 118" x 96" x 39"
Courtesy Sidney Janis Gallery, New York

SHAHN, Ben (1898–    )
*The Passion of Sacco and Vanzetti,*
1931–32                    **5-14**
From the Sacco-Vanzetti series of 23 paintings
Tempera on canvas, 84½" x 48"
Collection Whitney Museum of American Art, New York, Gift of Edith and Milton Lowenthal in memory of Juliana Force

SHEELER, Charles (1883–    )
*Chrysanthemums,* 1912          **3-4**
24" x 20"
Collection Whitney Museum of American Art, New York, Gift of the artist
Photograph Oliver Baker Associates

*Barns,* 1917                   **4-18**
Conté crayon on paper, 6" x 8¹⁵⁄₁₆"
Albright-Knox Art Gallery, Buffalo, N.Y., Gift of A. Conger Goodyear

*Barn Abstraction,* 1918        **4-19**
Black conté crayon on casein paper, 17¾" x 24¼"
Philadelphia Museum of Art, Louise and Walter Arensberg Collection

*Classic Landscape (River Rouge Plant),*
1931                            **4-23**
25" x 32¼"
Collection Mrs. Edsel B. Ford, Detroit, Mich.

*American Interior,* 1934       **4-22**
31½" x 30"
Yale University Art Gallery, New Haven, Conn., Gift of Mrs. Paul Moore

SHINN, Everett (1876–1953)
*Sixth Avenue Elevated After Midnight,*
1899                            **1-10**
Pastel on paper, 8" x 12½"
Collection Mr. and Mrs. Arthur G. Altschul, New York

*Revue,* 1908                   **1-11**
18" x 24"

Collection Whitney Museum of American Art, New York

SKIDMORE, OWINGS & MERRILL
Lever House, New York, 1952    **10-16**

SLOAN, John (1871–1951)
*The Cot,* 1907                 **1-9**
36¼" x 30"
Bowdoin College Museum of Art, Brunswick, Me., bequest of George Otis Hamlin

*Hairdresser's Window,* 1907    **1-4**
31⅞" x 26"    .
Courtesy Wadsworth Atheneum, Hartford, Conn.

*The Wake of the Ferry,* 1907   **1-12**
26" x 32"
The Phillips Collection, Washington, D.C.

*Sunday, Women Drying Their Hair,*
1912                            **3-2**
25½" x 31½"
Addison Gallery of American Art, Phillips Academy, Andover, Mass.

SMITH, David (1906–65)
*Blackburn—Song of an Irish Blacksmith,* 1950                   **9-13**
Steel and bronze, 38½" x 40¾"
Estate of the artist
Courtesy Marlborough-Gerson Gallery, Inc., New York

*Hudson River Landscape,* 1951  **9-14**
Steel, 75" l.
Collection Whitney Museum of American Art, New York
Photograph Geoffrey Clements

*Zig VII,* 1963                 **9-15**
Painted steel, 94¾" x 100⅜"
Courtesy Marlborough-Gerson Gallery, Inc., New York

*l. to r.: Cubi XIX,* 1964; *Cubi XVII,*
1963; *Cubi XVIII,* 1964        **9-16**
Stainless steel, 113⅛" h.; 107¾" h.; 115¾" h.
Courtesy Marlborough-Gerson Gallery, Inc., New York

SOYER, Raphael (1899–    )
*Office Girls,* 1936            **5-2**
26" x 24"

Collection Whitney Museum of American Art, New York

SPENCER, Niles (1893–1952)
*Erie Underpass,* 1949    **4-27**
28″ x 36″
The Metropolitan Museum of Art, New York, Arthur H. Hearn Fund, 1950

STAMOS, Theodoros (1922–    )
*Archaic Vista,* 1947    **6-10**
Oil on board, 24″ x 30″
Courtesy André Emmerich Gallery, New York
Photograph Eric Pollitzer

STANKIEWICZ, Richard (1922–    )
*Kabuki Dancer,* 1956    **9-32**
Iron and steel, 84″ h.
Collection Whitney Museum of American Art, New York, Gift of the Friends of the Whitney Museum of American Art

STELLA, Frank (1936–    )
*Ifafa II,* 1964    **8-18**
Metallic powder in acrylic emulsion on canvas, 89″ x 155″
Collection Mr. and Mrs. Robert C. Scull, New York
Courtesy Leo Castelli Gallery, New York

STELLA Joseph (1880–1946)
*Battle of Light, Coney Island,* 1914    **4-4**
76″ x 84″
Yale University Art Gallery, New Haven, Conn., Collection Société Anonyme

*Brooklyn Bridge,* 1917–18    **4-30**
Oil and lithographic crayon on sheet, 84″ x 76″
Yale University Art Gallery, New Haven, Conn., Collection Société Anonyme

*Portrait of Walt Whitman,*
*ca.* 1920    **4-28**
Silverpoint, 8¾″ x 7¼″
Collection Mr. and Mrs. Robert J. Schoelkopf, New Canaan, Conn.
Courtesy Zabriskie Gallery, New York

*Collage #11, ca.* 1921    **4-12**
11½″ x 17″
Collection Mr. and Mrs. Morton Baum, New York

Courtesy Zabriskie Gallery
Photograph John D. Schiff

*Song of Barbados,* 1938    **4-29**
58″ x 37″
Collection Bernard Rabin, Newark, N.J.
Courtesy Zabriskie Gallery, New York

STERNE, Maurice (1878–1957)
*Bali Bazaar,* 1913–14    **4-1**
36½″ x 39″
Collection Whitney Museum of American Art, New York
Photograph Oliver Baker Associates

STILL, Clyfford (1904–    )
*1943-A*    **7-6**
Oil on blue cloth, 35½″ x 30″
Collection the artist, Westminster, Md.
Photograph Eric Pollitzer

*Jamais,* 1944    **7-5**
65″ x 31½″
Collection Peggy Guggenheim, Venice

*1948-D,* 1948    **7-7**
92″ x 80″
Collection Professor William Rubin, New York

STORRS, John (1885–1956)
*Seated Gendarme,* 1925    **9-4**
Bronze, 18″ h.
Courtesy Zabriskie Gallery, New York

SUGARMAN, George (1912–    )
*The Shape of Change,* 1964    **9-30**
Laminated wood, 72″ h.
Collection Arnold H. Maremont, Chicago
Courtesy Stephen Radich Gallery, New York

TAYLOR, Henry Fitch (1853–1925)
*Guitar Series, ca.* 1914    **3-16**
32″ x 20″
Courtesy Noah Goldowsky
Photograph John D. Schiff

TOBEY, Mark (1890–    )
*New Life (Resurrection),* 1957    **7-1**
Tempera, 43⅜″ x 27¼″
Collection Whitney Museum of American Art, New York, Gift of the Friends of the Whitney Museum of American Art

TOMLIN, Bradley Walker (1899–1953)
*Number 20*, 1949                    **7-20**
86" x 70¼"
Collection The Museum of Modern Art,
New York, Gift of Philip Johnson

TWORKOV, Jack (1900–    )
*Watergame*, 1955                    **7-19**
69" x 59"
Collection Mr. and Mrs. Lee V. Eastman,
New York
Courtesy the artist, New York


WALKOWITZ, Abraham (1880–1965)
*Bathers*, 1910                      **2-7**
Water color, 13½" x 18½"
Collection Mr. and Mrs. Lawrence B.
Karter, New York
Courtesy ACA-Heritage Gallery
Photograph Geoffrey Clements

*New York*, 1917                     **2-8**
Water color, ink, and pencil, 30⅝" x
21¾"
Collection Whitney Museum of American Art, New York, Gift of the artist
in memory of Juliana Force

*Dance Rhythms, ca.* 1920       ,    **2-9**
Water color, 20" x 14"
Courtesy Zabriskie Gallery, New York

WEBER, Max (1881–1961)
*Figure Study*, 1911                 **2-3**
24" x 40"
Albright-Knox Art Gallery, Buffalo,
N.Y., Charles W. Goodyear Fund

*Chinese Restaurant*, 1915           **2-5**
40" x 48"
Collection Whitney Museum of American Art, New York

*Rush Hour, New York*, 1915          **4-3**
36" x 30"
Courtesy The Downtown Gallery, New
York
Photograph Geoffrey Clements

*Spiral Rhythm*, 1915                **9-2**
Bronze, 24½" h.
Collection Joseph H. Hirshhorn, New
York

*Adoration of the Moon*, 1944        **2-6**
48" x 32"

Collection Whitney Museum of American Art, New York

WOOD, Grant (1892–1942)
*Stone City, Iowa*, 1930             **5-7**
30¼" x 40"
Joslyn Art Museum, Omaha, Neb.

WRIGHT, Frank Lloyd (1867–1959)
Robie House, Chicago, 1909           **10-1**

Midway Gardens, Chicago, 1913    **10-4**
Courtesy The Museum of Modern Art,
New York

Kaufmann House ("Falling Water"),
Bear Run, Pa., 1936                  **10-2**

Johnson Wax Administration Building,
Racine, Wis., 1939
Interior view                        **10-6**

Johnson Wax Administration Building,
Racine, Wis., 1939
Exterior view                        **10-7**

Price Tower, Bartlesville, Okla.,
1955                                 **10-5**
Reproduced by permission of Horizon
Press from *A Testament* by Frank
Lloyd Wright. Copyright 1957

The Solomon R. Guggenheim Museum,
New York, 1959                       **10-3**
Exterior, viewed from Fifth Avenue
The Solomon R. Guggenheim Museum,
New York

WYETH, Andrew (1917–    )
*Christina's World*, 1948            **5-17**
Tempera on gesso panel, 32¼" x 47¾"
Collection The Museum of Modern Art,
New York

YOUNGERMAN, Jack (1926–    )
*Anajo*, 1962                        **8-13**
74" x 72"
Courtesy Betty Parsons Gallery, New
York

ZORACH, William (1887–1966)
*Floating Figure*, 1922              **9-5**
African mahogany, 9" x 33¼" x 7"
Albright-Knox Art Gallery, Buffalo,
N.Y., Room of Contemporary Art
Fund

# Index of Names

Agostini, Peter, 264
Albers, Josef, 146, 148, 156, 157, 216, 224
Albright, Ivan, 129, 130, 266
Anderson, Karl, 68
Anshutz, Thomas, 13–14
Apollinaire, Guillaume, 90, 91, 113
Archipenko, Aleksandr, 112, 161, 258
Arensberg, Walter, 78, 79, 96, 97
Arp, Hans, 148, 161, 165, 209, 247
Ault, George, 106
Avedisian, Edward, 234
Avery, Milton, 134–36, 200

Balla, Giacomo, 161
Banham, Reyner, 294
Bannard, Darby, 232, 234–35
Barnes, Albert, 24, 79
Barnes, Robert, 237
Barr, Alfred H., Jr., 143
Baziotes, William, 163, 166, 207, 208, 209
Beal, Jack, 237
Beckmann, Max, 132
Behrens, Peter, 279
Bell, Clive, 112
Bell, Larry, 268
Bellows, George, 25, 26, 27–28, 29, 71, 75, 80, 96, 124, 129
Benn, Ben, 80
Benton, Thomas Hart, 83, 93, 94, 100, 113, 114, 116, 117, 119–22, 123, 153
Biddle, George, 125, 126
Bischoff, Elmer, 237
Bishop, Isabel, 116, 117
Bladen, Ronald, 268
Blanc, Charles, 91
Blashfield, Edwin, 85
Bliss, Lillie P., 79
Bloom, Hyman, 126, 136
Bluemner, Oscar, 36, 37, 39, 40, 75
Blume, Peter, 106, 128–31 *passim*

Böcklin, Arnold, 29
Bohrod, Aaron, 119
Bolotowsky, Ilya, 146, 157, 158, 160
Bonnard, Pierre, 74
Bontecou, Lee, 264
Borglum, Gutzon, 68, 75, 238
Bouguereau, Adolphe, 13, 14, 17
Bourke-White, Margaret, 128, 279
Bourne, Randolph, 39
Brancusi, Constantin, 35, 74, 77, 161, 240–41, 246, 259
Braque, Georges, 37, 42, 71, 78, 87, 88, 102, 148
Breton, André, 160, 161, 168
Breuer, Marcel, 156, 286, 287, 290
Brinley, D. Putnam, 68
Brinton, Christian, 75, 83, 113
Brook, Alexander, 116
Brooks, James, 206
Brown, Milton, 78
Browne, Byron, 145
Bruce, Edward, 125
Bruce, Patrick Henry, 25, 37, 75, 94–95, 100, 124
Bunshaft, Gordon, 288
Burchfield, Charles, 61, 100, 119, 123, 124
Burlin, Paul, 75, 150
Burnham, D. H., 271–72, 281
Byrne, Barry, 273

Cabanel, Alexandre, 13
Cadmus, Paul, 130
Caffin, Charles, 76
Cage, John, 149, 211, 216, 221, 222, 235
Cahill, Holger, 98, 125
Calder, A. Stirling, 17, 238
Calder, Alexander, 17, 163, 238, 247–49, 259
Cannon, Gilbert, 84, 100
Carles, Arthur B., 36, 37, 75, 150
Cavallon, Giorgio, 145, 146, 208

Cézanne, Paul, 14, 18, 21, 30, 31, 32, 37, 41, 52, 57, 59, 68, 71, 79, 88, 102, 169
Chagall, Marc, 44, 159, 163
Chamberlain, John, 149, 263
Chase, William Merritt, 19
Clarke, John Mowbray, 68
Cobb, Henry Ives, 272
Coleman, Glenn O., 25, 75
Conner, Bruce, 266
Cornell, Joseph, 209, 265–66
Corot, Camille, 71
Couard, Alexander P., 94
Courbet, Gustave, 71, 128
Covert, John, 37, 99, 100, 113
Cox, Kenyon, 76
Cram, Ralph Adams, 285
Cramer, Konrad, 86
Craven, Arthur, 98, 113
Craven, Thomas, 119, 120
Crawford, Ralston, 106
Cross, Henri (H. Delacroix), 71
Curry, James Steuart, 116, 119, 121, 122–23

Dabo, Leon, 68
Dalí, Salvador, 129, 160, 168, 214
Dasburg, Andrew, 37, 75, 85, 94, 113
Daugherty, James, 94
Daumier, Honoré, 71, 128
Davidge, Mrs. Clara Potter, 68
Davidson, Jo, 239
Davies, Arthur B., 24, 25, 29, 31, 36, 42, 50, 68, 69–70, 71, 74, 77, 78, 79, 81, 82, 85–86, 94, 238
Davis, Edward, 17
Davis, Gene, 226
Davis, Ron, 234
Davis, Stuart, 17, 25, 29, 86, 90, 110, 113, 114, 117, 118–19, 124, 126, 128, 137–43, 151, 152, 214, 249
De Chirico, Giorgio, 109, 163

De Kooning, Willem, 126, 127, 146, 149, 153–54, 156, 166, 167, 173, 182–86, 187, 189, 190, 192, 205, 207–10 *passim*, 212, 214, 215, 217, 222, 224, 263
De la Fresnaye, Roger, 71
Degas, Edgar, 24, 31
Delacroix, Ferdinand, 71
Delaunay, Roger, 74, 90, 91, 92, 94, 95, 161
Dell, Floyd, 117
Demuth, Charles, 38, 65, 96, 102–6 *passim*, 110, 112, 138, 139, 214
Denis, Maurice, 74
Derain, André, 37, 62, 71
Di Suvero, Mark, 263
Dickinson, Edwin, 133, 134
Dickinson, Preston, 37, 88, 106
Diebenkorn, Richard, 237
Diller, Burgoyne, 146, 157, 160
Dimmock, Edith, 21
Dine, Jim, 221, 222, 223
Doesburg, Petra van, 161
Doesburg, Theo van, 161
Dove, Arthur, 36, 38, 40, 46, 47, 50, 51, 58–62, 65, 83, 87, 99, 113, 118, 164, 217, 244, 246
Dow, Arthur Wesley, 42, 46
Downing, Tom, 226
Dreier, Katherine, 79, 113, 157
Duchamp, Marcel, 9, 50, 69, 71, 75, 79, 83, 87, 89, 96, 97, 101, 103, 161, 217, 219, 264
Duchamp-Villon, Raymond, 69, 78, 240
Dufy, Raoul, 71
Duncan, Isadora, 49, 96
Duveen, Joseph, 78
Duveneck, Frank, 19
Dzubas, Friedel, 224

Eakins, Thomas, 13, 238
Eames, Charles, 282
Eberle, Abastenia St. Leger, 239
Eddy, Arthur Jerome, 79
Eidlitz, Leopold, 270
Elmslie, George Grant, 273

Ernst, Max, 113, 160, 161, 163, 165
Evergood, Philip, 128, 131–32

Feininger, Lyonel, 103, 156
Ferber, Herbert, 254, 256–57, 258
Ferren, John, 145
FitzGerald, Charles, 21, 24, 70
Flannagan, John B., 239, 246–47
Flint, Ralph, 115–16
Flint, Randolph, 39
Follett, Jean, 264
Francis, Sam, 224
Frank, Waldo, 38, 39
Frankenthaler, Helen, 224–26
French, Daniel Chester, 238, 244
Freud, Sigmund, 164
Frey, Albert, 289
Fried, Michael, 231
Friedman, Arnold, 94
Friesz, Émile, 71
Frost, Arthur Burdett, 94, 113
Fry, Roger, 70, 112
Fuller, Buckminster, 149, 289, 294

Gabo, Naum, 156, 258
Gallatin, A. E., 79, 148, 157
Gatch, Lee, 134
Gauguin, Paul, 18, 32, 37, 71, 86
Giacometti, Alberto, 163, 249
Gilbert, Cass, 280
Gill, Irving, 287, 291
Glackens, William, 14–18, *passim*, 24, 25, 27, 30, 31, 49, 68, 71, 75, 79
Glarner, Fritz, 146, 158, 160
Gleizes, Albert, 71, 87, 88
Goldberg, Michael, 209
Gonzales, Julio, 163, 238, 249, 267
Goodnough, Robert, 213
Gorky, Arshile, 126, 127, 142–43, 146, 149, 150, 151, 153, 156, 165, 166, 167, 168–73, 182, 183, 184, 186, 190, 209, 263

Gottlieb, Adolph, 126, 134, 163, 164, 167, 189, 197, 200–201, 207, 224
Goya, Francisco, 18, 31, 71
Grafly, Charles, 14
Graham, John, 9, 114, 143, 150, 249
Graves, Morris, 126, 133, 134
Greenberg, Clement, 149, 152, 211, 212, 224, 233, 235
Greene, Balcomb, 145
Greene, Charles Sumner, 290
Greene, Gertrude, 145
Greene, Henry Mather, 290
Greene, Stephen, 132
Gregg, F. J., 70, 77
Griffin, Walter Burley, 273
Grippe, Peter, 208
Gris, Juan, 148
Grooms, Red, 222
Gropius, Walter, 156, 282, 285, 286, 287, 290, 292
Gropper, William, 126, 128, 129
Gross, Chaim, 239
Grosz, George, 117, 128, 137, 159
Guggenheim, Peggy, 79, 160–64, 174, 180
Guglielmi, Louis, 129
Guston, Philip, 126, 189, 206, 209

Haag, Charles, 239
Hague, Raoul, 239, 259–60
Halpert, Edith Gregor, 65
Halpert, Samuel, 37, 42, 75
Hambidge, Jay, 63
Hapgood, Hutchins, 76
Hare, David, 163, 208, 254–55, 256
Hartigan, Grace, 209
Hartley, Marsden, 35, 36, 40, 46, 47, 53–55, 57–58, 65, 66, 75, 83, 87, 89–90, 96, 103, 113, 118, 119, 126, 150, 164, 246
Hartmann, Sadakichi, 51–52
Hassam, Childe, 17
Haviland, Paul, 39, 105
Hawthorne, Charles, 19
Held, Al, 213, 229, 231, 263
Helion, Jean, 148, 149
Helmholtz, Hermann, 91

317

Henri, Robert, 11–32 passim, 35, 36, 38, 39, 40, 67, 68, 70, 76, 81, 82, 116–17, 120, 129, 137–38, 142, 151
Herbin, Auguste, 149
Higgins, Eugene, 75
Hinman, Charles, 234
Hirsch, Stefan, 106, 128
Hitchcock, Henry-Russell, 285
Hofmann, Hans, 9, 150, 152–53, 163, 190, 207
Holty, Carl, 145
Holtzman, Harry, 157, 158
Homer, Winslow, 13, 16
Hood, Raymond, 282, 283
Hopper, Edward, 25, 29, 80, 121, 124–25, 129, 137, 142, 214, 220
Howells, John Mead, 282
Hulsenbeck, Richard, 209
Hunt, Richard Morris, 272
Huntington, Anna Hyatt, 238
Huot, Robert, 234

Indiana, Robert, 221
Ingres, Jean Auguste, 71
Irwin, Robert, 234

Jenney, William Le Baron, 281
Johns, Jasper, 216, 217–21, 224, 235
Johnson, Philip, 285, 287, 290
Jones, Joe, 119
Judd, Donald, 268

Kahn, Albert, 279, 280
Kahn, Ely Jacques, 283
Kahn, Louis, 292, 293–94
Kandinsky, Wassily, 54, 55, 59, 61, 74, 112, 143, 148, 150, 158, 161, 169, 170, 249
Kaprow, Allan, 222
Karfiol, Bernard, 37, 75
Kelly, Ellsworth, 229–31, 248, 267
Kent, Rockwell, 21, 25, 29
Kepes, Georgy, 286
Kienholz, Edward, 265, 266
Kiesler, Frederick, 9, 161, 294

Kirchner, Ernst, 74
Kitson, Henry Hudson, 244
Klee, Paul, 112, 158, 163, 179, 191
Kline, Franz, 149, 189, 203–5, 207, 208, 209, 212, 263
Knaths, Karl, 145
Kocher, Lawrence, 289
Koerner, Henry, 129
Kohn, Gabriel, 259, 260–61
Kramer, Hilton, 254
Krasner, Lee, 146
Kroll, Leon, 75
Krushenick, Nicolas, 231
Kuhn, Walt, 25, 68, 69–70, 71, 74, 75, 78, 79, 80
Kuniyoshi, Yasuo, 25, 116, 117, 126, 137
Kupka, Frank, 91, 92, 101

Lachaise, Gaston, 65, 75, 238, 242–45
Lassaw, Ibram, 147, 254, 255
Laurent, Robert, 240–41
Lawrence, Jacob, 129
Lawson, Ernest, 21, 24, 25, 27, 68, 70
Le Corbusier, 157, 285, 286, 291, 293, 294
Léger, Fernand, 71, 101, 112, 140, 143, 148, 149, 152, 157, 161, 215, 224
Lehmbruck, Wilhelm, 74, 75
Leslie, Alfred, 209
Levine, Jack, 126, 136–37
Levy, Julien, 169, 265
Lewandowski, Edmund, 106
Liberman, Alexander, 267
Lichtenstein, Roy, 221, 223, 224
Lie, Jonas, 68, 75
Lipchitz, Jacques, 161, 239, 240, 258
Lippold, Richard, 258
Lipton, Seymour, 254, 256, 258
Lissitsky, Eliezer, 161
Loos, Adolf, 291
Loringhoven, Elsa von, 98
Louis, Morris, 224, 226
Lozowick, Louis, 106
Luks, George, 14, 15–16, 17, 18, 21, 24, 25, 29, 31, 68, 75

Macbeth, William, 24
McBride, Henry, 84, 112
McCausland, Elizabeth, 62
Macdonald-Wright, Stanton, 25, 36–37, 70, 75, 83, 90–91, 93, 94, 113
McFee, Henry Lee, 88
McGarrell, James, 237
MacIver, Loren, 126
McNeil, George, 145
MacRae, Elmer, 68
Magritte, René, 163, 215, 224
Maher, George W., 273
Maillol, Aristide, 74, 242
Malevich, Kazimir, 113, 120, 158, 161
Manet, Edouard, 11, 14, 17, 21, 24, 26, 30, 31, 32–33, 70, 71
Manship, Paul, 242, 244, 245, 246
Marc, Franz, 54
Marca-Relli, Conrad, 186, 208
Marées, Hans von, 86
Marin, John, 36, 37, 38, 40, 46, 47, 50, 51–52, 53, 58, 61, 65, 75, 83, 87, 107, 118, 119, 150, 164, 244
Marinetti, Emilio, 101
Marisol (Escobar), 221
Marquet, Albert, 71
Marsh, Reginald, 116, 117, 129, 203, 214
Mason, Alice, 146
Masson, André, 9, 148, 160, 168, 179
Mather, Frank J., Jr., 76
Matisse, Henri, 30, 35, 37, 70, 71, 77, 79, 86, 88, 93, 94, 134, 141, 148, 152, 175, 197, 200, 215, 224, 248, 249
Matta (Echaurren), Roberto, 9, 160, 163, 168, 172
Matulka, Jan, 150, 249
Maurer, Alfred, 36, 37, 38, 59, 62–65, 69, 71, 83, 99, 118
Maurer, Louis, 65
Maybeck, Bernard, 290
Mehring, Howard, 226
Meier-Graefe, Julius, 112
Mellquist, Jerome, 38

Mendelsohn, Eric, 291
Metzinger, Jean, 88
Mies van der Rohe, Ludwig, 156, 285, 286, 287–88, 290, 291, 292
Miller, Kenneth Hayes, 25, 116, 117
Millet, Jean François, 58
Miró, Joan, 113, 143, 150, 165, 169, 170, 179, 191, 197, 247, 248
Mitchell, Fred, 209
Mitchell, Joan, 209
Moholy-Nagy, Laszlo, 156, 286
Mondrian, Piet, 9, 113, 149, 157–60, 161, 222, 233, 247, 249, 255
Monet, Claude, 191
Moore, Charles, 292
Moore, James, 21
Morris, George L. K., 131, 147
Morris, Robert, 268
Motherwell, Robert, 149, 155, 163, 165, 174, 177–81, 186, 187, 189, 194, 204, 205, 207, 208, 209
Müller, Jan, 237
Mumford, Lewis, 39, 50, 97, 109, 128, 270, 279, 294
Murphy, Gerald, 110
Myers, Jerome, 24, 44, 68, 75, 77

Nadelman, Elie, 36, 40, 75, 239, 240, 241
Nakian, Reuben, 239, 245, 258, 264
Nathan, George Jean, 97
Neutra, Richard, 291
Nevelson, Louise, 259, 262–63
Newman, Barnett, 155, 187, 189, 192–93, 194–97 passim, 205, 207, 209, 224, 226, 233, 257
Noguchi, Isamu, 259
Noland, Kenneth, 149, 226–27, 244, 252

O'Keeffe, Georgia, 36, 40, 42, 46–49, 50, 51, 61, 65, 87, 105, 110, 112, 113, 118, 164, 244
Oldenburg, Claes, 221, 222–23, 268–69
Olitski, Jules, 229

Oliveira, Nathan, 237
Orozco, José Clemente, 126–27, 153
Oud, J. J. P., 285
Ozenfant, Amédée, 157

Pach, Walter, 25, 69, 70, 71, 75, 77, 78, 79
Park, David, 237
Park, Edwin Avery, 84
Parker, Raymond, 213
Pascin, Jules, 137
Pearlstein, Philip, 237
Pei, I. M., 292
Pène du Bois, Guy, 25, 69, 75, 80, 81, 124, 240
Pereira, I. Rice, 146, 157
Perkins, Dwight H., 273
Perrine, Van Dearing, 75
Peto, John F., 220
Pevsner, Antoine, 163
Phillips, Duncan, 79
Picabia, Francis, 35, 50, 71, 78, 87, 89, 94, 96, 101, 163
Picasso, Pablo, 30, 35, 37, 41, 64, 70, 71, 78, 79, 86, 87, 88, 102, 143, 146, 148, 149–50, 154, 156, 161, 163, 169, 179, 180, 183, 197, 221, 238, 240, 249, 264, 267
Pickens, Alton, 129
Pissarro, Camille, 57
Polk, Willis Jefferson, 287
Pollock, Jackson, 126, 149, 153–54, 163–64, 165, 167, 173–77, 186, 189, 190–91, 192, 193, 194, 205, 207, 208, 209, 212, 222, 224, 226, 233, 257
Poons, Larry, 229, 232–33
Porter, Fairfield, 237
Pousette-Dart, Richard, 163
Prendergast, Charles, 32
Prendergast, Maurice, 24, 25, 27, 30, 31–32, 75, 79
Preston, James, 17, 75
Purcell, William Gray, 273
Putzel, Howard, 163
Puvis de Chavannes, Pierre, 74

Quinn, John, 70, 71, 77, 78

Rauschenberg, Robert, 149, 216–17, 218, 221, 224, 235

Ray, Man, 79, 83, 89–90, 96, 163
Read, Sir Herbert, 161
Redfield, Charles, 17
Redon, Odilon, 74
Reed, Paul, 226
Refregier, Anton, 125
Reinhardt, Ad, 126, 145, 189, 196, 201–3, 207, 209, 224, 233
Renoir, Pierre, 21, 30, 31, 79
Resnick, Milton, 206
Rich, Daniel Catton, 80
Richardson, Henry H., 270, 286
Rimmer, William, 238
Rivera, Diego, 126
Rivera, José de, 267
Rivers, Larry, 224, 237
Robinson, Boardman, 75, 125
Roché, Henri Pierre, 95
Rodin, Auguste, 36, 50, 74, 239, 243, 244
Roosevelt, Theodore, 12, 26, 67, 75, 76
Root, John Wellborn, 271–72, 281, 283
Rosati, James, 208
Rosenberg, Harold, 189
Rosenfeld, Paul, 50
Rosenquist, James, 221, 223, 224
Ross, Denman, 136
Roszak, Theodore, 258
Rothko, Mark, 126, 134, 163, 164, 167, 187, 189, 192, 194, 195, 196–97, 207, 208, 209, 224, 226, 233, 257
Rouault, Georges, 30, 136
Rousseau, Henri, 35, 41, 74
Rowe, Colin, 294
Rubin, William, 194
Rudolph, Paul, 292, 293
Russell, Morgan, 37, 70, 75, 83, 90–95
Ryder, Albert, 54, 57, 70–71, 154, 173, 194

Saarinen, Eero, 282, 289, 293, 294
Saarinen, Eliel, 282
Sargent, John Singer, 19
Schamberg, Morton, 19, 75, 94, 97, 102, 104, 113

Schapiro, Meyer, 169
Schindler, R. M., 287, 291
Schuyler, Montgomery, 270,
    271, 272
Schwitters, Kurt, 99, 113,
    163, 217, 266
Scully, Vincent, 294
Segal, George, 221, 223
Segantini, Giovanni, 53–54,
    55
Seitz, William, 171
Seligmann, Kurt, 160
Seuphor, Michel, 146
Seurat, Georges, 17, 18, 31,
    32, 57, 71, 91
Severini, Gino, 35, 65, 88,
    161
Shahn, Ben, 128
Sharrer, Honoré, 130
Shaw, Charles, 145
Sheeler, Charles, 19, 38, 71,
    75, 83, 96, 102–3, 104–5,
    110, 112, 138, 279
Shinn, Everett, 13, 14, 16,
    18, 21, 24, 25, 26–27,
    31
Signac, Paul, 71
Simonson, Lee, 86
Siporin, Mitchell, 125
Siqueiros, David, 153
Sloan, John, 12, 14–19 pas-
    sim, 21, 24–32 passim,
    49, 50, 71, 75, 79, 80–
    81, 96, 116, 117, 121,
    137, 151, 214
Smith, David, 146, 238, 242,
    245, 249–54, 257, 267
Smith, Pamela Colman, 35
Smith, Tony, 268
Sorolla, Joaquín, 121
Soutine, Chaim, 136
Soyer, Isaac, 116
Soyer, Moses, 116, 128
Soyer, Raphael, 116, 117
Speicher, Eugene, 25
Spencer, Niles, 106
Sprinchorn, Carl, 21, 25, 75
Stamos, Theodoros, 166
Stankiewicz, Richard, 264
Steichen, Edward, 35, 36, 37
Stein, Clarence, 284
Stein, Gertrude, 37, 38, 46,
    62, 69
Stein, Leo, 38
Stein, Michael, 38

Stella, Frank, 229, 231–32,
    234
Stella, Joseph, 40, 47, 75,
    88, 94, 96, 99, 103, 106–
    8, 112, 118
Sterne, Maurice, 37, 85, 241
Stieglitz, Alfred, 8, 35–36,
    37, 38–42, 43, 46, 47, 50–
    51, 54, 58, 60, 62–67
    passim, 70, 74, 76, 78, 82,
    113, 119, 151, 153, 164,
    244, 247
Still, Clyfford, 163, 164,
    189, 192, 193–96, 209,
    257
Stone, Edward D., 292
Storrs, John, 241
Strand, Paul, 128
Sugarman, George, 263
Sullivan, Louis, 270, 271,
    273, 274, 276, 279, 281,
    282, 286
Swinden, Albert, 146, 147,
    158

Tanguy, Yves, 163, 168
Tatlin, Vladimir, 101
Taylor, Henry Fitch, 68, 81
Thiebaud, Wayne, 237
Thoreau, Henry, 13, 40, 61
Tobey, Mark, 134, 191, 192,
    201
Tomlin, Bradley Walker,
    165, 189, 206–8, 209
Tooker, George, 130
Torres-Garcia, 200
Toulouse-Lautrec, Henri de,
    35
Tucker, Allen, 68
Turner, Joseph Mallord Wil-
    liam, 123
Twachtman, John, 17, 24
Tworkov, Jack, 149, 206,
    208
Tzara, Tristan, 98

Valentin, Curt, 148
Valentiner, W. R., 112
Valloton, Suzanne, 74
Van Everen, Jay, 94
Van Gogh, Vincent, 32, 37,
    58, 71, 86
Vantongerloo, Georges, 163
Varèse, Edgard, 96
Venturi, Robert, 292

Vicente, Esteban, 206
Villon, Jacques, 69, 71, 112
Vlaminck, Maurice de, 37
Vollard, Ambroise, 70
Von Wiegand, Charmion,
    158
Vuillard, Jean, 32, 74

Walkowitz, Abraham, 36,
    40, 41, 44–46, 49, 59, 63,
    75, 83, 113
Warhol, Andy, 214, 221
Watson, Forbes, 111, 125
Weber, Max, 36, 37, 38, 40,
    41–44, 59, 69, 74, 80, 88,
    103, 113, 240
Weichsel, John, 83
Weinrib, David, 263
Weir, J. Alden, 17, 68, 70
Wesselmann, Tom, 221, 223
Westermann, H. C., 265
Weyhe, E., 64
Whistler, James McNeill,
    14–15, 24, 51, 62
Whitman, Robert, 222
Whitman, Walt, 11, 17, 24,
    25, 40, 66, 107
Whitney, Gertrude Vander-
    bilt, 36, 70, 239
Williams, Neil, 234
Wilson, Woodrow, 67, 76
Wood, Grant, 116, 119, 121,
    122
Wright, Frank Lloyd, 114,
    238, 253, 254, 270, 273,
    274–79, 282, 284, 285,
    291, 294
Wright, Henry, 284
Wright, Willard Hunting-
    ton, 43, 83, 95
Wyeth, Andrew, 130, 214

Xceron, Jean, 145, 249

Young, Mahonri, 62, 239
Youngerman, Jack, 229, 230
Yunkers, Adja, 206

Zayas, Marius de, 78
Zimmerman, Harold, 136
Zorach, Marguerite, 37, 86
Zorach, William, 37, 86,
    239, 241–42, 245
Zox, Larry, 234